Charleston District, South Carolina

Journal of the Court of Ordinary

1812–1830

By

Caroline T. Moore

Edited by

Brent H. Holcomb

SCMAR
2002

HERITAGE BOOKS
2022

HERITAGE BOOKS

AN IMPRINT OF HERITAGE BOOKS, INC.

Books, CDs, and more—Worldwide

For our listing of thousands of titles see our website
at
www.HeritageBooks.com

Published 2022 by
HERITAGE BOOKS, INC.
Publishing Division
5810 Ruatan Street
Berwyn Heights, Md. 20740

Copyright © 2002 Brent H. Holcomb
SCMAR
Columbia, South Carolina

Library of Congress Catalog Card Number: 2002114160

International Standard Book Numbers
Paperbound: 978-0-7884-2339-0

INTRODUCTION

Anyone who has done genealogical research in South Carolina will recognize the name of Caroline T. Moore (1907-1987) as the author of the three volumes of *Abstracts of the Wills of the State of South Carolina* (1670-1784), a fourth volume *Abstracts of the Wills of Charleston District 1783-1800*, and an additional volume *Abstracts of the Records of the Secretary of the Province 1692-1721*. These volumes have been monumental in South Carolina genealogical research and were published in the period 1960-1978. Aside from the *South Carolina Historical and Genealogical Magazine* (which began publication in 1900), there were few other publications of source material available for South Carolina before these five volumes. Mrs. Moore was truly a pioneer in such publications for the Palmetto State.

In 1980 or 1981 this journal of the court of ordinary was discovered in the Office of the Probate Judge in Charleston by Mrs. Moore, who immediately began the task of transcribing this record for publication. She recognized the importance of this record because of the information about wills and estates and especially the list of marriage licenses included in this volume. With few exceptions, the original loose wills and estates papers for Charleston District do not survive from this period. Therefore, much of the information in this record cannot be found elsewhere. As is the case with many records, there is information included from an earlier time, sometimes many years earlier. In "James Eden's Case" three marriages of his mother are referred to, two of them prior to the Revolution. Information on the Scannel family in Ireland is included in one case. A number of soldiers died in 1815, and people from other districts in South Carolina were called on to administer their estates.

I was honored when Mrs. Michael Salley, daughter of Mrs. Moore, contacted me earlier this year about publishing her mother's manuscript and turned it over to me for editing. Because Mrs. Moore was not able to complete the project, it was necessary that I obtain microfilm of this volume and to check and make certain corrections in Mrs. Moore's transcription. The volume is certainly not in perfect condition, and the pages as microfilmed are not in the proper order. I have done my best to put the pages in the correct order in this publication, making notations as to where the pages can be found on the microfilm. Microfilm of this volume is available at the South Carolina Archives and History Center in Columbia. I wish to express my appreciation to Ms. Susan L. King of the Charleston County Records Center (where the original is housed) for allowing me to purchase a copy of the microfilm for this project. My thanks to Mr. James D. McKain for his excellent job of indexing.

Brent H. Holcomb
August 21, 2002

THE PARISHES OF SOUTH CAROLINA

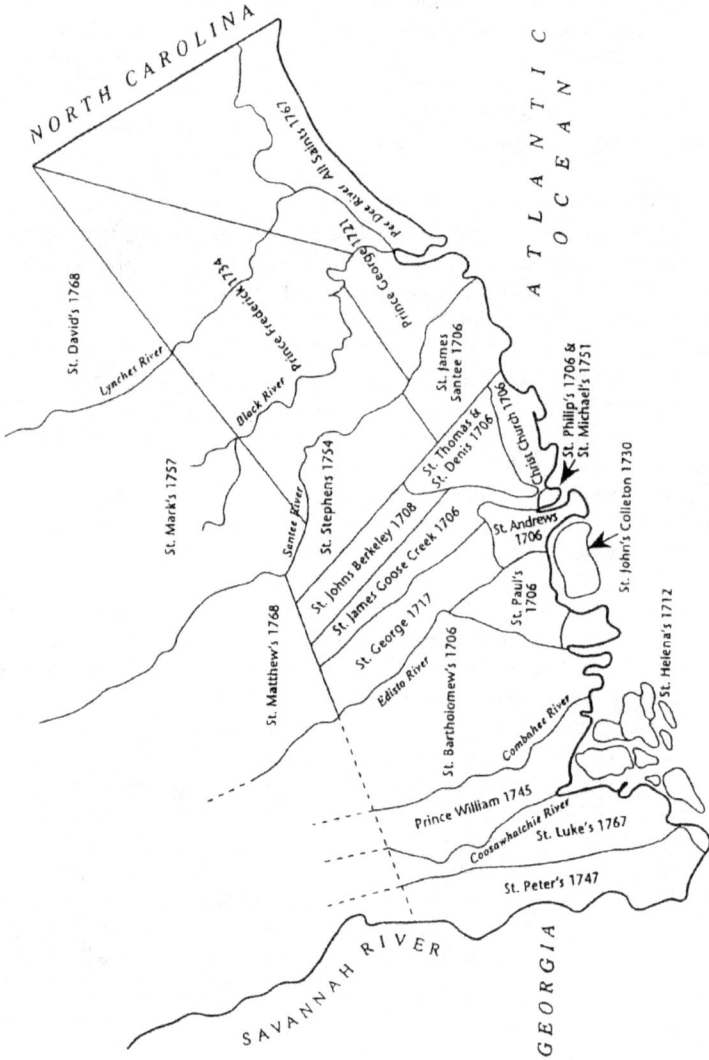

Map courtesy of the South Carolina Department of Archives and History.

CHARLESTON DISTRICT, SOUTH CAROLINA,
JOURNAL OF THE COURT OF ORDINARY
1812-1830

[N. B. Pages 1-2 are obviously out of order on the microfilm, coming just after page 174 of the original.]

[Page 1]

Proceedings and Minutes of the Court of Ordinary for Charleston District.

The Ordinary having qualified before his Honor, Judge Bay, one of the Associate Judges of the Superior Court, this twenty fourth day of December 1812.

In the Court of Ordinary. 24th December 1812.

Citation granted to Mary Watson, widow, and Elizabeth Morison to administer on the Estate and Effects of John Watson, late of Charleston, Cabinet maker, deceased, next of Kin.

Citation granted to Samuel Davenport of Charleston, to administer on the Estate of Roger Smyth, late of New Orleans, deceased, as next friend, proved the last Will and Testament of William Sheftliff, late of Charleston, Merchant, deceased, by the testimony of Benjamin Lufe of Charleston, Merchant, there being no subscribing witnesses thereto: and at the same time qualified James Houston and Charles Kiddell, the executors named therein.

In the Court of Ordinary 30 Dec. 1812. Proved the last Will and Testament [of] Mary Legg late of Charleston, widow, by the Testimony of J. W. Chitty, one of the subscribing witnesses, and at the same time qualified Joseph Legg, executor, named therein.

Proved the last Will and testament of Milliscent Colcock Junior late of Charleston, spinster, deceased, by the testimony of Mrs. Rebecca Bellinger, one [of] the subscribing witnesses thereto. and the Codicil and at the same time Mrs. Elizabeth M. Ferguson, executrix, named therein.

Proved the last Will and testament of William Loughton Smith, late of Charleston, attorney at Law, deceased, by the testimony of Henry H. Bacot, Esq., one of the Subscribing witnesses thereto: and the Codicil to the same by the testimony or the same Gentleman. There being no subscribing witnesses thereto.

1813 January 1st. Qualified Mary Watson, widow, and Elizabeth Morrison administratrixes of the Estate of John Watson, late of Charleston, Cabinet maker deceased.

Citation granted to William Broadfoot of Charleston, Merchant, to administer on the Estate of Isaac Legare Holmes, late of St. John's Colleton planter, deceased, as principal Creditor

[Page 2]

In the Court of Ordinary 2 January 1813. Proved the last Will and Testament of Susanna McPherson of the village of Hamsted, St. Philip's Parish, Widow, deceased, by the testimony of Catherine Davis, one of the subscribing witnesses thereto: and at the same time qualified Jane Hayden, executrix, named therein.

In the Court of Ordinary 8 January 1813. Qualified Samuel Davey, Administrator of the Estate of Roger Smyth, late of New Orleans, as next friend.

Alexander Mann. In the Court of Ordinary January, 1813. A Citation Case had been granted to Charistian Gradick of Charleston Neck, Butcher, to administer on the Estate [of] Alexander Mann, late of Charleston Neck Shop keeper, deceased, as principal creditor on the 27 November 1812; and a Caveat entered by J. B. White as Proctor for Alexander Stewart, and this day named by consent for hearing of the Case. Mr. Peyton appeared as Proctor for Christian Gradick; Each party produced their account duly attested. Mr. Peyton called Joseph Dickinson who was sworn and stated that the deceased, Alexd. Mann lived in the House of Mr. Gradick and died there: that his goods were in possession of Gradick: that the House was $50 quarterly: that deceased was punctual and clear of debt; that the House was Situated at the corner of St. Philips and Butcher Row and was two stories with four Rooms besides shed rooms; believes that Mr. Gradick paid for Coffin of value $35; that deceased would have been enterred in the strangers burial ground, but Gradick had him buried in the Methodist Church Yard. Mr. White in behalf of Stewart called John Hanahan who says that he was well acquainted with Stewart, and also with Mann before and at the time of his last illness. Stewart attached the store as clerk: Stewart was a Carpenter by trade: that Mann sent for Stewart from the Fort, where he was 'working and he afterwards saw Stewart at the House of Mann about a month or five weeks before his death. Mann said he meant to give Stewart a proportion of profits for his trouble and care: Stewart attended Mann night & day and acted as nurse to him: Gradick was sometimes with Mann, but never saw him set up with him; Some assistance was necessary to help Stewart as Mann was so low and Stewart particularly attentive and Mann is appeared attached to him.

[Page 3]

Did not see Gradie Grand at the funeral or after he was buried. Does it ___ an extravagant charge for attendance day and night on Mann, ____, and Hunhany to lay out deceased and paid the barber for shaving $2. heard Mann say he had money of Stewart's: that Stewart was a hard working industrious working man that decd. had a peculiar attachment to Stewart. The mulatto who stayed with deceased was a very attentive and perhaps as more useful as a nurse to Mann than Stewart was. Saw Stewart raise Mann to the pan and empty his pots for him. That demand was an honest man.

Mr. Joseph Dickinson called again never saw Stewart act as a clerk saw Stewart work at Walton's does not know that Stewart boarded at Mann's --- good nurses receive $3 p'r day.

Mr. Timothy Sullivan Sworn. He had frequent dealings with Mann and always found him punctual. Saw Stewart at Mann's House: they seemed familiar. Stewart bought articles from him he believes for Mann. Stewart seemed to have care of the Shop.

Mr. Crandell sworn. Stated that he became acquainted with Stewart at Mann's about 10 months ago: saw him at Mann's about a fortnight before his death: and appeared to have charge of the shop: Mann was then so sick that he dared not go out of doors: never was late enough then to know if Stewart attended at night. Stewart appeared as attentive as a brother and Mann called upon him almost every half hour. Mann seemed extremely fond of Stewart. Mann said he had sent for Stewart from the fort: one half cordwood, brought sawed and stored by Stewart apparently.

DECISION

The Ordinary after weighing the foregoing testimony decided as follows that from the face of the accounts and claims exhibited it appeared that Alexander Stewart was the greatest creditor: That it appeared also that Stewart was the intimate and confidential friend and in a manner the agent of the deceased and the person if he had made a Will, the deceased would have named him Executor under these considerations the Ordinary granted the Administration to Alexander Stewart in conformity to the sixteenth Section of the Act of Assembly of 1789 directing the manner of granting Probate of Will any better of Administration

[Page 4]

[In] the Court of Ordinary 12th Jany. 1813 Qualified Alexander Stewart _ Administrator of the Estate of Alexander Mann, late of Charleston Neck, Shopkeeper, deceased as principal Creditor, and next friend.
13 Jany 1813. Citation granted to Charles Bouchonneau of Charleston, Gentleman, to administer on the Estate of Charles Bouchonneau, late of Charleston, Gentleman, deceased, next of Kin with Will annexed.

Citation granted to Dr. Dyott to administer the Estate of Mr. Reverend Dr. William Best, decd., the said John Dyott having intermarried with a daughter of said deceased.

14th January 1813. Proved the last Will and testament of Daniel Lesesne, late of St. Thomas parish, planter, deceased, by the testimony of Dr. William Jenkins one of the subscribing witnesses thereto: at same time qualified Peter Lesesne, Executor named therein.

15 January 1813. Citation granted to Cato Ash Beckit and Elizabeth B. Lowery, widow, to administer the Estate of Henry Lowrey, late of John's Island, planter, deceased, as next of Kin.

15 January 1813. Qualified William Broadfoot administrator of the Estate of Isaac Legare Holmes, late of John's Island, planter, deceased.

19th. Proved the last Will and testament of Eliza Wiare, late of St. John's Parish, widow, deceased, by the testimony of Eliza Jackson one of the subscribing witnesses thereto: at the same time qualified Thomas Porcher, Executor named therein.

Proved the last Will and testament of Margaret Tousseger, late of Charleston, widow, deceased, by the testimony of Ann Ball one of the subscribing witnesses thereto: at same tine qualified Robert Verree Executor named therein.

20 Jany. 1813. Citation granted to Thomas Porcher to administer on the Estate of Samuel Nash Wiare, late of St. John's, planter, deceased, as next friend. 22 Jany. 1813. Qualified Dr. John Dyott, administrator of the Estate of the Reverend William Best, late of Charleston, deceased.

Qualified Cato Ash Beckit, administrator of the Estate of Henry Lowrey, late of John's Island, planter, deceased, the Widow Elizabeth B. Lowrey declined to qualifying.

25 Jany. 1813. Qualified William Yeadon administrator of the estate of Richard Yeadon, late of Charleston, watchmaker, deceased.

[Page 5]

23 Jany. 1813. Proved the last Will and testament of Samuel Thomas, late of Charleston, Physician, deceased, by the testimony of Thomas Hunt one of the subscribing witnesses thereto: at the same time qualified Mary G. Thomas, Executrix.

26 Jany. 1813. Proved the last Will and testament of Della Wyatt (a free Black Woman), late of Charleston, Washer, deceased, by the testimony of Robert Lang one of the subscribing witnesses thereto: at same time qualified William Eden, Executor.

28 Jan. 1813. Proved the last Will and Testament of Sarah Bouchonneau, late of Charleston, St. Philip's parish, Widow, deceased, by the testimony of Daniel Smith, one of the subscribing witnesses thereto.

27 Jany. 1813. Qualified Othneil John Giles, administrator of the Estate of Samuel Cole, late of Charleston, Gentleman, deceased.

22 Jan. 1813. Proved by Dedimus the last Will and testament of Esther Herring, late of St. John's Parish, Widow, deceased, by the testimony of Eliza Ann Cahusac, one of the subscribing Witnesses thereto.

27 January 1813. In the Court of Ordinary Qualified Othniel John Giles, Administrator of the Estate of Samuel Cole, late of Charleston, deceased.

Read the Petition of Jane Gates of Charleston Neck, Widow, praying to be appointed Guardian to his Grandson William Sims, a minor, whose father is about from and out the limits of the State.

February 4, 1813. Qualified Dr. Benjamin Howorth, Executor named in the last Will and testament of Esther Harring, late of St. John's Parish, Widow, deceased.

February 12, 1813. Proved the last Will and testament of James Bollough, late of Christ Church Parish, by the testimony or James Eden, one of the subscribing witnesses thereto: at the same qualified Mary Bollough, Executrix named therein.

February 13th 1813. Qualified Nash Roach, Executor named in the last Will and testament of Sarah Bouchanneau, late of St. Philip's parish, Widow, deceased.

Feby 13th 1813. Granted to Bartholomew Carroll, Esquire, a Citation to administer on the Estate of Susanna Quince, late of Charleston, as next friend in behalf of William Jerango Hesell / a son of the deceased / of North Carolina.

[Page 6]

February 15, 1813. Proved the last Will and testament of Alexander Nisbett by the testimony of Nicholas Harleston and George W. Chinners, two of the subscribing Witnesses to the same: on the same day qualified Abigail Nisbet, Executrix named therein.

16. Citation /Special/ granted to Joseph Cole, Shoemaker, of Charleston, one of the Securities to Elizabeth Billing, Administratrix of the Estate of Jane Billing, late of Charleston, Stable Keeper, decd., to cite the said Administratrix to apply on Friday.....February inst. to show cause why such order and decree as would be sufficient to grant him Relief should not be made.

19th. Citation granted to Stephen Thomas and Samuel Robertson to administer on the Estate of John Long, late of Charleston, Merchant, as next friend.

20. Citation granted to Charles Fraser to administer on the Estate of James Fraser, late of Charleston, Planter, deceased, as next of kin.

Proved the last Will and testament of Daniel Edwards, late of Charleston, deceased, by the testimony of Wisward Jones, one of the subscribing witnesses thereto: being almost being absent from out of the limits of the State: at the same time qualified Peter Ayrant executor named therein.

24. Dr. William Smith Stevens, and George Smith, Executors named in the last Will and testament of Charles Bouchonneau, late of Charleston, Gentleman, deceased, came into Court and renounced their Executorship to the said last Will: Whereupon qualified Charles Bouchonneau of Charleston, Gentleman (to whom a Citation had been granted on the 13 January 1813), Administrator with the Will annexed of Charles Bouchonneau, late of Charleston, Deceased.

26th. Qualified Stephen Thomas, administrator of the Estate of John Long, late of Charleston) Merchant.

March 1st, 1813. Proved the last Will and testament of Samuel Prioleau, late of Charleston, Merchant, deceased, by the testimony of William Dewees Jr. one of the subscribing Witnesses thereto: also the Codicil to said Will by the oath of Samuel Prioleau, Jr., one of the subscribing Witnesses thereto: at the same time qualified John Cordes Prioleau and Philip Gendron Prioleau, Executors named therein.

[Page 7]

March 3, 1813. Citation granted to Dorothy Marshall of Charleston, Widow, to administer on the Estate of Michael Bommer, late of Charleston, Butcher, deceased, as next of Kin with the Will annexed.

5. John Lloyd, Jr. and Francis Motte, two of the surviving Executors of those named in the last Will of Thomas Branford Smith came into Court and renounced their Executorship. J. Parsons came in Court and entered the following Caveat -- "If there should be any application for Letters of Administration ____ship on Ann Humphries' Estate, the subscriber will put in a Caveat against it" /signed/ "J. Parsons."

8th. Qualified Charlotte Wragg Smith named Executrix in the last Will and testament of William Loughton Smith, late of Charleston, Attorney at Law, deceased.

9. Proved the last Will and testament of John Smelie, late of Wadmelaw, Planter, by the testimony of Jonathan Reynolds, one of the Subscribing Witnesses thereto: at the same time qualified Benjamin Witter, Executor named therein.

11. Citation granted to Sarah Butler of Charleston Neck to administer on the Estate of Elizabeth Ladson, late of Charleston, Widow, deceased, as next of Kin.

Proved the last Will and testament of Marguerite Pigni Metivier, late of Charleston, Widow, deceased, by the testimony of Jean Gueriarino, one of the subscribing Witnesses thereto: at the same time qualified Francois Metivier, Executor named therein: NB. The original is in the French language but the Ordinary has translated and recorded it in the English language: a Copy of which translation is filed with the original.

12. Qualified Dorothy Marshall, Administratrix with the Will Annexed of Michael Bommer, late of Charleston, Butcher, deceased, as next of kin.

Citation granted to Francis Simmons of John's Island, planter, to administer on the Estate of Thomas Branford Smith, late of Charleston, Citizen, deceased, as next of Kin with the Will annexed.

13. Qualified Charles Fraser, administrator of Estate of James Fraser, late of Charleston, planter, deceased, as next of Kin.

[Page 8]

March 13. Citation granted to Durham Halls, of Charleston, Mariner, to administer on the Estate of John Bowman of Charleston, Esquire, deceased, as principal Creditor with the Will annexed.

16. Proved the last Will and testament of Robert Wilson, late of Charleston, deceased, by the testimony of Robert Henderson, one of the subscribing Witnesses thereto: at the same time qualified Edward Hughes, Executor named therein.

19. Qualified Sarah Butler, Administratrix. of the Estate of Elizabeth Ladson, late of Charleston, Widow, deceased; Agreeably to a special Citation issued in this Case; Mr. Billing appeared in Court and offered new Securities: the administration which had been granted to her on the 27th September 1811, was then revoked and a new one granted to the said Elizabeth Billing with other Securities; Thereupon Qualified Elizabeth Billing, of Charleston, Widow, Administratrix of the Estate of Samuel Billing, late of Charleston, Stable Keeper, deceased.

Proved the last Will and testament of John Crow, late of Charleston, Bookbinder, deceased by the testimony of Richard McCormick, one of the subscribing Witnesses thereto: at the same time qualified David Bell, Executor named therein.

21. Citation granted to Elnathan Haskell, Esquire, to administer on the Estate of Gersham Cohen, late of Charleston, Merchant, deceased.

24. Citation granted to Elizabeth Elbridge of Charleston, Widow, to administer on the Estate of Abner Elbridge of Charleston, Carpenter, deceased, as next of Kin.

25. Qualified Eliza Smith Mazyck, Administratrix of the Estate of Thomas Winstanly Mazyck, late of St. John's Parish, Berkeley, Physician, deceased.

Citation /Special/ granted to Joseph White and John Roche, Sureties to Mary Livingston, Administratrix of Meinard Griner, late of Charleston, Merchant, deceased, to cite the said Administratrix to appear on Tuesday the 30 of March at ten o'clock in the forenoon to show cause why such Order and decree as may be sufficient to grant them Relief should not be made.

[Page 9]

Proved the last Will and testament of Daniel Mazyck, late of Charleston, Esquire, deceased, by the testimony of John Johnson Junior, one of the subscribing Witnesses thereto: at the same Qualified Harriet Waring and Roger Heriot, Executrix and Executor named therein.

Proved the last Will and testament of Robert Lane, late of Charleston, Merchant, deceased, by the testimony of Mathew Thompson one of the subscribing Witnesses, then at the same time qualified Louise Lane, Executrix named therein.

30. Citation granted to Elizabeth Cambridge of Charleston, Widow, to administer on the Estate of Margaret Forshaw, otherwise called Margaret Jones, late of James Island, Widow, deceased, as next of Kin.

April 2. Citation granted to Mary Lindsay of Charleston, Widow, to administer on the Estate of Robert Lindsay, late of Charleston, Carpenter, deceased, as next of Kin.

Qualified Elizabeth Elbridge, Administratrix of the Estate of Abner Elbridge, late of Charleston, Carpenter, deceased.

Qualified Francis Simmons of John's Island, Planter, Administrator with Will annexed of Thomas Branford, late of Charleston, Citizen, deceased.

8. Citation granted to John A. Schroder of Charleston to administer on the Estate of Christopher Shultz, late of Charleston, Grocer, deceased, as next friend.

8. Caveat entered against any person obtaining Letters of Administration on the Estate of Christopher Schultz, late of Charleston, Grocer, deceased, in the following words: "to James D. Mitchell, Esq., Ordinary for Charleston Dist. Sir, I do hereby enter Caveat against any person obtaining Letters of Administration on the Estate of Christopher Schultz until I am heard before said Ordinary." /Signed/ "Richd. Fairweather."

Proved the last [Will] and testament of Thomas Harrison McCalla, late of Charleston, Physician, deceased, by the testimony of James Fisher Edwards, one of the subscribing Witnesses thereto: also the Codicil to said Will by the testimony of the same person, a subscribing Witness: at the same time qualified Mrs. Sarah McCalla named Executrix therein.

[Page 10]

9. Citation granted to Arthur Harper of Charleston Merchant, to administer on the Estate of John Strong Adams as principal creditor with Will annexed.

Citation granted to Peter Smith Senr. of Charleston, Factor, to administer on the Estate of Hannah Smiser, late of Charleston, Widow, deceased, as next of Kin.

Qualified Mary Lindsay, Administratrix of Estate of Robert Lindsay late of Charleston, Carpenter, deceased.

Caveat entered this day in the following words _ "To James D. Mitchell, Esq., Ordinary for Charleston Dist. Sir, I so hereby enter a Caveat against any person taking Letters of Administration on the Estate and Effects of Mrs. Margaret Forshaw, late of James Island, Widow, until I am heard before the Ordinary. April 9, 1813," /Signed/ "James T. Bruckner."

12 Caveat entered as follows _ "To James D. Mitchell, Esq. Ordy. of Charleston Dist. Sir, I do hereby enter a Caveat against any person whatsoever taking out Letters of Administration on the Estate and effects of Christopher Schultz, deceased, before I am heard before the Ordinary. /signed/ J. Carrigan[?].

12. Proved the last Will and testament of Mary Whaley, late of Charleston, Widow, by the testimony of Othniel John Giles one of the subscribing Witnesses thereto.

13. Qualified Jervis Henry Stevens, Executor named in the last Will and testament of Mary Whaley, late of Charleston, Widow, deceased.

Citation granted to Mary Moore, Widow, to administer on the Estate of Henry Herbert Moore, late of Charleston, Schoolmaster, deceased, as next of Kin.

14. Qualified Elnathan Haskell administrator of the Estate of Gersham Cohen, late of Charleston, Deceased, Merchant.

In the Court of Ordinary, Whitefoord Smith who had obtained Administration on the Estate of Thomas Gordon, late of Charleston, Gentleman, deceased, as next friend, came into Court and Surrendered his Letters of administration in favor of Kenneth Gordon, the brother of the deceased, who was absent from out of the limits of the State at the time of granting Administration to Whitefoord Smith; and the said Kenneth Gordon, having appeared and new Securities, the Administration was accordingly revoked: therefore Qualified Kenneth Gordon as Administrator of the Estate of Thomas Gordon, late of Charleston, Gentleman, deceased.

[Page 11]

16. Qualified Peter Smith Senr., Administrator of the Estate of Hannah Smiser, late of Charleston, Widow, deceased.

22. Qualified Major Thomas Porcher, Administrator of the Estate of Samuel Nash Wiaco, late of St. John's Parish, Berkeley, physician, deceased.

23. Qualified Mary Moore, Administratrix of the Estate of Henry Herbert Moore, late of Charleston, Schoolmaster, deceased.

28. Christopher Fitzsimons and John Stoney, Executors in this State of the last Will and testament of John Strong Adams, late of Charleston, Merchant, deceased, came into Court and renounced their Executorship to the same: and Arthur Harper who had on the 9 inst. obtained a Citation to Administer with the Will annexed on the Said Estate came into Court and declined the Administration in favor of Peter Thomas Ryan another Creditor, and the said Peter Thomas Ryan having furnished competent Securities the Administration was granted to him: Whereupon, Qualified Peter Thomas Ryan Administrator with the Will annexed as a principal creditor of the Estate of the said John Strong Adams, late of Charleston, Merchant, deceased.

29. Citation granted to John Henry Ward of Charleston, Bricklayer, to Administer on the Estate of Daniel Ward, late of Charleston Gentleman, deceased, as next of Kin.

[Pages 11-12]

Christopher Schultz's Case. In the Court of Ordinary 3 May 1813. This day being appointed to hear the above case, John A. Schroder, with his Proctor Mr. Geddes, appeared, produced the Citation certified as also Richard Fairweather and Mr. McCormick his Proctor and J. C. Morgan with Mr. Prioleau his Proctor, both of whom had entered Caveats, after some time occupied in the examination of several witnesses it was moved to adjourn the Court until Monday next at eleven o'clock.

Proved the last Will and Testament of Ann Eleanor Walker, late of Charleston, Spinster, deceased by the testimony of Richard Cameron, one of the subscribing Witnesses thereto.

4. Qualified Joseph Gaultier Executor named in the last Will and testament of Ann Eleanor Walker, late of Charleston, Spinster, deceased.

13. Citation granted to Catherine Ehney of Charleston, Widow, to administer on the Estate of Jacob Ehney, late of Charleston, Gentleman, deceased, so far as they were left unadministered by William Frederick Ehney, late of Charleston, deceased, by Citation granted to Catherine Ehney of Charleston Widow, to administer on the Estate of William F. Ehney, late of Charleston, Gentleman, deceased, as next of Kin.

14. Citation granted to Catherine Freeman of Wadmalaw, Widow and Isham Lowrey of Edisto [Island] to Administer on the Estate of Benjamin Furman, Senr., late of Wadmalaw, planter, deceased, as next of Kin.

13. Proved the last Will and testament of Sarah Barton, late of St. John's Parish, Berkeley, by the testimony of Elias Couturier, one of the Subscribing Witnesses to the same. At the same time qualified Dr. Samuel Dwight, Executor named therein.

17. Benjamin B. Smith, Esq., this day withdrew the Caveat entered by James T. Buckner against Administration being granted to any person on the Estate and effects of Margaret Forshaw, late of James Island, Widow, deceased, in the following words "This Caveat is withdrawn. Benj. B. Smith, Proctor for Jas. T. Buckner. 17th May 1813."

Christopher Shultz's Case. The Court which had adjourned to meet on Monday 10 inst. resumed the examination of witnesses which being gone through and the council of each claimant heard, the Ordinary gave the following Decision

[Pages 12-13]

In reviewing the testimony of this Case the Ordinary perceiving that his decision may be reduced to a very narrow Compass. It will be necessary to take a view of the pretensions of the Several claimants. And first Mr. Morgan stated his Claim to the Administration on his right as a Creditor: but as it appears that Mr. Fairweather's claim far exceeds his, it is probable that Mr. Morgan would not have felt himself disposed to have such an application unless under the impression that Mr. Fairweather would be excluded as an alien enemy. So Mr. Fairweather's strong objections have then made as an alien enemy. No law is more incontrovertible than that of an alien enemy cannot be heard as a Suitor in our Court of Justice in time of open and declared War. It becomes necessary therefore to examine the Evidence which has been given particularly applicable to that Subject. Mr. Bevens swore that he was on duty with Fairweather at Haddrell's Point when he heard Fairweather say that he was born in England; that he had been in an engagement under a British Admiral, and that one of his companions had been injured by the bursting of a gun which he Fairweather had overcharged and for which he had been reprimanded: the witness further stated that he thought Fairweather serious when he made the declaration. This is the evidence offered to Prove him an alien enemy. On the other hand this testimony is in some measure counter balanced by the evidence of Mr. Fitz, who declared that he had known Fairweather for five years, during which time he had conducted business here and that he had understood from Fairweather that he was born at the Northward; to which we must add the Protection from the Collector of New York: and the circumstances of his not having availed himself of the Plea of being an Englishman to exonerate himself from duty at Hadderell's Point, when it had become so irksome as to induce him to offer a substitute who was refused because he was lame: all these corroborating circumstances induces the Ordinary not to view him as an alien enemy: altho it must be conferred he labors strongly under the Suspicion of being so. Admitting however, that he is not inadmissible on the ground of his being an alien enemy: yet there is an objection which weighs strongly against Mr. Fairweather with the Ordinary:

[Page 14]

It appears that there had been intimate transactions between the deceased Mr. Shultz and Mr. Fairweather; so much so as to induce the latter to set up claim as copartner; now it also appears shortly before the death of Shultz a serious misunderstanding had taken place between them and that Shultz declared that altho he had been a friend to Fairweather, that Fairweather had been an enemy to him from which it is to be inferred, that Shultz had taken strong exceptions to the conduct of Fairweather which propriety, therefore, would be in placing the Estate of the deceased under the control of him, whom he had declared to be his enemy, so shortly before his death: who would there be then to make objection to changes which probably had been the cause of dissatisfaction to Shultz; now if Mr. Fairweather were invested with the Administration he would have the Privilege of allowing what changes he pleased. Another consideration which must be made by the Ordinary on this occasion is that if admitted on all sides that the Estate is perfectly solvent, the Creditors will all obtain their full legal rights; it is not therefore necessary for them to be vested with the Administration to secure them; but there is another class of persons entitled to the surplusage after payment of debts is namely the Kindred of the deceased in Germany; and as they are all absent the Ordinary must be attentive to their rights from the Evidence it appears that. Mr. Schroder was the companion of Mr. Shultz in their passage to America: that he knows the place whence he came and is probably acquainted with the best manner of transmitting a knowledge of their rights to the relatives of the deceased: In addition to which it is in evidence that he repeated and declared that Schroder was his best and only friend he had here; and he would probably have made Mr. Schroder his Executor if he had made a Will; which circumstances always has great weight with the Ordinary in his inquiry as to the propriety of granting an Administration. The Act regulating the manner of granting Administration has given discretionary power to the Ordinary to decide between persons claiming as Creditors and friends; yet they must not be an arbitrary or capricious exercise of authority, but must be guided by a due regards to the rightful claim of Creditors; and therefore always when an Estate if likely to be insolvent the admor is granted to Creditors because they will make the best of it: but when an Estate is perfectly solvent, other motives may govern some of which have actuated on this occasion; Under these impressions the Ordinary feels it his duty to grant the Administration to Mr. Schroder upon his giving good and sufficient security - 14th May 1813. Whereupon Qualified John Adolphis Schroder Administrator of the Estate and effects of Christopher Shultz, late of Charleston, Grocer, deceased.

[Page 15]

May 21. Qualified Catharine Eheny of Charleston, Widow, Administratrix of Jacob Eheny, late of Charleston, Gentleman, deceased. Qualified Catharine Eheny of Charleston, Widow, Administratrix of William Frederick Eheny, late of Charleston, Gentleman, deceased.

Qualified Catherine Freeman and Isham Lowrey of Wadmalaw, widow, Administratrix and Admor. of Estate of Benjamin Freeman Senr., late of Wadmalaw, planter, deceased.

June 1st. Qualified Elizabeth Cambridge, Widow, Administratrix of the Estate of Margaret Forshaw, late of James Island, Widow, deceased.

May 28th. Citation granted to Henry Bennett of Charleston, Planter, to administer on the Estate and effects of Mary Bennett, late of Charleston, Widow, deceased, as next of Kin.

June 3. Citation granted to John McKinley, late of Charleston, Merchant, deceased, as next of Kin.

Citation granted to Charles Johnston of Charleston, Gentleman, to administer on Estate & Effects of Susanna Johnston, late of St. Thomas Parish, Widow, deceased, as next of Kin.

4th. Qualified Henry Bennett of Charleston, Planter, administrator of the Estate and Effects of Mary Bennett, late of Charleston, Widow, deceased.

[Page 16]

June 7. Citation [Special] granted on the Petition of John Roche and Joseph White, Sureties to Mary Livingston, Administratrix of the Estate of Meinard Griner, Merchant, deceased, to cite the said Admix. to appear Friday the tenth inst. at 11 o'clock to show Cause why such order and decree should not be made as would be sufficient to give Relief to the said Petitioner: the former Citation granted not having been duly returned.

9. Proved the last will and testament of Elizabeth Christian, late of Charleston, widow, deceased, by the testimony of Francis Thomas, one of the subscribing witnesses thereto.

Proved the last Will and testament of James O'Hear, late of Charleston, Accountant, deceased, by the testimony of James A. Sperin, one of the Subscribing witnesses to the same: at the same time qualified Joseph O'Hear, otherwise called Joseph Faban O'Hear, Executor.

10. Qualified Charles Christian, Executor named in the last Will and Testament of Elizabeth Christian, late of Charleston, deceased.

Proved the last Will and testament of Richard Fowler, late of Christ Church parish, planter, deceased, by the testimony of William Roach one of the subscribing witnesses thereto.

11. Qualified Nash Roach, Executor named in the last Will and Testament of Richard Fowler, late of Christ Church Parish Planter, deceased.

Qualified John McKinlay of Charleston, Merchant, administrator of Dugald McKinlay of Charleston, Merchant, decd.

18. Proved the last, Will and testament of Francois Figuiere, late of Charleston formerly of Lyons, in France, Comb Maker, deceased, by the testimony of Charles Rotieriau, one of the subscribing witnesses thereto - at the same [time] Qualified Jean Baptiste Perodin, Executor named therein.

Citation granted to Hugh Livingston of Charleston, Mariner, to administer on the Estate of William Livingston, late of Charleston, Mariner, deceased.

29th. Mary Manton, late Mary Livingston, having appeared agreeably to the Citation issued on the 7th instant and having offered new Securities whereupon the old Administration on the Estate and effects of Maniad Griner was revoked and a new one granted to the said Mary Manton.

1813 July 1st. Proved the last will and testament of Edward Creighton late of Charleston, Hairdresser, deceased, by the testimony of William Logan, one of the subscribing witnesses thereto. At the same time qualified George Logan executor named therein.

2d. Granted Citation to David Oliphant of Charleston, painter, to administer on the estate and affects of John Davidson, late of Charleston, Gentleman, deceased, as next of kin.

Proved the last will and testament of Marianne Lafferte, late of Charleston, by the testimony of Antoniette Loqueinst Arnaud, there being no subscribing witness thereto. At the same time qualified John Blome executor named therein. The will was presented in the French language and a translation by the ordinary and filed with the original will.

3d. Citation granted to hannah Edwards of Charleston, widow, to administer on the estate and effects of Isam Edwards, late of Charleston, Factor, deceased, as next of kin.

Citation granted to Peter Rowe of Orangeburg District to administer on the estate and effects of James Quin, late of Ch--, Deputy Sheriff, deceased.

9. Qualified Susannah Edwards of Charleston, Widow, administratrix of the estate and effects of Isom Edwards, late of Charleston, Factor, as next of kin.

Citation granted to Mary Hutchinson, of Charleston, Widow, to administer on the estate of Thomas Holland[?] Hutchinson, late of Charleston, planter, deceased, as next of kin.

16. Citation granted to Susanna Eason of Charleston, widow, to administer on the estate and effects of William Eason, late of Charleston, Blockmaker, deceased, as next of Kin.

Proved the last will and testament of Elias Smerdon, late of Charleston, Merchant, deceased, by the testimony of John Plumeau, there being no subscribing witness thereto. Same time qualified Priscilla Smerdon executrix in the said will.

Qualified John Henry Ward of Charleston, Bricklayer, administrator of the Estate & Effects of Daniel Ward, late of __, Gentleman deceased, as next of kin.

[Page 18]

July 16. Qualified David Oliphant administrator of the Estate & Effects of John Davidson, late of Charleston, Gentleman, deceased, as next of kin.

17. Proved the last will and testament of William Gunn, late of Charleston, Gunsmith, deceased, by the testimony of J. Jessop, one of the subscribing witnesses thereto; at the same time qualified William Gray executor named therein.

24. Citation granted to John Le Sage of Charleston, Carpenter, to administer on the estate and effects of Michel Foucaut, late of Charleston, Carpenter, as creditor and next friend.

27. Qualified Susanna Eason administratrix of the Estate and Effects of William Eason, late of Charleston, Blockmaker.

28. Caveat entered by Louis Chupein of Charleston, Hairdresser, against the proving of certain papers purporting to be a Codicil to the last will and testament of John Francis Schem until he is heard before the Ordinary.

29. Special Citation granted to Dr. Plem Joseph More to cite and summon Louis Chupein to produce a certain instrument of writing purporting to be the last will & testament of John Francis Schem and to shew cause why a certain paper purporting to be a Codicil to said last will and testament should not be proved and allowed by the court.

30. Qualified John Le Sage of Charleston, carpenter, administrator of the estate and effects of Michael Foucant, late of Charleston, carpenter, deceased.

August 2d. Proved the last will and testament of The Reverend Francis Wilson, late of Charleston, Minister of the Gospel, deceased, by the testimony of Thomas Lee, attorney at Law, there being no subscribing witness thereto.

3. Qualified Francis Thomas an executor named in the last will and testament of Thomas Turner, late of Charleston, Esquire, deceased.

Agreeably to the special citation issued on the 29th ult. Mr. Louis Chupein with Henry DeSaussure his Proctor and Dr. Peter Joseph More with Keating Lewis Simons his Proctor appeared in Court. Mr. DeSaussure produced the will of John F. Schem and moved

[Page 16]

that it be proved which was accordingly done by the testimony of William Payne one of the subscribing witnesses thereon. Mr. Simons then tendered the Codicil and moved that it should be proved also; whereupon Mr. DeSaussure objected and stated that the testator was not in a frame of mind to make a testamentary act at the time of the execution of the said Codicil. Mr. Simons then moved the Court that the subscribing witnesses thereto be sworn; upon which Ph: Messeray the first subscribing witness was sworn and stated that he had not seen the testator for a twelve month before the time of signing the codicil.

Mr. Simons then moved the Court that the subscribing witnesses thereto be sworn; upon which Ph. Messery the first Subscribing witness was sworn - and states that he had not seen the testator for a twelve month before the time of signing the Codicil that when he entered the Room the testator asked witness how he was and knew his perfectly: that testator walked from his bed and put his signature to the paper as soon as the other witnesses were present: all of the witnesses saw him sign and did also sign at his request: testator told witness that he had sent for him to witness his Will and asked for the other witnesses and said "to act till the other gentlemen arrive:" he appeared properly in his senses, had full time to read the will and was strong enough to have read it: but did not see him read it: testr. appeared to know that he was about and to understand the content of the   Codicil. Believe that it was executed of his own accord and thinks the testr. could not have been improved upon; would not have witnessed it if he thought that the dec. did not know what he was about. X Saw no other paper at the time of signing the Codicil: had not seen Schem for any length of time; he took witness by the hand and requested him to witness his will: Does not know that he read the Codicil. No comments were made on it. It was the 18th July, he thinks about 10 o'clock A.M. and confident that it was the 18th; but sure it was not. on a Sunday. Testator was perfectly sober at the time period.

Timothy Ford, Esq., sworn in behalf of Mr. Chassein. Waited on dec. about business and found him exceedingly weak evidently in body and thinks in mind also: had to repeat what he said to testr. understand; thought testr. too feeble to transact business of any importance and ought not to do so with persons likely to take advantage of him; witness doubted whether testator would live until the time of Sale about which he went to consult with him. X Testr. appeared to understand witness; expressed himself, many persons calling on him; witness believes it was in June that he was with testr. but the date of Sale ascertains within a day or two the time; Dr. More called on witness and requested him to have the House Sold for Cash which witness thought improper under the pressure of the times; had no conversation with dec. about any person.

Nicolas Poulnot second subscribing witness sworn. Saw Shem sign the Codicil which was doubled or folded up which witness believes was done because the table was small. Testr. upon being asked how he was, said he was middling well that day, took the paper from the small table and placed it on a large table where he signed it: was sober and all the witnesses signed in his presence; Schem. asked him to sign as witness but not say it was his will and said he would not keep him from his work; witness acquainted five or six years with Schem and believed him then as much in his senses as at any former period. Thinks that testr. knew the contents of the paper; and told witnesses to put their names to it; Codicil was signed on the 20th July about 10 o'clock A. M. testr regretted that he had taken Poulnot from his work Dr. More cited no solicitation to .make testr. sign; the other witnesses were there before him.

J. F. Sandoz, 3d. subscribing witness; lived with Schem signed the Codicil as witness at the request of testr. in his presence and in the presence of all of the other witnesses; that Schem was then as much in his senses as witness; Testr. had previously mentioned that he intended to make Dr. Moore Co-executor with Mr. Chupein. Here the testimony closed: When Mr. DeSaussure stated to the Court that Mr. Chupein had been induced to institute the foregoing inquiry from some information he had received which inclined him to believe that his testator had been imposed on at the moment, when he was unfit to transact any testamentary act; but from the evidence which had been detailed

Mr. Chupein was now satisfied that no undue advantage had been taken of his testator; he therefore withdrew his objections to the proving of the Codicil; Whereupon,

Proved the last Will and testament of John Francis Schem, late of Charleston Watchmaker, deceased, by the testimony of William Payne, one of the subscribing witnesses to the same; and also proved the Codicil thereto by the testimony of the three subscribing witnesses. Attested same Ph Messeray, Nicolas Poulnot, and J. F. Sandoz: at the some time qualified Louis Chupein and Dr. Pierre Joseph More, Executors named therein.

August 10. Mr. Thomas Warnock in behalf of Peter Rowe of Orangeburg District who had Attained Citation to administer on the Estate and effects of James Quin, late of Charleston, Deputy Sheriff, dec. Came into Court and stated that the person whose Estate he intended to obtain administration was William Quin son of the said James Quin, but that since obtaining Citation he had been informed that William Quin is still alive altho absent from the State. See page 44 under date of 20 Jany. 1814 Original Book.

13. Citation granted to Mrs. Mary C. Thomson of Charleston to administer on the Estate and effects of Henry Cuhun, late of Charleston, shopkeeper, deceased, as next friend to the children of the said deceased.

17. Proved the last [Will] and testament of Edward Weyman, late of Charleston, Gentleman, deceased, by the testimony of Charles Kershaw, one of the subscribing witnesses thereto: at the same time qualified Catherine Weyman, executrix named therein.

20. Qualified Mary C. Thomson, Administratrix of the Estate and effects of Henry Cuhum, late of Charleston, Shopkeeper, deceased.

27. Citation granted to Mary McHugh of Charleston, widow, to administer on the Estate and effects of Francis McHugh, late of Charleston, Carpenter, deceased, as next of Kin.

28. Citation granted to Anne Legge, of Charleston, Widow, to administer on the Estate and effects of John Henry Legge, late of Charleston, Factor, deceased.

[From inner edge of page 21 of Original Book.] 21st August 1813. Dedimus granted to Robert Porter, Esq., President of the Third Judicial District of the Commonwealth of Pennsylvania, to qualify John Wilson and William Craig, Executors named in the last Will & testament of Francis Wilson, late of Charleston, Minister of the Gospel, decd.

27. Proved the last Will and testament of Charles Lining, late of Charleston, Attorney at Law, deceased, by the testimony of John Stock one of the subscribing witnesses thereto: and the Codicil by the testimony of Margaret

Blake, one of the subscribing witnesses thereto: at the same time qualified Polly Blake Executrix named therein.

Sept. 2. Citation granted to Arnold Harvey of St. James Parish Goose Creek, planter to administer on the Estate & effects of Sarah Taylor, late of St. John's Parish, Berkeley, as next of Kin.

3. Qualified Mary McHugh, Widow, Administratrix of the Estate & effects of Francis McHugh, late of Charleston, Carpenter, deceased.

[Page 22]

1813 September 3. Citation granted Eliza Hepburn of Charleston, Widow, to administer on the Estate & effects of John S. Hepburn, late of Charleston, Shoemaker, deceased, as next of Kin.

6. Qualified Ann Legge of Charleston, Widow, Administratrix of John Henry Legge, late of Charleston, Factor, deceased, as next of Kin. Citation /special/ granted to Jacob Frederick Boyer to cite Charles Dukes, administrator of the Estate & effects of Frederick Dukes to appear on Wednesday the 8th inst. at 10 o'clock in the forenoon to cause if he has not made a return of the Warrant of appraisement and exhibited an acct. of the said Estate.

Citation / Special/ granted to Mary Spencer, a creditor to cite to Lewis Philips Descondus and Peter Crovat, administrators of Jonah Rhodes, late of St. James Parish Goose Creek, to [shew] cause why he hath not made account of his administration.

7. Qualified John Wilson and William Craig / by Dedimus/ executors named in the last Will and testament of Francis Wilson, late of Charleston, Minister of the Gospel, deceased.

8. Proved the last Will and testament of James Nisbett, late of Charleston Neck, Gardner, deceased, by the testimony of William Kunhardt, one of the subscribing witnesses at the same time qualified Patrick Duncan and James Nicholson, executors named therein.

10. Proved the last Will and testament of Johannes Otzell, late of Charleston, Grocer, deceased. by the testimony of George McKay and David Henry Nipper, two of the subscribing witnesses thereto: at the same time qualified Jacob Eckhard Senior, and John Frederick Cutter, Executors named therein.

Sarah Taylor's Case. This day came into Court Arnold Harvey who had obtained a Citation to administer on the Estate and effects of Sarah Taylor, late of St. John's Parish, Berkeley, and presented the Citation duly certified: when John Bee Holmes, Esquire, entered a Caveat against the said administration being granted to said Harvey in behalf of John Taylor who claimed as the son of the deceased: It was denied that Harvey was the legitimate son of

Sarah Taylor, and after some discussion of the case the parties agreed to take the administration jointly; therefore qualified Arnold Harvey of St. James Goose Creek and

[Page 23]

Sept. 10, John Taylor of St. John's Parish, Berkeley, administrators of the Estate and effects of Sarah Taylor, deceased.

Citation granted to John Maynard Davis of Charleston, Merchant, to administer on the Estate & effects of John Bowman, late of Charleston, Gentleman, deceased so far as they were left unadministered by Sabina Bowman, deceased with the Will annexed as principal Creditors. Danham Hall came into Court at same time and declined qualifying in favor of Mr. Davis.

Citation granted to Samuel Holman of St. James Parish Santee to administer on the Estate and effects of Samuel Holman, late of Great Britain, Mariner, deceased, as next of Kin.

14. Citation granted to Clinton Crozier of Charleston, Tavernkeeper, to administer, on the Estate and effects of Henry Anderson, late of Charleston, Mariner, deceased, as principal Creditor and next friend.

16. Caveat entered by John Gadsden, Esq., against any person whatever taking out letters of Administration on the Estate and Effects of John Bowman, late of Charleston, Gentleman, deceased, until he is heard before the Ordinary as Proctor for John Bowman Lynch.

Caveat entered by Henry Laurens, Esq., against administration of the Estate and effects of Samuel Holman, late of Great Britain, Mariner, dec., until he is heard before the Ordinary.

Citation granted James Myer Jacobs of Charleston, Gentleman, to administer on the Estate and effects of Irael Davis, late of Charleston Merchant, deceased, as Principal Creditor and next friend.

Citation granted to Myer Jacobs of Charleston, Gentleman, to administer on the Estate and effects of Judith Davis, late of Charleston, Widow, deceased as next of Kin.

17. Citation granted Benjamin Phillips, late of Charleston, Shoemaker, to administer on Estate and effects of John S. Hepburn, late of Charleston, Shoemaker, deceased as principal Creditor. N. B. The Citation granted to Eliza Hepburn on the 3 Sept. 1813 was destroyed and never published.

[Page 24]

September 17th [1813]. Keating Lewis Simons, Esq., in behalf of Mr. Henry Laurens who had entered a conditional Caveat withdrew the same and stated that he held a Will of Samuel Holman, late of Great Britain, Mariner, decd., which on perusing it made apparent that Samuel Holman was not entitled to admon, the decd. having disposed of his property, a regularly formed Will & appointed Executors who had qualified and acted. Whereupon Samuel Holman who had obtained the Citation states that he was unaware of the existence of such a Will and withdrew his pretensions.

18. Proved the last Will and Testament of Edmund Green, late of Charleston, Factor, deceased, by the testimony of William Burgoyne, one of the subscribing witnesses thereto; at the same time qualified Elizabeth Green, Executrix named therein.

20. I hereby enter a Caveat against any person taking out Letters of Administration on the Estate and Effects of Irael Davis, late of Charleston, Merchant, deceased, until I am heard before the Ordinary. s/ Simon Mairs

I hereby enter a Caveat against any person taking out Letters of Administration on the Estate of Judith Davis, late of Charleston, Widow, deceased, until I have been heard by the Ordinary. s/Simon Mairs.

21. Proved the last Will and testament of Isaac Pool, late of Charleston, Storekeeper, deceased, by the testimony of George Timmons, one of the Subscribing Witnesses thereto: at the same time qualified Jacob Clava Levy Executor named therein.

Citation granted to John Magrath of Charleston, Merchant, to administer on the Estate and Effects of John Campbell, late of Charleston, Merchant, deceased, so far as they were left unadministered by John Strong Adams, deceased, as principal Creditor or rather agent to Creditor.

Citation granted to Richard Wall of Charleston, Storekeeper, to administer on the Estate & Effects of Sarah Grifen of Charleston, a Sole dealer, as Trustee and next of friend.

Caveat. Benjamin Fanuel Hunt, Esq., entered a Caveat against administration being granted to any person on the Estate & Effects of Ichabod Bruster, late of Wadmalaw, physician, deceased, until he is heard before the Ordinary.

[Page 25]

Proved the last Will & Testament of Montague Simons, late of Charleston, Merchant, deceased, by the testimony of D. Leitch one of the subscribing Witnesses thereto: at the same time qualified Samuel Simons and Simon Magwood, executors named therein.

23. Caveat entered by Eliza Hepburn, Widow, against Benjamin Phillips or any other person taking out letters of Admor on the Estate & Effects of John S. Hepburn, late of Charleston, Shoemaker, decd.

Irael Davis & Judith Davis Case.

24. Jacob Meyers with H. H. Bacot, Esq., his Proctor, appeared and produced the Citation which he had obtained on the 16th inst., duly certified; also I. Warnock, Esq., a Proctor for Simon Mairs who had entered a Caveat on the 20th inst. and petitioned for further time to which Mr. Bacot acceded. Whereupon ordered the hearing of Irael Davis and of Judith Davis Cases be postponed until Tuesday next the 28th inst. at 10 o'clock in the forenoon.

25. Citation granted to James Caveneau Miles of Charleston, Physician, to administer on the Estate and Effects of George Carter, late of Charleston, Physician, deceased, as principal Creditor.

27. J. P. White and L. H. Kennedy the former as Proctor for Mr. Benjamin Philips as is the latter for Mrs. Eliza Hepburn. Mr. White stated that he had no objection to the Widow of the deceased taking out Letters of Administration, but urged that there was a necessity for her doing it immediately as there were grounds for belief that if it was delayed until Friday next /the time asked for/ considerable injury would accrue to the Creditors he therefore asked that the time to be allowed should be as short as possible as there had already been a system of delay injurious to the rights of the Creditors. Mr. Kennedy stated that he rebut by affidavit the grounds of supposed injury, and only wished for time because Mrs. Hepburn was a stranger and could not therefore so readily obtain Security. The Ordinary after hearing the reasons alleged on both sides made the following order and Decree. That it was proper that Mrs. Hepburn being a stranger should be allowed a reasonable time to produce her Security

[Page 26]

but as considerable time had elapsed since she took out a Citation so as to induce a Creditor to believe that she meant to abandon and thereby caused him to obtain a Citation so as to bring his forward, the Ordinary deemed it necessary as the Property was not under legal care to limit the indulgence to Wednesday next, the 29th inst. Therefore ordered that Eliza Hepburn to produce her Securities on Wednesday next the 29th inst. at 12 o'clock in the forenoon.

28th. Judith Davis Case. Mr. Warnock in behalf of Simon Mairs who entered a Caveat on the 29 inst. withdrew his objections and consented that the Administrations should be granted to Myer Jacobs who obtained the Citation.

Irael Davis Case. Myer Jacobs and H. H. Bacot, his Proctor - and Mr. J. Warnock as Proctor for Simon Mairs appeared in Court and after progressing in the investigation of the Case it was necessary to adjourn to enable Mr. Mairs to support his account which was not sworn to and objected to by Mr. Bacot.

29th. Myer Jacobs with H. H. Bacot approved his proctor, and Simon Mairs with J. Warnock, his proctor, appeared. Mr. Bacot claimed as greatest Creditor and exhibited and assigned Judgment for $200. The Bond upon which the above judgment was obtained was given by Grace Davis in his lifetime to Philip Cohen in settlement of an account against Davis of $1052 and to secure Cohen against injury by endorsement for Davis; acct. from the President of the Planters & Mechanics Bank was produced amounting to Seven hundred and twenty nine dollars Sixty seven cents making $1781.67 - these items were introduced to show that the Judgment was for valuable consideration and not as was objected to secure Cohen against such injury as endorser alone. The $1781.67 was actually paid and furnished. The judgment was obtained by Cohen assigned to Myer Jacobs who applies for Admor as Creditor on the judgment. Mr. Warnock exhibited Simon Mairs account sworn to the amount of $1593.22, being the balance due him and produced the Cash Books or Journal of Simon Mairs to support the several items. Articles of agreement were also produced which it appears that Grace Davis was to have half of the profits of the Store for his Services and no other compensation. Simon Mairs paid a Note he endorsed for Davis $243 and held the balance of $100 on Irael Davis' note in his hand still due.

[Page 27]

Mr. Ottolingue sworn in behalf of Meyer Jacobs - Lived with Irael Davis and took an Inventory of his goods previous to the establishing the Store in the Country with Simon Mairs' goods and amt'g to about 375 dollars, assisted also in taking Inventory of Simon Mairs goods and supposed about $11.00 worth of goods. Sent up to the store in the Country by Mairs. Know of no other shipment. Witness then went to Georgetown and Irael Davis to the store near Belleville on the Congaree. Witness understood Davis, that he had sold about $13 a short time after he went up: After the death of Davis, Simon Mairs told witness he had more than two thousand dollars in the Stock. Mairs sold such goods as were inconvenienced to be brought down but to what amount Witness cannot tell. Pool sold the goods for Mairs and sent account of them on the 2 August. Mairs informed them that the Goods arrived from the Country, which was sent to Auction to be sold by Witness, and after sale Mairs stated that $660 or thereabouts was the balance due him. Sale of the goods worth more than original cost. Mairs credited goods at cost - List of debts due to the Store was sent from the Country by Pool. Adjourned until Tuesday at 10 o'clock the 5th instant.

29. Mr. John Phillips White appeared in behalf of Benjamin Phillips and moved that Eliza Hepburn who had entered a Caveat should produce her Sureties on tomorrow the 30th inst. at 10 o'clock in the forenoon. Therefore ordered that Eliza Hepburn do produce her Sureties tomorrow the 30th inst.

at 10 o'clock in the forenoon or admon be granted Benjamin Phillips on the Estate and Effects of John S. Hepburn, late of Charleston, Shoemaker,

30. Mrs. Hepburn failing to attend in person or by Proctor, qualified Benjamin Phillips administrator of the Estate and effects of John S. Hepburn, late of Charleston, Shoemaker, deceased.

30. Citation granted to John Williams of Charleston, Boarding House Keeper, to administer on the Estate and effects of James Harris, late of Charleston, Mariner, deceased as principal Creditor.

October 1. Citation granted to James Watson of Charleston, Inn Keeper, to administer on the Estate and Effects of John Izzy, late of Charleston, Mariner, deceased as next friend.

Caveat entered by Robert Limehouse against administration being granted to James Cavaneau Miles, physician, until he is heard before the Ordinary on the Estate & effects of George Carter, late of Charleston, physician, decd.

[Page 28]

October 1. Proved the last Will and testament of Sophie Faures of Charleston, Widow, by the testimony of Robert Clark one of the subscribing witnesses to the same: and also the Codicil to the said Will by the Testimony of Payenne-ville a subscribing Witness to the same. At the same time qualified James Joseph Delesse, executor, named therein. Dr. Jean Dumaine also accepted his appointment of guardian by the Will of said deceased to the person of Pierre Charles Auguste le Vasseur, a mulatto boy named in said Will & Codicil - the original Will and Codicil being in the French language, a translation thereof was presented by Mr. Delesse the executor and sworn to by Frederick Delesse who translated it.

Qualified Richard Wall administrator on the Estate and effects of Sarah Griffin, late of Charleston, sole dealer, as next friend and trustee in the absence of the husband.

Qualified John Magrath administrator de bonis non of the Estate and effects of John Campbell, late of Charleston, decd., as principal Creditor - so far as they were unadministered by John Strong Adams, decd.

2d. Proved the last Will & testament of John Filbin late of St. James Parish Goose Creek, Carpenter, deceased by the testimony of Joseph Hardy one of the subscribing Witnesses thereto.

4. Proved the last Will and testament of Jean Sudrie, late of Charleston, Ship-Carpenter, deceased, by the testimony of Dominique Dison one of the subscribing witnesses thereto: at the same time qualified Jean La Fons

executor named therein: The Will was presented in the French language with a translation by James Joseph Delesse duly sworn to.

7. Caveat entered by Thomas Flynn of Charleston, Grocer, against administration being taken out by any person on the Estate and effects of John Tommy, late of Charleston, Carpenter, deceased.

Citation granted to James Leman of Charleston, Merchant, to administer on the Estate and effects of John Smyth, late of Charleston, Merchant, deceased, as next of Kin.

Irael Davis Case. Myer Jacobs with H. H. Bacot, Esq., his proctor, and Simon Mairs with B. B. Smith, his proctor, appeared. The Court proceeded to the examination of the Case: when it appeared that Myer Jacobs

[Page 29]

substantiated his claim to the amount of $1781.67 and Simon Maire to $1593.22 and the question in dispute being who was the greatest Creditor, Mr. Smith admitted the amount and consequently that administration should be granted to Myer Jacobs. Wherefore qualified Myer Jacobs administrator of the Estate and effects of Judith Davis, late of Charleston, Widow, deceased, as next of Kin and, Qualified Meyer Jacobs administrator of the Estate & Effects of Israel Davis, late of Charleston, Merchant, decd.,

8. Citation granted to Thomas Flyn of Charleston, Grocer, to administer on the Estate & Effects of John Tommy, late of Charleston, Carpenter, deceased, as principal Creditor.

Citation granted to Benjamin Fanuil Hunt of Charleston, Attorney at Law, to administer on the Estate of Ichabod Bruster, late of John's Island, Physician, deceased.

12. Proved the last Will and testament of William Winbourne, late of Charleston, Soldier, in the First Regiment of United States Artillery, deceased by the testimony [of] John Kenny one of the subscribing witnesses thereto - at the same [time] qualified John Spence executor therein named.

14. Proved the last Will and testament of Peter Pye, late of St. John's Parish, Blacksmith, deceased, by the testimony of James Byrd, one of the subscribing witnesses thereto: At the same time qualified William Pye and Stephen Pye executors named therein.

Proved the last Will and testament of William McClure, late of Charleston, Merchant, deceased, by the testimony of Alexander Brown, one of the subscribing witnesses to the same.

15. Qualified Clinton Cregier, administrator of the Estate and Effects of Henry Anderson, late of Charleston, Mariner, deceased.

Qualified Thos Flyn, administrator of Estate and Effects of John Tommy, late of Charleston, Carpenter, deceased

18. Granted to George Dantzman Letters ad Coleigendum bona of the Estate of George Steinert, late of St. Stephen's Parish, Storekeeper, deceased, and Citation to administer to the said George Dantzman and Conrad Frederick Marthieson, both of Charleston, Merchants, on the Estate & effects of the said deceased as principal Creditors.

[Page 30]

1813. Mr. James Hall of Charleston, Stonecutter, came into Court and accepted the appointment of Guardian to the child Pierre Charles Auguste Le Vasseur, named in the last Will and Testament of Sophie Faures, late of Charleston, Widow, deceased, and requested the same to be recorded.

Citation granted to Daniel Ravenel of Charleston, Attorney at Law, to administer on the Estate and Effects of Damaris Elizabeth Ravenel, late of St. John's Parish, Berkeley, Widow, deceased, so far as they were left unadministered by Daniel Mazyck with the Will annexed, as next of Kin.

19. Qualified James Leman administrator of Estate & Effects of John Smyth, late of Charleston Merchant, deceased.

Citation granted to Jacob Malvey, Esquire, Spanish Counsul, to administer on the Estate & Effects of Jose Vidal, late of Charleston, Merchant, deceased, as next friend.

21. Proved the last Will and Testament of Helen Perry, late of Charleston, Widow, deceased, by the testimony of Amelia H. McCall one of the subscribing witnesses thereto: at the same time qualified Sophia T. Shepheard, executrix and William Trescot, executor named therein.

Proved the last Will and Testament of Alexander McBride, late of Christ Church Parish, Overseer, deceased, by the testimony of Plowden Weston, Esquire, one of the subscribing witnesses thereto: at the same time qualified William Smith, otherwise called William Mason Smith, executor named therein.
22. Citation granted to Joaquin Jose of Charleston, Mariner, to administer on the Estate & effects of Joaquin de Silva, late of Charleston, Mariner, deceased, as next of Kin.

23. Citation granted to John Gibbes of Charleston, Planter, to administer on the Estate and effects of Ann Gibbes, late of Charleston, deceased, as next of Kin.

Citation granted to Eleanor Douglass of St. James Parish, Widow, to administer on Estate and Effects of John Filbin, late of same place, Carpenter, deceased, in behalf of herself and of George Douglas her son, a minor, the said Eleanor and George being the sole legatees and next of Kin with Will annexed.

[Page 31]

October 27th. I hereby enter a Caveat against any person taking out Letters of Administration on the Estate and Effects of Jose Vidal, late of Havana, Merchant, deceased, until I am heard before the Ordinary. Wm. Frean

Proved the last Will and Testament of Samuel William Smith, late of Charleston, Attorney at Law, deceased, by the testimony of John S-- Trescot one of the subscribing witnesses to the same and on 28th Qualified Mary G. Smith, executrix named therein

29. I hereby enter a Caveat against any person or persons taking out Letters of Administration on the Estate and effects of George Stinert, late of St. Stephen's Parish, Storekeeper, decd., until I am heard before the Ordinary. Alex'r. Black

Qualified Joaquin Jose of Charleston, Mariner, Administrator of Joaquin de Silva, late of Charleston, Mariner, deceased.

Qualified Jacob Mulvey, Esq., Spanish Consul, administrator of Jose Vidal, late of Charleston formerly of the Havana, Merchant, deceased.

Citation granted to Elizabeth Beard of Charleston, Widow, to administer on the Estate & Effects of Ann Collis, late of Charleston, Spinster, deceased, as next of Kin.

Qualified William Muir, executor named in the last Will and testament of William McClure, late of Charleston, Merchant, deceased.

30. Citation granted Honora Pyne of Charleston, Widow, to administer on the Estate and Effects of John Pyne, late of Charleston, Planter, deceased, as next of Kin.

Citation granted Daniel Henderson of Charleston, Gunsmith, to administer on the Estate & effects of James Holton, late of Charleston, Gentleman, deceased as

Citation granted to Anna Caroline Lesesne of Charleston, Widow, to administer on the Estate and Effects of Thomas Lesesne, late of Charleston, Planter, deceased, as next of Kin.

Qualified John Gibbes of Charleston, Planter, Administer of Ann Gibbes, late of Charleston, deceased.

30. I do hereby enter a Caveat against any person taking out Letters of Administration on the Estate and effects of George Steinert, late of St. Stephens Parish, Storekeeper, decd., until I am heard before the Ordinary. P. de Condres & Co.

[Page 32]

Nov. 5. Citation granted Francis Sylvester Custer to administer on the Estate & Effects of John Filben, late of St. James Goose [Creek], as next friend in behalf of Eleanor Douglas & Charles Douglas, The P. Eleanor has returned the Citn. granted on the 23rd unpublished.

Nov. 6. Citation granted William Gilchrist and John Gilchrist, Roberson County, North Carolina, farmer, to administer on the Estate & Effects of Archibald Lusk, late of St. John's Parish, Taylor, deceased, as next of Kin,

Nov. 5. Citation granted to Mary Pyne Hutchinson, to administer on the Estate & Effects of Thomas Holland Hutchinson, late of Charleston, Planter, deceased; The Citation granted 13 July 1813 and lost and never published.

Qualified Ann Caroline Lesesne, Administratrix of Thomas Lesesne, late of Charleston, planter, deceased.

8. Proved the last Will and testament of Ann Timmons, late of Charleston, Widow, deceased, by, the testimony of Charles C. Chitty, one of the subscribing witnesses to the same: at the same time qualified Jacob Sass and James Drummond, executors named therein.

12. Qualified William Gilchrist of Robeson County, North Carolina, administrator of the Estate & Effects of Archibald Lusk, late of St. Stephen's Parish, Taylor, decd.

13. Qualified Francis Sylvester Curtis administrator of the Estate & Effects of John Filbin, late of St. James' Goosecreek, Carpenter, decd., with his Will annexed.

15. Qualified Elizabeth Beard of Charleston, Widow, Administratrix of the Estate & Effects of Ann Collis, late of Charleston, Spinster, deceased, as next of Kin.

18. Proved the last Will & Testament of Samuel Guilow, late of Charleston, Taylor, deceased, by the testimony of William Miller, one of the subscribing witnesses thereto: at the same time qualified Jane Guilow and Benjamin Cudworth, executrix and executor named therein.

19. Qualified Mary Pyne Hutchinson of Charleston, Widow, Administratrix of Estate and Effects of Thomas Holland Hutchinson, late of Charleston, Planter, deceased, as next of Kin.

20. Qualified Anson Brewster of Hartford, Connecticut, administrator of the Estate and Effects of Ichabod Brewster, late of Wadmalaw, Physician, deceased, as next of Kin: Benj'n Fanuiel Hunt to whom a Citation had been granted on the 8th Octr. last, came into Court and acknowledged he said Anson Brewster to be the brother of the said Icabod Brewster and declined in his favor.

[Page 33]

George Steinert's Case. 30th Octr. 1813 in the Court of Ordinary Mr. Holmes in behalf [of] George Dantzman and Conrad Frederick Malthiessen who had obtained the Citation on the 18 instant to administer jointly on the Estate of George Steinert, late of St. Stephen's Parish, Storekeeper, deceased, together with the above persons, and Mr. Codgell in behalf of Philip Louis DeCoudries who had entered a Caveat against administration being granted to any person before he was heard before the Ordinary, all appeared in Court. Mr. Holmes moved that administration should be granted Dantzman and Malthiessen, they having returned the Citation duly published. Mr. Cogdell opposed the same on the grounds that De Coudres was a greater Creditor than Maltheissen; and that DeCoudres ought to be joined in the administration with Dantzman in preference to Malthiessen because Maltiessen was really a Creditor only to the amount of about $300: for that the Note if $3,800 upon which he claimed jointly with Dantzman was the property of Dantzman and only placed in his hands as a collateral Security for the return of Note lent to Dantzman to the amt. of $300; which De Coudres was actually a Creditor to the amount of $912. Mr. Holmes then took another ground and insisted that Malthiessen whom it was attempted to deprive of any participation in the administration, was entitled to it in preference to every other Claimant, being the holder of the Note of $3,800 drawn by Steinert in his lifetime and made payable to George Dantzman or order which Note was endorsed by Danzman and passed to Malthiessen; and being negotiable and being in the possession of Mr. Mallheissen made him the greatest Creditor.

Mr. Cogdel denied that the Note was negotiable in as much Dantzman had in his possession (which was produced in Court and admitted by Matthiessen) and is acknowledgment in Matthiess's own hand writing in which he recognized distinctly the right of Dantzman to the said Note and engage expressly to return it on Dantzman's retiring the Note of $300 above mentioned for the return of which the Note of $3800 was placed in the hands of Matthiessen as collateral security only - Mr. Holmes again insisted that the Note was negotiable upon the face of it and that the Court had no right to go further into evidence to ascertain who was the real owner of the Note, and that Maltiessen being in possession was the ostensible Creditor, and therefore entitled at

[Page 34]

least to a participation in the administration.

The Case was then submitted to the Court when the following Decision was made. The Ordinary is of opinion from a review of the Case that George Dantzman and Philip Louis DeCoudres are the two greatest Creditors. Mr. Mallhiessen has no claim on the estate of Stinert but of $300 - His holding the Note of $3,800 ought not to avail him, since he has under his own hand declared that he had no claim to the Note but that it was the property of Danzman and only held as collateral Security for the return of Note to the Amount of $300 which Notes have been tendered to him and he has declaimed receiving the Ordinary therefore grants the admor to George Dantzman and Philip Louis De Coudres as the two greatest Creditors.

George Steinert's Case. 31 Octr 1813. In the Court of Ordinary. after the above decision, Mr. Washington Potter came into Court and requested that if Letters of Administration had not been issued to Dantzman that the Ordinary would revoke the decision and suspend the business and have the Case open for further discussion for that the Note upon which Dantzman had claimed the Admor had together with all his other property been to assigned - - - right of himself and of a Mr. Clark of Philadelphia for whom he was agent and that therefore, under such circumstances it would be highly improper that Dantzman should have any participation in the Admor and that he wished Mr. Mallhiessen to be his representative. As the Case seemed to require investigation the Court consented to let the Case stand open.

George Steinert Case. 6 Novr. 1813. In the Court of Ordinary upon further investigation it was found that the Note above mentioned was returned by Dantzman to satisfy several other Creditors - Mr. Potter therefore consented that Admor should be granted conformably to the above decree: the Case being open Mr. Mallhiessen again renewed his application but a Caveat was entered by S. Bidgood who had a claim of $1176 - against Mallhiessen but Consented that the De Coudres should be appointed.

[Page 35]

The following day was then named to give an opportunity to all parties to come to some conclusion: when Mr. DeCoudres appeared in Court and stated that he had bought up the claim of Mallhiesses and Dantzman that they had consented to his being appointed alone. Whereupon

November 19. Qualified Philip Louis DeCoudres administrator of the Estate and effects of George Stienert late of St. Stephen's Parish, Storekeeper. deceased.

24. Proved the last Will and testament of James Smith late of Charleston, Carpenter, deceased, by the testimony of Henry Alexander DeSaussure, Esq.,

one of the subscribing witnesses thereto: at the same time qualified Henrietta Smith, executrix named therein.

Qualified William Wightman of Charleston, Jeweler, administrator of the Estate and Effects of Ann Paul Emanuel Sigismend de Montmorency, Luxembourg, late of Paris, Gentleman, deceased, William Craft Esq., the former administrator having some time since come into Court and surrendered his Letters of Administration on the Estate in favor of Elnathan Haskell who declined Qualifying in favor of Whiteman.

Proved the last Will and testament of James Houlton, late of Charleston, deceased, by the testimony of William Austin, Jr., one of the subscribing witnesses thereto, and also the Codicil to the Will by the testimony of the same person, one of the subscribing witnesses thereto: on the same day qualified Richard Baker North, executor therein named.

[in margin]

25. Letters ad. Colligendum, bona granted to Joseph Johnson of Charleston Physician, on the Estate & Effects of Peter Freneau, late of Charleston, Gentleman, decd., & Citation to the said Joseph Johnson to administer on the Estate as Principal auditor.

26. Citation granted to Honoria Pyne of Charleston, Widow, to administer on the Estate & effects of Obrien Smith, late of Charleston, Planter, deceased, as next of Kin with the Will annexed.

Citation granted to Josiah Taylor of Charleston, Factor, to administer on the Estate and Effects of James Wilson, late of Charleston, Merchant, deceased as principal Creditor. Citation granted to Nicholas Dovergne of Charleston, Mariner, to administer on the Estate and effects of Lege Lenude, late of Charleston, Mariner, deceased, as next of Kin.

December 3d. Qualified Josiah Taylor of Charleston, Factor, administrator of the Estate & effects of James Wilson, late of Charleston, Merchant, deceased.

[Page 36]

December 3d Qualified Joseph Johnson of Charleston, Physician, administrator of the Estate & Effects of Peter Freneau, late of Charleston, Gentleman, deceased.

John Parks Case. In the Court of Ordinary 6 December 1813.

Henry Findley the uncle of Sarah Parks, a minor daughter of John Parks, late of Charleston, Shoemaker, late of Charleston, deceased, came into Court and petitioned for a prohibition to stop the sale of certain property under an order of this Court as the property of Samuel Parks, the said property belonging to the Estate of John Parks in which his niece, the said minor, was interested: upon investigation the Court discovered the estates were blended and had not been divided by any proper authority & no account had been returned of either of the said Estates, therefore Ordered the sale to be suspended until the parties were heard and the matter properly examined.

8th. John S. Richardson Esq., Proctor for Henry Findley, and J. P. White as Proctor for Maria Jacques, late Maria Parks, approved in Court Mr. White stated that an order having arrested the sale of the Estate of Samuel Parks in consequence of a belief that the Property of John Parks was implicated, he moved that time be allowed to make a return of the Estate of John Parks. Mr. Richardson opposed the motion on the ground that there were strong reasons to take up the business, should be brought on and therefore moved that a. Citation be granted in the name of Henry Findley as next of Kin, in order to make a legal representation of the Estate of John Parks. Mr. White apprehended that there was no occasion to take the Estate out of the hands of the admin. of Samuel Parks who was invested on his own right and in the right of Sarah Parks, the minor as her guardian. Mr. Richardson urged that there ought to be some process to take possession of the Estate of John Parks as there was no legal representation of the Estate.

The Ordinary decided that there was no need of any process issuing as the admin. of Samuel Parks was liable and his Security for the Estate of Samuel Parks who must acct. for John Parks Estate _____ he having been admor but that a Citation should issue to make a legal representation of John Parks' Estate to whom the Admin. of Saml. Parks may acct. therefore the suspension of the sale must continue until administration be granted on John Parks: accordingly.

[Page 37]

8th. Citation granted Henry Findley to administer on the Estate Effects of John Parks, late of Charleston, Shoemaker, deceased, as next of Kin, so far as they were left unadministrated by Samuel Parks, decd.

December 7. Qualified Nicholas Douergne, administrator of the Estate & Effects of Lege Simide, late of Charleston, Mariner, decd.

13. Caveat entered by Philip Moore, Cabinetmaker, & William Henderly, Bell Hanger, both of Charleston against any person taking out Letters of Administration on the Estate & Effects of Philip Echills, late of Charleston, Storekeeper, deceased, until they are heard before the Ordinary.

15. Qualified Ann Morris, late Ann Evans & executrix named in the last Will and testament of Daniel Evans, late of James Island, deceased.

Citation /special/ granted to Louise Aiquier, a Creditor to cite Jean Joseph Durban, admor of Jerome Lardil to appear on Friday next the 17 instant to show cause why he had returned an inventory & appraisement and made an acct. of his admor.

17. Proved the last Will & testament of Andre Antoine Charles Lechay late of Charleston, deceased, by the testimony of Benoist Vinesse, one of the subscribing witnesses at the same time qualified Jaquelin Francois Pibarte Courtin Lechais executrix named therein. Will was produced in the French language and the translation attested by Mr. Chaneognes who translated it.

Proved the last Will and testament of Hannah Forsby, late of Charleston, Spinster, deceased, by the testimony of James P. Carroll one of the subscribing witnesses of the same.

Jerome Lardil's Case. Mr. Charles Elliott appeared with Mr. Dunbar, the administrator of Jerome Lardil who had been cited to appear this day to show cause why he had not returned as Inventory and appraisement and made an account of the administration, and stated that it was entirely through ignorance that he had not done so: that he made an appraisement regularly as the time but being a foreigner did not know the course he ought to have pursued: he now tendered the inventory and appraisement and moved for further time to make his acct. which with consent of person appearing for Mr. Arquier was granted.

[Page 38]

1813 December. The Ordinary therefore named Tuesday the 21 Dec. inst: for the said administrator to account.

Citation granted to Samuel A. Greenland and Esther Susanna, his wife, to administer on Estate and Effects of Susanna Johnson, late of [St.] Thomas Parish, Widow, deceased, as next of Kin.

18. Citation granted to Philip Moore, Cabinet Maker, and William Hedderly, House Bell Hanger, to administer on the Estate and effects of Philip Echells, late of Charleston, Storekeeper, deceased, as next friends.

Citation granted to Jacob Pruit of the 18th Regiment of Infantry in the United States Army to administer on the Estate and effects of Peter Pruit, dec., a soldier in the said Regiment, as next of Kin.

20. We hereby enter a Caveat against Philip Moore and William Hedderly and all others taking out Letters of Administration of the estate and effects of Philip Echells, or Hanckells, until we can be heard before the Ordinary. McCall & Hayne, Proctors for L. Wright.

John Parks Case. In the Court of Ordinary 20 Dec. 1813.
Henry Findley who had obtained a Citation to administer on the Estate of John Parks appeared with Richardson his Proctor and produced the Citation

regularly published. Mr. Richardson moved that Letters of Administration be granted to Mr. Findley when Mrs. Jacques, late Maria Parks, by Mrs. J. P. White, her Proctor opposed the granting of Administration on the following grounds & that Mrs. Jacques was the admix of Samuel Parks who was admor of John Parks and was of consequence more capable of giving an acct. than any other person. 2nd that she was the legal representative of Sarah Parks, the minor, who was entitled to a part of the Estate of John Paris: and 3rd. because she was entitled to a distributive part of the Estate of John Parks and witness stated that she was a creditor. After entering into argument in support of the claim of Mrs. Jacques. Mr. Richardson in reply stated that the admix. of Samuel Parks having intermeddled since the admor had been granted, it was therefore workable at the decretion of the Ordinary and on this occasion there was Particular reasons for such a revocation as this intermarriage was with a stranger: this was urged not with a view to deprive her of the admor of Samuel Parks, but to show that she was not on that acct. entitled to the admor of

[Page 39]

John Parks' Estate. She further urged that minor objections then might be there was one which he deemed insurmountable, namely that she was femme covert and could not without the assent of her husband enter into Bond: her husband being now absent from and out of the limits of the State. She having intermarried with Mr. Jacques of New York: he admitted that his client Findley was no creditor and contended that Mrs. Jacques could not at present be considered as one that Mr. Findley although of no kin to John Parks yet he was the uncle to Sarah Parks, the minor, and therefore interested in her behalf and it was only on her acct. he wished for the Administration. Mr. Mouzon was sworn and proved that Mr. Findley was a respectable free holder in Charleston District and could give good security and concluded that Mr. Findley was the proper person to be appointed - Mr. White in reply stated that altho Mrs. Jacques was a femme covert she had a power of attorney which would enable her to give Bond and it was not deemed sufficiently explicit one more ample could be obtained from New York and that the administration of the Estate was such that it would not receive injury by the delay: that Mr. J. Richardson a respectable freeholder would join in her Bond These were briefly the arguments urged by the Council on both sides after which the case was submitted to the Court.

Decision - In adverting to the circumstances of the Case the first point which came to the consideration of the Court is whether Mrs. Jacques as Admix of Saml. Parks was entitled to the Admon of Saml Parks' Estate. That an executor is the Exor of all the Estate, to which his testator was Executor is a settled point, because in legal implication the testator is supposed to have Confidence in the Executor of his own appointment and may therefore be supposed to extend that confidence to his Executor, but the law varies with respect to Admor when the Admor being the creditor of the Ordinary no Confidence can be implied from the decd. to Admor and much less to his successor and because Administrations are revocable and grantable according to the exegences of each case at the discretion of the Ordinary. The 3d point is whether Mrs. Jacques is competent to receive the Admor. The Common doctrine that a wife cannot bind the

[Page 40]

husband for anything but the necessaries without his assent is not to be questioned: yet the practice of this Court and I think the law varies when she gives bond as Admix. It is not necessary however to decide on this point at present, as there are other motives which induce the Ordinary: the avowed purpose of Mrs. Jacques marrying and being about to leave the State to reside at New York is alone sufficient to induce the Ordinary either to withhold Admor from her or to join some other person with her in the Administration agreeably to the directions of the Act: which it might be proper to do in the present case, were it not inadvisable to join two persons in an administration where the parties are likely to be struggling against each other. Under all the circumstances of the Case, it appears to me that Mr. Findley is the most proper person to take the Administration because he is the uncle of the minor who is entitled to them jointly of the Estate of John Parks: because he was acquainted with the property of John Parks before Saml. Parks took possession and can therefore discriminate better than Mrs. Jacques who has innocently and inadvertently, in administering her late husband's Estate, blended the two Estates: and moreover because there ought to be some person disinterested in the Estate yet interested in the welfare of the minor to receive an acct. from the Admins. of Samuel Parks. The Ordinary therefore feels it his duty to grant Admor to Mr. Findley upon his giving good and sufficient Security.

22. Citation granted to Jane Elizabeth Page of Charleston, Widow, to administer on the Estate & effects of William Page, late of Charleston, a Soldier in the 1st Regiment of Artillery in the service of the Unites States. deceased, as next of Kin.

24. Citation granted Robert Gibbs of James Island, Planter, to administer on the Estate and Effects of Mary Gibbs, late of same place, Widow, deceased, as next of Kin.

Philip Echells or Hackells Case. In the Court of Ordinary 24 Dec. 1813 George W. Cross in behalf of Philip Moore and William Hedderly who had Jointly obtained a Citation on the 18th. instant to administer on the Estate and Effects of Philip Echells or Hackells returned

[Page 41]

the same duly published; and moved that Letters of Administration be granted to William Hadderly. Philip Moore having declined in favor of the former, when Mr. McCall in behalf of Lochlin Wright moved for a postponement having entered a Caveat on the 20th instant, and stated that the only ground he had for a postponement was that he had not seen his client since the time when the Caveat was entered and that he did not fully communicate the nature of his claim to the Administration further than he stated generally that he was a creditor but did not say to what amount: Mr. Cross objected to the postponement because he had evidence to produce that Lochlin Wright so far from being a creditor was a debtor to Heckells he having obtained a judgment against Wright for Hackell not long since which being judgment up & 2 Executions issued one of fi fa and the other of La. Ca. were returned N. E. J. and Nulia bona: and more over it was stated that there had been an attempt to rob the premises of the deceased and the holiday approaching it was absolutely necessary that some person should take possession and guard the house. Upon which the Case was submitted to the Court. Decision.

The Court is always disposed to give time when there is a reasonable ground for such indulgence: but the time allowed by law having expired and Lochlin Wright not appearing nor instructing his Proctor on the merits of his Claim: and from the evidence produced that a judgment had been obtained so lately against him by the deceased rendered it very improbable whether he could support his claim as creditor: and there being a necessity from the frequent robberies lately committed, that the property should be in legal custody this being the day before the Christmas Holidays. The Court determined that it would [be] more to the advantage of all concerned that the Administration should be immediately granted to Mr. Hadderly. Whereupon qualified William Hadderly of Charleston, House Bell Hanger, administrator of the Estate and Effects of Philip Hackell, late of Charleston, Storekeeper, as next friend.

[Page 42]

December 28, 1813. Citation granted to Samuel Nobbs of Charleston Neck to administer on the Estate and Effects of Richard Henry Peyton, late of Charleston, Attorney at Law, deceased, as next friend.

29. Qualified Samuel Ashley Greenland of St. James Parish Goosecreek, Planter, to administer on the Estate and effects of Susanna Johnson, late of St. Thomas Parish, Widow, deceased.

30. Proved the last Will and testament of John Fowler Percy, late of [St.] James Parish Santee, Planter, deceased, by the Testimony of Jacob Mitchell one of the subscribing witnesses thereto, at the Same time qualified Joseph D. Legare executor therein named.

31. Proved the last Will and testament of Susanna Wilson, late of Charleston ton, Spinster deceased, by the testimony of James Drummond: the only Subscribing witness, William Lee being dead. At the same time qualified Thomas Drayton, Esq., executor therein named.

Jose Vidal's Case. In the Court of Ordinary 1st January 1814. Mr. Molvey, the Spanish Counsul who had taken out Letters of Administration of the Estate and Effects of Jose Vidal, late of Havana, Merchant, deceased, came into Court and surrendered his administration to Ramon Videl the Copartner and creditor of Jose Vidal: and having exhibited an Acct. of his transactions which being to the satisfaction of the Ordinary; Whereupon qualified Ramon Vidal of Havana, Merchant, Administrator of the Estate and effects of Jose Vidal, late of Havana, Merchant, deceased:

1814 January 3. Proved the last Will and testament of Alexander Forbes, late of Charleston, Merchant, deceased, by the testimony of George Lusher, one of the subscribing witnesses thereto: at the same time qualified William Smith, executor therein named.

5th Proved the last Will and testament of William Sparkman, late of St. John's Parish, Berkeley, Overseer, deceased, by the testimony of S. S. Owens, one of the subscribing witnesses to the same. At the same time qualified Anne Sparkman, executrix therein named.

Proved the last Will and testament of McMillan Campbell, late of Charleston, Auctioneer, deceased, by the testimony of Thomas Millikin one

[Page 43]

of the subscribing witnesses thereto: at the same time qualified Henrietta Campbell, executrix therein named.

January 8th. Citation granted to John Cordes Prioleau of Charleston, Factor, to administer on the Estate and Effects of Mary Grimbal, late of Charleston, Widow, as next of Kin.

11. Qualified Samuel Nobbs of Charleston Neck, Esquire, to administer on Estate & Effects of Richard Henry Payton, late of Charleston Attorney at Law, deceased.

Citation granted to William Taylor of St. Thomas Parish, planter, and Sarah Taylor, late Sarah Jaudon, his wife to administer on the Estate & Effects of Daniel Jaudon, late of St. Thomas Parish planter, deceased.

Citation granted to John Roche of Charleston, Grocer, to administer on the Estate & Effects of Oliver Eckland, late of Charleston, Mariner, deceased, as principal Creditor.

13. Qualified Henry Findly administrator of Estate & Effects of John Parks, late of Charleston, Shoemaker, deceased.

12. Proved last Will and testament of Christopher Williman, late of Charleston, deceased, by the testimony of John M. Schnieble as subscribing witness

to the same; also the Codicil to the said Will by the same witness & on the same day qualified Mary Peters, Margaret Bethune and Gilbert Davidson executrixes & executor therein named.

14. Citation granted to John Smith Dorrill, Mariner, and Josiah James Dorrill, Gentleman, both of Charleston, to administer on the Estate and Effects of Edward Dorrill, late of Charleston, Merchant, deceased, as next of Kin, so far as they were left unadministered by Richard Robinson Stowe who is absent from and out of the limits of the State.

15th. Citation granted to Thomas Jones Horsey to administer on the Estate & Effects of Thomas Horsey, late of St. Philip's Parish, Gardner, deceased, with the Will annexed.

14th. Proved the last Will and Testament of Rebecca Smith, late of Charleston, Widow, by the testimony of William Ladson, one of the subscribing witnesses thereto; at the same time qualified James William Gadsden Executor named therein.

[Page 44]

January 17, 1814. In the Court of Ordinary. The Honorable William Johnson, Junior, came into Court and renounced his Executorship of the Estate of Thomas Horsey, late of St. Philip's Parish, gardener, deceased.

Miss Mary B. Johnston enters a Caveat against any order of sale being granted on the Estate & Effects of Susanna Johnston, late of St. Thomas' Parish, deceased, until she is heard before the Ordinary.

20. Qualified Peter Rowe of Orangeburg, Administrator of the Estate and Effects of James Quin, late of Charleston Deputy Sheriff, deceased. N.B. Mr. Rouse stated that he never authorized Mr. Thomas Warnock to say that he did not wish the administration: See Page 21 of the minute Book under date of the 10th. August 1813.

22, Citation granted to Martha Broer of Charleston, Widow, to administer on the Estate and Effects of Thos. Broer, late of Christ Church Parish, Ship-Carpenter, deceased, as next of Kin.

21. Qualified Thomas Jones Horsey administrator with the Will annexed of Thomas Horey, late of St. Philip's Parish, Gardner, deceased.

24. Caveat entered by William Clement in behalf of the Widow & Children of David Johnston against any order of sale being granted to Saml. A. Greenland of the Estate of Susanna Johnston, until he is heard before the Ordinary.

Caveat entered by Charles Johnston to the same effect.

26. Citation granted to Elias Couturier and Robert James Kirk[?] of St. John's Parish, Berkeley, planter, to administer on the Estate & Effects of Isaac Couturier, junior, late of same place, planter, deceased, as next of Kin.

Qualified John Cordes Prioleau of Charleston, Factor, Administrator of the Estate and Effects of Mary Grimball of Charleston, Widow, deceased.

27. Proved the last Will and Testament of Isaac Couturier, late of St. John's Parish, Berkeley, planter, deceased, by the testimony of Frances Marion, one of the subscribing witnesses to the same: at the same time qualified Elias Couturier and Joseph Couturier executors named therein.

[Page 45]

1814 January 28th. Qualified Martha Broer of Charleston, Widow, administratrix of the Estate and Effects of Thomas Broer, late of Christ Church Parish, Ship-Carpenter, deceased.

Proved the last Will and Testament of the Reverend Doctor Isaac Shockton Keith, late of Charleston, one of the Pastors of the Independent or Congregational Church of Charleston, deceased, by the testimony of Thomas Wright Bacot, Esq. one of the subscribing witnesses of the same.

31. Citation granted to Maurice Harvey Cooper of St. Stephen's Parish, Planter and administrator or the Estate & Effects of Jane Cooper, late of same place, Widow, deceased, as next of Kin.

Citation granted to William D. Shaw to administer on Estate & Effects of Frances Palmer, late of Charleston, deceased / a free person / as principal Creditor.

Feb. 7. Citation granted to Polly Jennings of Charleston /a free person of Color/ to administer on the Estate and Effects of Jacob Smith, late of same place, Mariner, deceased, as principal Creditor

8. Citation granted to Ann Morgan of Charleston, Widow, to administer on the Estate & Effects of Abraham DeCosta, late of Savannah, Georgia, Merchant, deceased, as next of Kin.

Qualified John Axson an executor named in the last Will & Testament of John Fowler Percy, late of St. James' Parish Santee, planter, deceased.

Citation granted to Anthony Preston of St. George's Parish, Planter, deceased, as next of Kin, so far as they left unadministered by John Smyth, deceased.

9. Citation granted to William Burrows Foster of Chas., Gentleman, on the Estate & Effects of Mary Foster, late of Charleston, Widow, as next of Kin.

11. Qualified William D. Shaw administrator of the Estate & Effects of Francis Palmer, late of Charleston, a free dealer, deceased.

Proved the last Will & Testament of John Parker, late of Charleston, Wine Merchant, deceased, by the testimony of James Carson there being no subscribing witness thereto at the same time William Drayton & Jacob Eberhard August Steinmetz executors named therein.

[Page 46]

1814 Feb. 11. Citation granted to Robert Wood, Boarding House-keeper, of St. Andrew's Parish, to administer on the Estate & Effects of Ann Shearwood, late of St. Andrew's Parish, Widow, deceased, as principal Creditor.

Qualified Elias Couturier & Robert James Kirk both of [St.] John's Berkeley, planter, Administrators of the Estate & Effects of Isaac Couturier, junior, decd.

Susanna Johnston's Case. In the Court of Ordinary 12 February 1814. Mr. William Clements in behalf of Charles Johnston, Mary B. Johnston, John Wm. Johnston & Eleanor Johnston, Widow, of David Johnston deceased, appeared in Court and presented a petition that the Administration be granted on the twenty-ninth day of December 1813, to Samuel Ashley Greenland be revoked and that no order of sale be granted to the said Administrator for the reasons set forth in the Petition. Mr. John B. White appeared in behalf of Mr. Greenland, and objected to the revocation of the Administration on the grounds that it was regularly obtained, the Citation having been published and Bond with good security having been executed by Mr. Greenland the Administrator and contended that the Administrator was the best Judge whether a sale was necessary or not and that no one else could pretend to have the requests information on the business of the estate so fully as he whom the Ordinary had authorized to investigate the matter; and that Admor had stated in his petition that the Estate was indebted & property unproductive wherefore he prayed for leave to sell and concluded by saying the party asking a revocation had slept on their rights and ought now to obtain the purpose of their prayer.

Mr. Clements admitted that the party asking a revocation were blameable in not having earlier attended to the business but that this was a Court of Equity and this was a fit subject of discretion for the Ordinary: That the Citation had been obtained in the Name of Samuel A. Greenland & Susanna his wife late Susanna Johnston, but that the Admor had been granted to Saml. A. Greenland alone without his wife joining with him in whose right he claimed which the Johnstons contend was a Surprise: for that which they may not have objected to Greenland when joined his wife in the Bond, yet they did now object and would have done so at the time, had they been aware of the circumstances, to Greenland taking it alone: That there was

[Page 47] [large portion of this page missing]

... qualified Peter Laurans named executor therein The Will was produced in the French Language with translation attested Fredk. Tavil.

11. Citation granted to John Calvitt of St. Stephen's Parish, Planter to Administer on the Estate & Effects of Edward Calvitt, late of the same place, Planter, decd. as next of Kin.

8. Qualified Ellis Smith, a Soldier in the Regiment of Infantry in the United States Service, administrator on the Estate & Effects of Isaac Smith, a Soldier in said Regt., deceased..

10. Qualified John Ruberry of Charleston, House Carpenter, to Administer on the Estate & Effects of William Ruberry, late of Charleston House Carpenter decd.

Qualified Catherine Caborne of St. Andrew's Parish, Widow, Administratrix on the Estate & Effects of George Caborne, late of same place, Planter, deceased.

Qualified James Mackie, an executor named in the last Will & testament of William Moer, late of Charleston, Cooper, deceased.

Qualified John McIntosh of Charleston, Mariner, administrator of Estate & Effects of Rebecca Morrill of Christ Church Parish, Widow, decd.

[Page 48] [large portion of this page missing]

was now so short she was not prepared with her Surities. The Ordinary informed the parties that he had agreed to indulge Mr. Clements until Friday next, but that when he did so, he expected that the other party would have been informed of the Postponement so as to prevent Mr. & Mrs. Greenland from attending at Court under every inconvenience, and as they had received no notice of the Postponement & considering the inconvenience, they had been put to in attending, the Ordinary was strongly disposed to qualify them and grant them the Administration: but Mr. Clements is absent and he might not have understood that he was to give notice to the opposite party, the Ordinary adjourned the Court to Friday the 22d. inst; at 11 o'clock in the forenoon; at which time if Miss Mary B. Johnston and some other person who signed on the petition for revocking (sic) former Admor do not take out Admon, Mr. & Mrs. Greenland shall be instantly qualified.

19. Qualified Maurice Harvey Cooper of St. Stephen's Parish, administrator of Estate & Effects of Jane Cooper, late of same place, Widow, decd.,

Proved the last Will & Testament of William Brown, late of

[Page 49] [part of page missing]

Charleston, Mariner

22. Qualified John Calvitt administrator of Estate & Effects of Edward Calvitt of St. Stephen's Parish, planter, decd.

Susanna Johnston Case. Samuel Ashley Greenland appeared in Court at 11 o'clock with his Surety and observed that as no other person had yet appeared and the time fixed, being past, he moved that he be immediately qualified as Admor and entered in Bond accordingly.

Miss Mary B. Johnston appeared about from fifteen to twenty minutes after the time, but Mr. Greenland had availed himself of his priority and the failure of the other party, and as Miss Johnston had been in a special manner warned by the Ordinary that if she and her Surities were not ready Mr. Greenland & Mrs. Greenland who were equally entitled would be Qualified and it was upon this express Condition that a postponement had been granted, after such frequent adjourning. Therefore qualified Samuel Ashley Greenland and Esther Susanna Greenland admor and admix of the Estate & Effects of Susanna Johnston, decd.

Mr. Clements then gave notice that he would appeal from the decision.

25. Citation granted to Isaac Mendes Seixas of Charleston, Merchant, to administer on the Estate & Effects of Richae Siexas, late of Charleston, Widow, deceased as next of Kin.

[Page 50] [part of page missing]

...Testament of Jones Emerson
...Henry Gradick ...administer on Christian Gradick late of

...Effects of William Smith, late of Elliott Street, Charleston, Merchant, Deceased, with Will annexed

30. Citation granted to Henry Criscey Barr of Charleston, Shop-keeper to administer on Estate & Effects of Albert Myer, late of Charleston, a Soldier in the 2d. Regiment of Artillery, deceased, as principal Creditor.

May 4. Proved the last Will and testament of James LaRoche, late of Wadmalaw Island, Planter, deceased, by the testimony of Richard Jenkins one of the Subscribing witnesses thereto; at the same time qualified Mary LaRoche and John LaRoche, executrix and executor named therein.

6. Citation granted to Thomas Smith, of St. Paul's Parish, Planter, to Administer on the Estate and Effects of Daniel Smith, late of Charleston Gentleman, deceased, as next of Kin.

Citation granted to Mary LaRoche of Wadmalaw Island, Widow, to Administer on the Estate and Effects of Mary Ann Waight, late of John's Island, Spinister, deceased, as next of Kin.

Qualified Henry Cliscey[sic] Barr, of Charleston, Shopkeeper, administrator of Estate and Effects of Albert Myers, late of Charleston, a Soldier in the 2d. Regiment of Artillery, deceased.

[Page 51] [part of page missing]

11. Citation granted to ..... Dr. David ... wife, late Sarah

13. Proved the last Will and testament of Mary Fowke, late of Charleston, Widow, deceased, by the testimony of Beekman McCall, one of the subscribing Witnesses thereto: at the same time qualified Stobo Richard Perry, executor, named therein,

[in margin]: 13 May 1814. Caveat by Stobo Perryagainst any person admr. on the estate of James Stobo the elder.

Citation granted to James Anderson of Christ Church Parish, Gentleman, to administer on the Estate & Effects of Mary Anderson, late of same place, Widow, decd., as next of Kin with the Will annexed de bonis non.

17. Citation granted to Charles Rivers Stone of Charleston, Gentleman, to administer on Estate & Effects of Elizabeth Rivers Scott, late of James Island, Widow, decd., as next of Kin.

Citation granted to Rebecca Elizabeth Frink of Charleston, Widow, to administer on the Estate & Effects of Thomas Frink, late of Charleston, Merchant, deceased, as next of Kin.

318. Qualified Isaac Mendes Seixas, of Charleston, Merchant, admor of the Estate and Effects of Richar Seixas, late of Charleston, Widow, deceased, [See p. 65]

19. Qualified Edward Lynah of Charleston, Physician, administrator of Estate of Eleanor Lynah, late of same place, Widow, decd.

Qualified Sarah Sarzeda and David Sarzeda of Charleston, Physician, Administratrix and Admor of the Estate of Abraham Da Costa, late of Savannah, Merchant, decd.

20. Citation granted to Margarete Carmand des Jardins of Charleston, Widow, to Administer on the Estate & Effects of Jean Adrien des Jardins, late of Charleston, Merchant, decd., as next of Kin.

Dedimus granted to William Joyner, Esquire, to prove the last Will and Testament of Sarah Farr, late of Charleston Widow, decd., equally the exor. therein named.

[Page 52] [part of page missing]

Mary Anderson, late of Christ Church Parish...

of
Stephen Dunham, late of ... by the testimony of James Mays to the same... at the same time Broun, executor, named therein.

26. If application for administration on the Estate of James Stobo, the elder, should be made, the Ordinary is requested to inform Mr. Lance, the Proctor, for Stobo Richard Perry.

Proved the last Will & Testament of David Virtue, late of Charleston, a Soldier in the 1st. Regt. of Artillery, deceased, by the testimony of George Briggs, one of the subscribing witnesses to the same & qualified Thomas Seed[?] Executor therein named.

27. Qualified Marguerite Carmand des Jardins of Charleston, Widow Administratrix of the estate of Jean Admren des Jardins, late of Charleston, Merchant, deceased.

Qualified Thomas Smith, Junior, of St. Paul's Parish, Planter, Admor of the Estate & Effects of Daniel Smith, late of Charleston, Gentleman, decd.

[in margin.] 13 May 1814. Caveat by Stobo Perry against any person Admor on the Estate of James Stobo, the Elder.

[in margin] 30 May. Proved the last Will & testament of Sarah Farr, late of Charleston, one of the subscribing witnesses by virtue of a dedimus before W. M. Jones, Esq.; at the same time qualified William Robertson, executor.

Citation granted to William Jones of Charleston, Tavern-keeper, to administer on the Estate & Effects of George Miles late of Charleston, Mariner, decd., as principal Creditor

Qualified Mary Pyne of Charleston, Widow, admix. of the Estate & Effects of John Pyne, planter, decd.

June 1. Qualified Samuel McGinley of Charleston Blacksmith, admor of Estate of James Hamilton Cambridge, late of Charleston, Vendue Master, decd.

[Page 53] [part of page missing]

Citation granted to Mary Simmons English to administer on the Estate & Effects of ... of the same place, planter, deceased.

7. Proved the last Will and testament _____ Harvey, late of Charleston Neck, Planter, deceased, by the testimony of Charles S. Tucker, one of the subscribing witnesses to the same at the same time qualified Susanna Frances Harvey, executrix, named therein.

10. Citation granted to Elizabeth Johnston of Charleston, Widow, to administer on the Estate & Effects of John Johnston of Charleston, Carpenter, deceased, as next of Kin.

Proved the last Will & testament of Mary Edwards of Charleston, Spinster, deceased, by the testimony of James Fisher Edwards of Charleston, Planter, there being no subscribing witnesses thereto.

Citation granted to John William Schmidt of Charleston, Physician, to administer on the Estate & Effects of Alexander Crawford, late of Charleston, Painter, deceased, as principal Creditor so far as they were left unadministered by Joseph Emas admor, decd.

Citation granted to Harleston Simons of Charleston, Widow, to administer on the Estate & effects of the Reverend James Dewar Simons, late of Charleston, Rector of St. Philips Church, deceased, as next of Kin.

Qualified George Morgan Gibbes of Charleston, Planter, admor de bonis non of Thomas Stanyarne Gibbes, late of St. Bartholomew's Parish, planter, decd.

Qualified Dorothy Phillips of Charleston, Widow, admix of Arthur Honeywood of Charleston, Blacksmith, decd.

[in margin] 14 June. Qualified Mrs. Jane Keith, executrix named in last Will & testament of the Rev. Isaac Stockton Keith, late of Charleston, Minister of the Gospel, deceased.

[Page 54] [part of page missing]

Livingston and Mary his [wife]... cite Betji Henrickson to appear

Reverend Dewar Simons, late of ... Philip's Church, deceased
                                                        granted to
Mathew Fleming and Ann, his wife, late Ann McCormick, one of the daughters of William McCormick, late of Charleston, Merchant, deceased, to cite Richard Brenan & Thomas Blackwood to appear on Friday, the 24th of June inst.: to show cause why the Letters of Administration granted to them

on the fourteenth day of February 1812 should not be revoked and the same granted to them and Mathew Fleming cojointly.

22. Caveat. Mrs. Mary Rose, widow of William Rose, late of John's Island, Planter, deceased, enters a caveat against any person taking out Letters of Administration on the Estate & effects of her husband,

William McCormick's Case. In the Court of Ordinary, 24 June 1814.

Mr. Geddis in behalf of Mr. Blackwood came into Court agreeably to a Special Citation granted to Mathew Flemming on the 21st. inst., and stated that in consequence of the absence of Mr. Richd. Brenan, one of the Admors the parties had agreed to postpone the case until the return of Brenan: Mr. McCormick on behalf of Mr. Fleming at the same time appeared and concurred therein.

24. Qualified Mary LaRoche of Wadmalaw, Widow, Administratrix of the Estate & Effects of Mary Ann Waight, late of John's Island, deceased.

[Page 59]

1812 June 27th. proved the last Will and Testament of Elizabeth Harvey, late of Charleston, widow deceased, by the testimony of Thomas Winstanlay one of the subscribing witnesses to the same; at the same time qualified Anne Legge executrix therein named.

July 1st. Citation granted to Honora Pyne of Charleston, widow, to administer on the Estate & Effects of Aedimus Burke, late of Charleston, Esq., deceased, as next friend with the Will annexed so far as they were left unadministered by O'Brien Smith, executor, deceased.

2nd. Citation granted June Scouler of Charleston, widow, to administer on the estate & Effects of Thomas Scouter, late of Charleston, watchmaker, deceased, as next of Kin.

7. In the Court of Ordinary Mr. Alexander Mazyck came into Court and renounced the Executorship of the Estate of Charlotte Izard, late of Charleston, Widow, deceased. See 14 Eu No. 6

Citation (special) granted to Robert Walker, one of the sureties for William Murdock admor to David Kinmont, to cite the said Admor to appear on Tuesday next the 12 inst. at 11 o'clock in the forenoon to show cause why such order & decree as shall give relief to the sd. Robert Walker should not be made.

8. Qualified Jane Scouler of Charleston, widow, admix of the Estate & Effects of Thomas Schouler, late of Charleston, watchmaker, deceased.

11. Citation granted to Susannah Nelson of St. James Parish Goose Creek Widow, to Administer on the Estate & Effects of Isaac Nelson, late of the same place, planter, deceased, as next of Kin.

12. Citation granted to Rachel Moses of Charleston, widow, to administer on the Estate & Effects of Joseph Moses of Charleston, storekeeper, deceased, as next of Kin.

Citation granted to Thomas Price, Sergeant in Capt. Hawkin's Company of Artillery, stationed at Fort Moultrie, to administer on the Estate & Effects of Michael Seagraves, late of same regt., dec., as principal creditor

Proved the last Will & testament of Daniel Brown late of Charleston, merchant, dec., by the testimony of John Ling one of the subscribing witnesses to the same.

[Page 60]

1814 July 13. Citation granted to Marguerite Wall, widow, to administer on the Estate & Effects of William Wall, late a Soldier in the 2nd Regt. of Artillery stationed at Fort Moultrie, deceased, as next of Kin.

Dedimus to Thomas Handy, Esq., of New Port, Rhode Island, qualified the executrix named in the last Will & testament of Daniel Broun, late of Charleston, merchant, dec.

14th. Citation granted to James Mackie of Charleston Gentleman, to administer with the Will annexed on the Estate & Effects of James Allison, late of Savannah, Georgia, cooper, dec., as principal creditor (De bonis non) so far as they were left unadministered by William Smith, executor, dec.

15. Proved the last Will and Testament of Paul Prichard, Senior, late of Charleston, shipwright, dec., by the testimony of Francis Coram, one of the subscribing Witnesses thereto.

14. Proved the last Will and Testament of William Hall, late of Charleston, mariner, dec., by the testimony of William Trescot, one of the subscribing witnesses to same.

16. Special citation granted to George Arthur to cite Thomas Townsend admor, of Stephen Townsend to appear on Tues. the 9th day of August next to render an account of his Admor of said estate.

19th. Qualified Honora Pyne of Charleston, widow, admix with the Will annexed and de bonis non of Adner Burke late of Charleston, Esq., deceased.

Citation granted to William Hall of Charleston, physician, to administer on the Estate & effects of William Hall late of Charleston, mariner, deceased, as next of Kin with the Will annexed.

Proved the Will and Testament of Mary Elliott Shubrick, late of Charleston, spinster, deceased by the testimony of Robert Hasell Quash, one of the subscribing witnesses thereto.

20. Citation granted to Eliza Carr of Charleston, widow, to administer on the Estate & effects of Dale Carr, late of Charleston, mariner, deceased as next of Kin.

[Page 61]

July 1814 21. Citation granted to Thomas Fitzgerald Quin to administer on the Estate and Effects of Myles Gerrill, late a Soldier in a Company of Artillery stationed at Fort Moultrie, deceased, a principal Creditor.

Qualified Roger Pinckney, an Executor named in the last Will & testament of Mary Elliott Shubrick, late of Charleston, Spinster, deceased.

22nd. Qualified Thomas Price of Warren County, North Carolina, Sargent, in Capt. Hawkins' Company of Artillery stationed at Fort Moultrie -----Admor of Michael Seagraves, late a Soldier in Cant. Hawkins' Company of Artillery deceased. Qualified Margaret Wall of Orange County, North Carolina, widow, Admix. of the Estate and Effects of William Wall, late a soldier in the Regt. of Artillery stationed at Fort Moultrie, deceased. Qualified Susanna Nelson of St. James' Parish, Goose Creek, Widow, Admix of the Estate & Effects of Isaac Nelson, late of same place, planter, dec. Qualified Rachael Moses of Charleston, widow, admix. of Joseph Moses, late of Charleston, Storekeeper. deceased.

23. Qualified James Mackie of Charleston, Gentleman, admor with the Will annexed of James Allison late of Savannah, Georgia, Cooper, dec. so far as they were left unadministered by William Smith, Executor, deceased

25. Citation granted to Jane Scouler of Charleston, Widow, to administer on the Estate & Effects of Thomas Scouler, late of Charleston, watchmaker, decd., as next of Kin with his will annexed.

26. Citation granted to Robert Griggs, a Corporal in Capt. Hawkins' Company of Artillery stationed at Fort Moultrie to administer on the Estate & Effects of Sion Parrish, late a private in the Company, dec., as next friend.

Citation granted Denson Pilkenton, a private in Capt. Hawkins' Company of Artillery, stationed at Fort Moultrie, to Administer on the Estate & Effects of Kintcher Pilkenton, late of the same Company, dec., as next of Kin.

28. Paul Hamilton, Esquire, renounced his Executorship to the Will & Testament of William Hall, late of Charleston, mariner, deceased, see Renun: filed with original Will

[in margin] 27 July 1814. Citation granted to Lyon Levy of Charleston, Gentleman, to administer on the Estate & Effects of Jacob L. Levy, late of Charleston, dec., as next of Kin.

[Page 62]

1814 July 29. Proved the last Will & Testament of Charles Rottenbury, late of St. James' Goose Creek, planter, deceased, by the testimony of Ezekiel Smyth, one of the subscribing witnesses to the same: at the same time qualified Catherine Rottenbury, Executrix, named therein.

Qualified Thomas Fitzgerald Quin, of Charleston, Grocer, Admor of the Estate & Effects of Myles Gerrill, a Soldier in a Company of Artillery stationed at Fort Moultrie, dec.

Qualified Eliza Carr of Charleston, widow, admix of the Estate & Effects of Dale Carr, late of Charleston, Mariner, deceased.

Citation granted to John Dunn of Charleston, Grocer, to administer on the Estate & Effects of Charlotte Duggan, late of Charleston, widow, deceased, as principal Creditor.

Special Citation granted at the instance of John Claney to cite Charles Graves to appear on Monday the 1 August next at 10 o'clock A. M. to make a just & true acct. of the admor of the Estate of Michael Clancy, late of Charleston, grocer, deceased.

30. Qualified William Hall of Charleston, physician, Administrator cum testamento annexo, of William Hall of the same place, mariner, deceased.

Aug. 4 Caveat entered by Thomas Duggan of Charleston, Bricklayer, against Letters of Administration being granted to John Dunn of Charleston, Grocer, (until he is heard before the Ordinary) on the Estate & Effects of Charlotte Duggan.

4. Proved the last Will & Testament of Edward Marlen of Charleston, Taylor, by the testimony of Catherine Norton, one of the subscribing witnesses thereto: at the same time qualified David Thwing [Hewing?], executor, named therein.

5. Qualified Robert Griggs, Corporal in Capt. Hawkins' Company of Artillery, stationed at Fort Moultrie, administrator of the Estate & Effects Lion (sic) Parrish, of the same Company, dec.

Qualified Denson Pilkenton of Capt. Hawkins' Company of Artillery stationed at Fort Moultrie Admor of the Estate & effects of Kintchen Pilkenton of the same Company, dec.

Proved the last Will & Testament of Thomas Scouler, late of Charleston, gunsmith (and Watchmaker), deceased, by the testimony of William Colden junior, there being no subscribing witness thereto.

[Page 63]

1814 Aug. 5 Qualified Lyon Levy of Charleston, Gentleman, admor of the Estate & Effects of Jacob C. Levy, late of Charleston, Saddler dec.

Qualified Jane Scouler, Administratrix, of Thomas Scouler, late of Charleston, gunsmith, deceased, with his Will annexed. N.B. In the Citation the dec. was called watchmaker, but Mrs. Scouler said he was also a gunsmith and she wished the dec. styled by the latter appellation.

9th. Stephen Townsend's Case, George Arthur, who had obtained a special Citation to Summond Thomas Townsend admor of Stephen Townsend to appear on this day and give an account of his administration, came into Court and informed the Ordinary that the said Thomas Townsend was unable to attend being confined in Goal at present.

10th. William Windham Trapier of Georgetown, So. Ca., planter, obtained a Citation on behalf of Mary Belin to administer on the Estate & Effects of Peter Roberts as next friend to the said Mary Belin who was next of Kin of, dec. So far as they were left unadministered by Lynch Roberts, admix dec.

11th. [Note in margin: see March 5, 1813.] Francis Motte an Executor named in the last will of Thomas Branford Smith, late of Charleston, Gentleman, deceased, who had renounced his Executorship in favor of Francis Simmons, Esquire, came into Court and stated that in consequence of the death of the said Francis and his administration thereby ceasing; he would now take upon himself the Execution of the said Will: Whereupon qualified Francis Motte, Executor, named in the said Will and Citation granted the said Francis Motte to administer with the testament annexed of the said Thomas Branford Smith.

16. Citation granted to Ruben Grady of Capt. Hawkins' Company of Artillery, Drummer, to administer on the Estate & Effects of Asa Stillwell, late a private in the said Company, dec., as principal Creditor.

[Page 64]

1814 August 16. Charlotte Duggan's Case In the Court of Ordinary 16 Aug. 1814. This day appeared in Court Mr. Craft in behalf of Mr. Dunn who had obtained a Citation on the 29th ult'o to administer Estate & Effects of Charlotte Duggan, late of Charleston, widow, deceased, and also Mr. Geddes

& Mr. Richardson in behalf of Thomas Duggan who had entered a Caveat on the 4th inst. against admor of the said Estate being granted to said Dunn. After examining the witnesses hearing Council on both sides, the circumstances of the case appeared to be: That Thomas Duggan was neither relative, Creditor, nor friend of the deceased and that his only claim to the admor was on the grounds of the desire of Miss Charlotte Duggan, daughter of the deceased, that she would not be fourteen until November next, consequently not old enough to receive the admo'n or appoint her Guardian, and Mr. Duggan was not her legal representative: that Mr. Duggan was probably indebted to the Estate, at least a bill had been filed against him in Equity by the late Mr. Duggan for a discovery & acct. of his Brother's Estate to a proportion of which she was entitled on the other hand Mr. Dunn appeared to be a Creditor to about the sum of $668 & produced an assignment from Mrs. Duggan in her lifetime of so much of her Proportion of her husband's Estate as she would be entitled to, in payment of money lent her by Mr. Dunn: it appeared also that Mr. Dunn had been at some expense to educate & Board the child [in] Charlotte. This the Case of discretion the Ordinary deemed it proper to appoint Mr. Dunn the only Creditor during the minority of the child to administer the said estate.

17. Qualified John Dunn Admor. of Charlotte Duggan, late of Charleston, widow, dec.

18. Citation to James Richbourgh of St. John's Parish, Berkeley, planter to administer on the Estate & Effects of Samuel Isaac Little, late of the same place, planter, deceased, as next friend.

19th. Citation granted Charles Lee Edwards of St. Thomas' Parish, physician, to administer on the Estate & Effects of John Jones Edwards of late a lieutenant in the Navy of the United States, deceased, as next of Kin.

[Page 65]

1814 August 19th. Citation granted to Bridget Jones of Charleston, widow, to administer on the Estate & Effects widow, of William Jones, late of Charleston, mariner, deceased, as next of Kin.

26th. Citation granted to Richard Greneker, tavern keeper, Charleston, to administer on the Estate & Effects of Oliver Salvidore, mariner, deceased; as next friend & principal Creditor.

Qualified Ruben Grady, Drummer, Capt. Hawkins' Company of Artillery, administrator of the Estate & Effects of Asa Stillwell, late of same Company a private, dec.

Qualified Bridget Jones, widow, of Charleston, Administratrix of the Estate & Effects of William Jones, late of Charleston, mariner, dec.

27. Citation granted to Duthe Desmottes of Charleston to administer on the Estate & Effects of Michonne Coudougnan, late of Charleston, widow, deceased, as next of Kin.

29. Granted to Thomas Fitzgerald Quin of Charleston, Grocer, letters of Administration ad colligendum bona of Daniel Henderson, late of Charleston, Gunsmith, deceased, and at the same Citation to administer on the Estate & Effects of the said Daniel Henderson, dec., as principal Creditor.

30. Qualified Charles Lee Edwards of St. Thomas' Parish, physician, Administrator of Estate & Effects of John Jones Edwards of St. Thomas' Parish, late Lieut. in the Navy of the United States, dec.

Rufus Howard enters a Caveat against Administration being granted on the Estate of Daniel Henderson being granted to Thomas Fitzgerald Quin of Charleston, Grocer, or to any other person before he is heard before the Ordinary.

31. Special Citation granted to Morris Goldsmith, one of the sureties of Isaac Mendes Seixas, admor of Richae Seixas to cite him to appear on tomorrow at 10 o'clock in the forenoon 1st Sept. to show cause why he should not be relieved.

Citation granted Sarah Sampson of Charleston, widow, to administer on the Estate & Effects of Henrich Gramoke, late of Charleston, mariner, dec. as principal Creditor.

September 2. Citation granted to Michael Watson Perry of Capt. Butler's Company of Infantry to administer on the Estate & Effects of Abner Carter, late a private in the same Company as principal Creditor.

[Page 66]

1814. September 2. Citation granted to James Humpreys of Capt. Donoho's Company of Artillery stationed at Fort Moultrie, to administer on the Estate & Effects of Hardy Jones, late a private in the same Company as principal Creditor.

Citation granted to James Humpreys of Capt. Donoho's Company of Artillery to administer on the Estate & Effects of Luke Wilson of the same Company, deceased, as principal Creditor to Richd. Greneker of Charleston, tavern keeper, admor. of the Estate & Effects of Oliver Salvedore, late of same place, mariner.

Richae Seixas' Case. Mr. Bay with Isaac M. Seixes admor appeared and asked to be indulged until Monday next at ten o'clock to produce sureties which with the concurrence of Mr. Grimke who appeared in behalf of those interested was granted.

Proved the Last Will & testament of Thomas Hall, late of Charleston, Planter, deceased, by the testimony of Christian M. Logan, one of the Subscribing witnesses thereto: at the same time qualified James Jervey and James Broun, Executors named therein.

6. Citation granted to Charles Rogers of St. Stephen's Parish, farmer, to Administer on the Estate & Effects of William McKay, or Mcay, late of same place, farmer, dec., as next of Kin.

Qualified Duthe Desmottes of Charleston, administrix of Michonne Coudougman, late of Charleston, widow, dec.

8. William Austen's Case. Caveat entered by Mr. Heath on behalf of William Austen, Junior, against the Probate of the Will of Wm. Austen, Senr., until he has been heard before the Ordinary.

Citation granted to John Hancock Willis of Charleston, Factor, to administer on Estate Effects of Russell Bessett, late a Lieutenant in the Navy of the United States of America, deceased, as next Friend

Proved the last Will and testament of Alexander Inglis, late of St. Paul's Parish, planter, deceased, by the testimony of John Ramsey and M. M. I. Clitherall, two [of] the subscribing witnesses thereto: also the Codicil to the same by the testimony of M. M. I. Clitherall, one of the subscribing witnesses there to at the same time.

[Page 67]

Qualified Mary Inglis, executrix, named therein Dr. Ramsey stated that Mr. Inglis had for the two last years of his life lived in Charleston which was the known place of his residence lately and died there.

13 September. Citation granted to Margaret Leaumont of Charleston, Widow, to administer on the Estate & Effects of Marie Robert Leaumont, late of Charleston musician, dec., as next of Kin.

Richae Seixas Case. 10th. Sept. in the Court of Ordinary After several days of hearing of objections from time to time to the sureties offered by Isaac M. Seixas it was considered by the Gentlemen concerned for Mrs. Harris who was a daughter of the deceased that, the Surety when he cast off there was no objection to be made: the armor was thus confirmed to tell Seixas on Bond.

September 9. [See Page 65, 66 of Original Book.] Qualified James Humphreys of Capt. Donoho's Company of Artillery, Admor of Hardy Jones of the same Company, dec. Qualified the said James Humphreys admor of Luke Wilson of Capt. Donoho's Company afore said dec.

Qualified Michael Watson Perry of Capt. Butler's Company of Infantry admor of Abner Carter of the same Company, dec.

Citation granted to Samuel Amburn to administer on the Estate Effects of Jacob Rose, dec., and of John Rose, dec., all of them of Capt. Donoho's Company of Artillery as next friend to John Rose and as Principal Creditor Jacob Rose.

Sept. 15. Citation granted to Sarah Ann Legare of Charleston, spinster, to administer on Estate & Effects of Alice Legare, late of Charleston, widow, dec., so far as they are left unadministered by Thomas Savage Legare, Esq., dec., as next of Kin with her Will annexed.

Sept. 16th. Qualified John Hancock Willis, admor. of Russell Basset, late Lieut. in the Navy of the United States.

[Page 69]

The Case of Daniel Henderson in the Court of Ordinary, Sept. 14th. 1814. This is a case of discretion and depends greatly upon the evidence it will therefore be necessary for the Ordinary to review such part of the testimony as have relation to the two points under consideration by Creditor and next friend. Mr. Quin obtained the Citation and claims the admor solely as Creditor and exhibits an account amounting to $94.18 3/5. Mr. Howard entered Caveat and claims in the double capacity of Creditor and next friend. Mr. Quin to support his claim produced Mr. Stoll who in substance swore that he presented an Act. to Henderson about three months before his death amounting to $94.18 3/5. That Henderson acknowledged then, and had previously in Quin's Store acknowledged before Witness the $85 and requested remaining to be added when he would pay them together.

There is nothing further relative to Mr. Quin's Claim until we arrive at the testimony of James Nicholson who among other things says that Henderson mentioned or spoke lightly of money and made nothing of calling $80 or $100 a trifle. We all therefore to presume the demand of Quin as proved to the amt. of $94.18 3/5. The rest of the witnesses who were examined for Quin have stated generally that Howard after the death of Henderson, declared that he had no claim against his Estate except for his Services and as to that he hoped to be done to as well by others; that he only wanted admor on acct. of Henderson's Children; It was further stated that Howard had sold several articles belonging to Henderson before his death and offered to sell some of them after his death: These I believe are fairly the leading features of Mr. Quin's application for Admor. Mr. Howard's claim founded on an acct. for services rendered to the amount of $175 in support of which Dr. Robert Wilson was produced who thought that the rate of his charge was reasonable; that nurses who were likewise fed received $2 per diem. with respect to his claim as next friend a number of witnesses proceeded

[Page 69]

to show his repeated acts of friendship to the deceased. Dr. Wilson said that Howard was always fair when he went to visit Henderson both early and late and remained there at the risk of his life; that he remained there when Henderson was deserted by everyone else; that Howard's attention he was convinced had saved the life of Henderson's child whom he nursed. Dr. Prentice attended Henderson also and said that Howard was frequently there and came to witness for medicine for Henderson that Howard acted the part of a friend and even performed menial Services for Henderson.

Mr. Footman stated that he visited Henderson who declared that to him that he did not know what he would have done without Howard; that his attention to his child had saved its life that he owed much to Howard (meaning gratitude) for his services assisted when all had abandoned him. Some of the 'Witnesses proved that Howard took care of Henderson's children and had them with him, but do not occur as to the length of time.

Mr. Stevens stated that there on four weeks before Henderson's death that Howard came to him and complained of Henderson's destitute situation and Mr. Stevens advised Howard to sell some small articles.

Mr. S. told Howard that if Henderson was in his senses to get his consent and to be cautious how he had laid out the money and advised him not to sell Henderson's horse and chair. Mr. Stevens said he was satisfied that the signature to the bill of sale to the horse and chair was not Henderson's writing. Mr. Hamet who kept Henderson's books for five years concurred with Mr. Stevens in saying that the signature was not Henderson's.

The bill of sale was there with drawn: Subscribing witnesses not being present such is the substance of the evidence offered to the Court from which the Ordinary is to draw his conclusion.

It would appear from comparing the accounts that Mr. Howard is the larger & as he has established his claim as next friend to the deceased, the Ordinary would therefore have felt it his duty to have committed the admor into his hands;

[Page 70]

were it not for some circumstances in the case which induced him to pause. After the repeated declaration on the part of Mr. Howard that he had no claim against Henderson. It would seem that this acct. was got up with a view only to secure the admor and of course cannot be viewed in so favorable a light as otherwise it might have been. Again that while Henderson was alive Howard might have been sanctioned in of disposing of the property by the necessity of furnishing Henderson with support and having partly his consent; but after his death that necessity excited [existed] no longer; it was therefore improper to have intermeddled with the Effects of the deceased selling or offering to sell them, both report of the bill of Sale as it has been withdrawn it would be uncandid to draw any inference. The Ordinary has only to add that under his present impression he deemed it proper to confirm the authority and granted to Mr. Quin by committing the admor. into his hands, Whereupon qualified Thomas Izzard Quin of Charleston, Grocer, admor of the Estate & Effects of Daniel Henderson, Gunsmith, dec.

Septr. 23. Qualified Sarah Sampson of Charleston, Widow, Admix. of Hendrick Gramake of Charleston, mariner, dec.

Citation granted to Christian Schmieser of Charleston, Grocer, to administer on the Estate & Effects of Frederick Schmieser, late of Charleston, Butcher, dec., as principal Creditor. (see page 65)

Citation granted James William Tinsley of Capt. Butler's Company of Infantry to administer on the Estate & Effects of Allen Cobb of the same Company, deceased, as principal Creditor.

24. (see pages 30, 31) Citation granted to George Morgan Gibbes of Charleston, Planter, to administer on the Estate & Effects of Ann Gibbes, late of Charleston dec., as far as they were unadministered by John Gibbes admor., dec., as next of Kin.

26. Proved the last Will & Testament of Justine (a free black woman of Charleston), by the testimony of Andre Boulineau, one of the subscribing witnesses thereto.

[Page 71]

Sept 26. Qualified Margaret Leaumont of Charleston, Widow, administratrix of the Estate & Effects of Marie Robert Leaumont, late of Charleston, musician, deceased.

28. Citation granted to John Halfrid of Charleston, Grocer, to administer on the Estate & Effects of Christian Drake, late of Charleston, Grocer, deceased, as next friend.

Qualified Jean Le Sage executor named in the last Will & Testament of Justin late of Charleston, (a free black woman), deceased. (see page 70) [in Original Book.]

29. Citation granted to George William Jones of Capt. Blount's company of Infantry to administer on the Estate & Effects of Asaph Bailey Johnston, late of Capt. Elmore's Company of Infantry, decd, as principal creditor.

30. Qualified George Morgan Gibbes of Charleston, planter, admor on the Estate & Effects of Ann Gibbes, late of Charleston, deceased. see page 70.

Qualified James William Tinsly, admor, of Allen Cobb, late of Capt. Butler's Company of Infantry, dec. (see page 70) [in Original book.]

Proved the last Will & testament of Charles Tepier, late of Charleston, mariner, dec., by the testimony of Francios Duboc, one of the subscribing witnesses at the same time Qualified Joseph Guerineau, otherwise called Joseph Garino[?], executor, named therein.

October 6. Qualified (by Dedimus to Thomas Handy, Esquire, of New Port of Rhode Island), Lydia Broun, Penelope Lawton, Mary Broun and Elizabeth Broun named executrixes of the last Will & testament of Daniel Broun, late of Charleston, Merchant, dec.

7. Qualified John Hilfrid admor of Christian Drake late of Charleston, Grocer, dec. (see page 60)

Qualified George W. Jones of Capt. Blunt's Company of Infantry, Admor. of Asaph Bailey Johnson, late a Sergeant in Capt. Elmore's Company of Infantry, dec. [see before this date]

14. Citation granted to Matthew Braid of Charleston, House carpenter, to administer on the Estate & Effects of Locklin Wright, late of Charleston, planter deceased, as next of Friend.

[Page 72]

1814 October 14. Citation granted to Ann FitzSimons, late of Charleston spinster, to administer on Estate & Effects of Mary FitzSimons, late of Charleston, spinster, as next of Kin.

15. Citation granted to Nathaniel Green Hillard of Charleston, Mariner, to administer on the Estate & Effects of Ann Henderson, late of Charleston, widow, deceased, as next of Kin.

Proved the last Will & Testament of Hannah Anderson, late of Charleston, Widow, deceased, by the testimony of Robert Ogden one of the subscribing witnesses to the same; at the same time qualified Thomas Mapier and Robert Anderson, executors named therein.

18. Citation /Special/ granted to Robert Walker, one of the Sureties of William Murdock, Administrator of David Kinmount to appear on Wednesday the 26th of October inst. to show cause why he should not render a true & faithful account of his administration.

20. Proved the last Will & testament of Benjamin Cudworth, late of Charleston, Merchant, by the testimony of William Cudworth, one of the subscribing witnesses thereto; at the same time qualified Charles John Steedman, Executor named therein.

21. Citation granted to Drury Coley, a private in Capt. Hendersin's Company of Artillery to administer on the Estate & Effects of John Burchet, late of the same company, dec., as next friend

Proved the last Will & testament of George Parker, late of Charleston, planter, deceased, also the Codicil thereto by the testimony of James Johnston, a subscribing witness. At the same time qualified Samuel Parker executor, named therein.

25. Qualified Mathew Braid of Charleston, House Carpenter, administrator of the Estate & Effects of Locklin Wright, late of Charleston, plasterer, dec. see page 71. [in Original Book.]

Robert Lindsay's Case. John Phillips of Charleston, Painter, came into Court & represented that he was in danger of being injured by his Suretyship to Mary Lindsay, admix. of Robert Lindsay. Whereupon Mary Lindsay appeared and offered new Security. (see page 10 & 9)

[Page 73]

28 October. Proved the last Will & testament of Gilbert Bernard Jacques Lapierre, late of Charleston, joiner, deceased by the testimony of Rene Goddard, one of the subscribing witnesses thereto: at the same time Qualified Thomas Le June, executor, named therein. N.B. The same being in the French language, a translation was exhibited which was sworn by John J. Leris to be a true & perfect one as far as the language would admit.

Citation granted to Hugh Monies of Charleston, Merchant, to administer on the Estate & Effects of James Carson, late of Charleston, Merchant, dec., as next friend and as far as they were unadministered by William Monies, admor, who is absent from & out of the limits of the State.

Proved the last Will & Testament of Thomas Campbell Cox, late of Charleston, Printer, dec., by the testimony of William Yeadon, Esq., one of the subscribing witnesses there to at the same time qualified Charles Edmondson and Taticitus Gaillare Skrine, executors, therein named.

Qualified Drury Coley, a private in Capt. Hawkins' Company of Artillery, admor of the Estate & Effects of John Burchet, late a private of the same Company, deceased.

November 3. Special Citation to Robt. Walker, one of the sureties for William Murdock, admor of David Kinmont, dec., to appear at 12 O'clock on tomorrow to show Cause why he should not render his acct., or in failure thereof why the admor granted to him on the 22nd of Augt. 1812 on the Estate & Effects of David Kinmont, dec., should be revoked and granted to Robert Walker.

4. Qualified Hugh Monies of Charleston, Merchant, admor de bones non of James Carson, late of Charleston, Merchant, dec.

David Kinmont's Case. Robert Walker who had obtained Special Citation to summon William Murdock, admor. of David Kinmont, dec., appeared in Court, but the said William Murdock did not appear, nor gave any account of his administration. The Ordinary at the insistence of Robert Walker revoked the admor on the Estate & Effects of David Kinmont which had

[Page 74]

been granted to the said William Murdock on the 22nd day of Augt 1812 and appointed the said Robert [Walker] admor of the said David Kinmont.

Whereupon qualified Robert Walker of Charleston, Cabinet maker, admor of the Estate & Effects of David Kinmont, late of Charleston, Blacksmith, dec.

November 4. Proved the last Will & Testament of Abraham M. Isaacs, late of Charleston, Merchant, dec., by the testimony of J. Heydenfeld, one of the Subscribing Witnesses to the same; at the same time qualified Philip Cohen, Executor named therein.

10. Qualified James Richbourgh of St. John's Parish, Berkeley, Planter, admor of the Estate Effects of Samuel Jarad Little, late of same place, planter deceased.

11. Proved the last Will & Testament of Leonard Prauninger, late of Charleston Neck, Butcher, deceased, by the testimony of Daniel Thompson, one of the subscribing witnesses thereto: at the same time qualified Elizabeth Prauninger, executrix named therein

Proved the last Will & Testament of James Gordon, late of Charleston, Bricklayer, deceased, by the testimony of John S. Cogdell, Esq., one of the subscribing witnesses thereto: at the same time qualified John Gordon, executor named therein.

Proved the last Will & Testament of Martha Cannon, late of Charleston, Spinster, deceased, by the testimony of James Nicholson, one of the subscribing witnesses thereto: Also the Codicil to the same by the testimony of Thomas B. Seabrook, one of the subscribing witnesses thereto:

Citation granted to Edward Brake Lining of Charleston, attorney at Law, to administer on the Estate & Effects of William Deitch, late of Charleston, Bricklayer, deceased, as principal Creditor.

Citation Special Granted to Joseph Pinch of Charleston, Merchant, one of the Sureties of Isaac Mendes Seixas, Admor of

[Page 74]

Richae Seixas late of Charleston, Widow, deceased, to cite the said admor to appear on Thursday next the seventeenth instant at eleven o'clock in the forenoon to show cause why he should not provide other security.

Proved the last Will & Testament of Richard Stiff, late of Charleston, Tavernkeeper, dec., by the testimony of Adolph Beckman, one of the subscribing witnesses thereto: at the same time qualified John Mitchell and Campell Douglass, Executors named therein.

Citation granted Jane Millar of Charleston, Widow, to administer on the Estate and Effects of William Millar, late of Charleston, Baker, dec., as next of Kin.

12th. Citation Granted to Peter Huxford of St. John's Parish, Berkeley, Farmer to administer on the Estate & Effects of Joseph Garlington, late of same place, Farmer, deceased, as the next friend.

Qualified Daniel Cannon Webb named executor in the last Will and testament of Martha Cannon, late of Charleston Neck, spinster, deceased.

14. Citation granted to William Edwards of Capt. Blount's Company of Infantry to administer on the Estate & Effects of Nathan Edwards, late a private in the Company, dec., as next of Kin.

Citation granted to William Brinn of Capt. Blount's Company. of Infantry, to administer on Estate & Effects of Richard Brinn, late a private in the same Company, dec., as next of Kin.

15. Proved the last Will & Testament of Joseph Brown, late of Charleston, Grocer, deceased, by the testimony of Richard McCormick, one of the subscribing witnesses to the same; at the same time qualified the Revd. Dr. Simon Felix Gallagher and Thomas Flyn, executors, named therein.

18. Qualified Hugh Patterson, an executor named in the last Will & testament of Samuel Cochran, late of Charleston, planter deceased.

Qualified Jane Miller admix of the Estate & Effects of William Miller of Charleston, deceased.

[Page 75]

1814 November 21, Citation granted to John Sand[ers] of St. Thomas' Parish, Overseer, to administer on the Estate & Effects of William Sanders, late of same place, Overseer, deceased, as next of Kin.

Qualified Frances Rogers, Admix of the Estate & Effects of William Plowden McCay, late of St. Stephen's Parish, farmer, dec., the said Frances Rogers being a daughter of the said dec. who married Charles Rogers, the latter took out the citation but wanted his wife to administer alone.

22. Qualified Christian Schneider of Charleston, Grocer, administer of the Estate & Effects of Frederick Schmiesser, late of Charleston, Butcher, deceased.

23. Proved the last Will & Testament of Thomas Corbett, late of Charleston, Merchant, deceased, by the testimony of Jn. F. Plumeau, one of the subscribing witnesses thereto: at the same time qualified Margaret Corbett and Thomas Corbett, executrix & executor named in the said Will.

24. Citation (Special) granted to (Michael Fronty a Creditor of the said Estate) to cite Jeremiah Wilcox, admor of George Flagg, junior, dec., to show cause why he should not make and render an account of his administration of said Estate, to appear on Friday the 10th day February 1815.

25. Qualified William Edwards admor of the Estate & Effects of Nathan Edwards, dec., both of Capt. Blount's Company of Infantry.

Qualified William Brinn of Capt. Blunt's Company of Infantry admor of Estate & Effects of Richard Brinn, late of the same Company, deceased.

Qualified Ann Fitzsimons Vos Admix of the Estate & Effects of Mary FitzSimons, late of Charleston, Spinster, dec.

Citation granted to Margaret Leaumont of Charleston, Widow, to administer on the Estate & Effects of Marie Leaumont, Threse Leaumont de Lomenie, late of Charleston, Widow, dec., as next friend so far as they were unadministered by Marie[?] Robert Leaumont, executor, dec. With her Will annexed.

24th. Proved the last Will & testament of Sarah Dickinson, late of Charleston, Spinster, deceased, by the testimony of Elijah Belcher,

[Page 76]

the subscribing witness thereto: at the same time qualified Francis Dickinson, executor, named therein.

Nov. 23. Citation granted to Marian Gendron Porcher, Widow, and Joseph Palmer, planter, both of St. John's Parish, Berkeley, to administer on the Estate & Effects of George Porcher, late of same place, planter, deceased as next of Kin.

30. Proved the last Will & testament of Samuel Desel, late of Charleston, Cabinetmaker, decd., by the testimony of Henry Muckenfuss, one of the

subscribing witnesses to the same: at the same time qualified Catherine Muckenfuss and Mary Desel executors named therein.

December 1. Citation granted to Joseph Finch, one of the Sureties of Isaac Mendes Seixas, Widow, decd., to appear on Tuesday the 6th instant to show cause why the Surety should not return.

2. Citation granted to Samuel Dorrill of Christ Church Parish, planter, to administer on the Estate & Effects of Joseph Dorrill, late of the same place, Planter, decd. as next of Kin.

Citation granted to Frederick Gallagher of Charleston, Store keeper, to administer on the Estate & Effects of William Smith, late of Charleston, mariner, decd., as principal Creditor,

Qualified Francis Motte of Charleston, Factor, admor of the Estate & Effects of Thomas Branford Smith, late of Charleston, Citizen, dec., with his [Will] annexed and de bonis non.

Citation granted to Abraham Gilbert Smith, Corporal in Capt. Fenner's Company of Infantry to administer on the Estate & Effects of James Crumwell, late of Capt. Clinton's Company of Infantry, decd., as principal Creditor,

Citation to John Gregg Flagler of Sumter District, farmer, to administer on the Estate & Effects of John Ellis, late a private in the 2d. Regt. of Dragoons in the service of the United States, decd., as next friend.

[Page 78]

1814 December 2nd. In the Court of Ordinary Jeremiah A. Yates and John R. Rogers, two of the Executors named in a certain paper purporting to be the last Will & testament of Buthel Threadcraft, late of Charleston, Watch-maker, deceased, appeared in Court and submitted Several instruments of writing for the Consideration of the Ordinary; which appeared to have been all intended as Wills of the decd.; two of the papers were regularly executed according. to the 2d sec. of the acts of Assembly, but the testator having afterwards intermarried and had a child by the present wife, the Ordinary felt no hesitation in saying that they were of no effect altho regularly executed; because of the 10th. Section of the act of Assembly directed the manner of granting Probate of Will be expressly that, "if any person making a Will shall afterwards marry and die leaving issue, it shall be deemed and taken to be a revocation of such Will to all intents & purposes whatsoever." Another paper was then exhibited purporting to be the last Will & testament of the said Bethel Threadcraft dated in July 1814 being sometime after his marriage with his present wife and after the birth of his last child; the paper was not Signed nor Sealed nor was it in the Hand Writing of the dec'd. The following witnesses were then produced & examined in support of it.

Mr. Charles P. Butler swore that the deceased Mr. Threadcraft told him that his friend, Mr. Gates, had drawn his Will at his request and then desired him, Mr. Butler, to take it and consider it; that after having the paper now under examination in his possession for some days, he returned it to Mr. Threadcraft with his approbation of its contents; that Mr. Threadcraft said that he (Mr. T.) was satisfied also and that he intended to execute it: That witness thought that he had executed it; that this occurrence happened about two months before Threadcraft's death; and that he never heard the deceased after that conference say anything which would induce witness to think that he was wavering or intended to alter the paper; but only that Mr. Threadcraft mentioned that his wife was not satisfied with it altho he was perfectly so and that he meant to execute it, that Witness was the intimate friend and near neighbor of the deceased. Mr. Robert Gibson swore, that Mr. Threadcraft

[Page 79]

had admitted that same paper to his consideration that he returned it with his approbation; That Mr. Threadcraft mentioned that his wife was not satisfied with it, she having made some objections as to the distribution of the property: but that still Mr. Threadcraft was perfectly satisfied with the Will and expressed his intention to execute it, and altho his intimate friend and near neighbor he never heard the deceased express any intention after, that conference, of altering the paper.

The Ordinary then declared the paper to be a testament and valid as to the personal Estate; there was no objection to this decision and the Widow having acquiesced therein; the Proved testament of Butel Threadcraft, late of Charleston, Watch maker, dec., by the oaths of Charles P. Butler and Robert Gibson, there being no subscribing witnesses thereto at the same time qualified John R. Rogers an Executor named therein.

December 5. Proved the last Will & testament of Mary Axson, late of Charleston, Widow, dec., by the testimony of John Lloyd, Jr., one of the subscribing witnesses to the same: at the same time qualified Samuel E. Axson, Executor therein.

7. Citation granted to Matthew McCuller of St. James' Goose Creek, planter, to administer on the Estate Effects of Charles Cock, late of St. John's Parish, Overseer, dec., as next friend of Sarah Cock, the only child of the dec. so far as they were unadministered by Mary Cock, Overseer, dec. as next friend of Sarah Cock the only child of the dec. so far as they were unadministered by Mary Cock.

8. I hereby enter a Caveat against Frederick Gallagher or any other person whatever taking out letters of Administration on the Estate and Effects of William Smith, late of Charleston, mariner, and gunner, deceased, until I am heard before the Ordinary. Lavinia (X) Smith.

Qualified Sarah Threadcraft an executrix named in the last Will & Testament of Bethel Threadcraft, late of Charleston, Watch maker, deceased.

Citation granted to John Hicks of Capt. Clinton's Company of Infantry, to administer on the Estate & Effects of Trueworthy S. Parker late of Capt. Taylor's Company of Infantry, deceased, as principal Creditor.

Citation granted to Bridget Jones, of Charleston, Widow, to administer on the Estate & Effects of James Welsh, late of Charleston, Mariner, deceased, as principal Creditor.

[Page 80]

1814 December 8. Citation granted to Francois Pineau of Charleston, Shopkeeper, to administer the Estate & Effects of Christian Phink, late of Charleston, deceased, as principal Creditor.

Citation granted to Francois Pineau of Charleston, Shopkeeper, to administer on the Estate & Effects of Francois Nicholas late of Charleston, mariner, deceased, as principal Creditor.

Proved the last Will & testament of Bernard Castagnon, late of Charleston, Blacksmith, deceased, by the testimony of Berd. Barnette, one of the subscribing witnesses thereto: at the same time qualified Emile Marie LeGrand Castagnon, executrix, named therein: N. B. The original Will was exhibited in the French Language and a translation thereof was tendered and sworn as a true translation by Jean Francis Plumeau, a translator.

9. Citation granted to John Morrison of Charleston, Boarding House Keeper, to administer on the Estate & Effects on the five following Seamen, to wit: John C. Scott, John Bramble, Peter Boubeck, Henry Lambert and Benjamin Cook, all of Charleston, mariners, deceased as principal Creditor.

Citation granted to Levinia Smith of Charleston, Widow, to administer on the Estate & Effects of William Smith, late of Charleston, mariner and gunner, deceased as next of Kin.

Proved the last Will and testament of William Calburn of Charleston, mariner, deceased, by the testimony of John Egleston, one of the Subscribing witnesses thereto: at the same time [qualified] Margant Chambers, executrix, named therein:

Qualified Frederick Gallagher of Charleston, Store keeper, admor of the Estate & Effects of William Smith, late of Charleston, mariner, & Prize master, deceased, N. B. The caveat against Frederick Gallagher was withdrawn it appearing that there were two William Smiths on board the Saucy Jack who died or were killed in the cruise and the Caveat was designed to act against William Smith, the gunner's Estate: the Ordinary did not know the circumstance of their being of the same name and therefore was not special enough in the citation.

[Page 81]

1814 December 9. Qualified Abraham Gilbert Smith of Capt. Finner's Company of Infantry', admor of the Estate & Effects of John Crumwell, late of Capt. Clinton's Company of Infantry, deceased.

10. Citation granted to Michael Watson Perry of Capt. Butler's Company of Infantry to administer on the Estate & Effects of John Cole, late of Capt. Taylor's Company of Infantry, dec. as next friend in behalf of Mary Cole, Widow, of the dec.

Citation granted to Bridget Jones of Charleston, Widow, to administer on the Estate & Effects of John Morro of Charleston, mariner, deceased, as principal Creditor.

Citation granted to William Bahot Craig of Capt. Donoho's Company of Artillery to administer on the Estate & Effects of James Cooper, late of the same Company deceased, as principal Creditor.

12th. I hereby enter a Caveat against John Morrison or any other person taking out letters of admor on the Est'a. of John Scot until I am heard before the Ordinary. J. Gadsden for S. Refoe.

I hereby enter Caveat against any persons whatever taking out letters of Guardianship for the children of Thomas Campbell Cox, late of Charleston, Printer, dec. until I have heard before the Ordinary (withdrawn). signed, T. G. Skrine.

13. I do hereby enter a Caveat against James Morrison or any other persons taking out letters of administration on the Estate of John Bramble, late of Charleston, mariner, dec., until I am heard before the Ordinary. Thos. Towle for Richd. Nelson.

15. Proved the last Will and testament of Mary Middleton, late of Charleston, Widow, deceased, by the testimony of Thomas Parker Esquire, one of the subscribing witnesses thereto; at the same time qualified Henry Middleton and John Izard Middleton, Executors named therein.

16. Qualified Francois Pineau of Charleston Shop keeper, admor of the Estate & Effects of Christian Phink, late of Charleston, mariner, deceased.

Qualified Francois Pineau, admor of Francois Nicholas, late of Charleston, mariner, deceased.

[Page 82]

1814 December 16. Qualified John Hicks of Capt. Clinton's Company of Infantry admor of the Estate & Effects of Trueworthy S. Parker; late of Capt. Taylor's Company of Infantry, deceased.

16. Qualified Bridget Jones of Charleston, Widow, admix of the Estate & Effects of James Welsh, late of Charleston, mariner, deceased.

Qualified the said Bridget Jones admix of the Estate & Effects of John Munro, late of Charleston, mariner, deceased.

Qualified Lavinia Smith of Charleston, Widow, admix of the Estate & Effects of William Smith, late of Charleston, mariner and gunner, deceased, N. B. The Caveat was withdrawn. The Widow having the exclusive right to the admor, she having given conclusive proof of her marriage, which the dec.

Qualified George William Jones of Capt. Blunt's Company of Infantry, admor of the Estate & Effects of John Bosworth, late of Capt. Robinson's Company of Infantry, deceased.

20. Proved the last Will and testament of William Frederick Griswold, late of Charleston, mariner, deceased, by the testimony of William Porter, Esquire, the only subscribing witness thereto: at the same time qualified George Riley, executor, named therein.

Proved the last Will & testament of Henry Lambert, late of Charleston, mariner, deceased, by the testimony of William Porter, the only subscribing witness thereto; at the same time qualified John Morrison, executor, named therein.

Proved the last Will & testament of John Scott, late of Charleston, mariner, deceased, by the testimony of William Porter, Esq., the only subscribing witness thereto: at the same time qualified John Morrison, executor, named therein.

Proved the last Will & testament of Adolphe Duprean Thomas, late of Charleston, mariner, deceased, by the testimony of William Porter, Esquire, the only subscribing witness thereto: at the same time qualified Elizabeth Thomas, executrix, named therein.

21. Proved the last Will & testament of John Bramble, late of Charleston, mariner, deceased, by the testimony of William Porter, Esq., the only subscribing witness thereto; at the same time qualified Richard Nelson, executor, named therein:

[Page 83]

1814 Dec. 21st. Proved the last Will and testament of Henry Ward, late of Charleston, mariner, deceased, by the testimony of William Porter, Esq., the only subscribing witness thereto: at the same time qualified Clinton Cregier, executor, named therein.

Proved the last Will & testament of Jackson Lapaus late of Charleston, mariner, deceased, by the testimony of William Porter, Esq., the only subscribing witness thereto: at the same time qualified Clinton Gregier, executor, named therein.

Citation granted to Clinton Cregier of Charleston, Tavern Keeper, to administer on the Estate & Effects of Samuel Gold, late of _____, mariner & carpenter's mate in the service of the United States, deceased, as principal Creditor.

Citation granted to Levi Wolfe, a sergeant in Lieut. Lissenhoff's Company of Light Dragoons to administer on the Estate & Effects of John Ellis, late of the same Company, deceased.

John Gigg Flagler who obtained a Citation to the same effect on the 2nd. instant, having since departed this life.

Proved the last Will & testament of Angus Bethune, late of Charleston, Merchant, deceased, by the testimony of Patrick Duncan, one of the subscribing Witnesses thereto: at the same time qualified Margaret Bethune, executrix, named therein.

22. Proved the last Will & testament of John Lane, late of Charleston, mariner, deceased by the testimony of William Palmer one of the subscribing witnesses to the same: at the same time qualified Sarah Sampson, named executrix therein.

Qualified John Sanders of St. Thomas Parish Overseer, admor of the Estate & Effects of William Sanders, late of same place, Overseer, deceased.

23. Citation granted to James Grady of Charleston, Grocer, to administer on the Estate & Effects of John Colvin, late of Charleston, mariner, deceased, as principal Creditor.

Qualified John Morrison of Charleston, Board House Keeper, admor of the Estate & Effects of Peter Boubeck late of Charleston mariner dec.

[Page 84]

1814 Decd. 23rd. Qualified John Morison [*sic*] of Charleston, Boarding House Keeper, admor of the Estate & Effects of Benjamin Cock, late of Charleston, mariner deceased.

Qualified Levi Wolfe of the 2nd. Regt. of Lt. Dragoons, admor of the Estate & Effects of John Ellis, late of the same Regt., dec.

Proved the last Will & testament of Felix Warley, late of Charleston Planter, deceased, by the testimony of James S. Bee, one of the subscribing witnesses thereto: at the same time qualified William Kern Warley, executor, named therein.

Qualified Margaret Leaumont of Charleston Widow, admix of the Estate & Effects of Marie Laurent Theresa Leaumont de L'ominie, late of Charleston, Widow, deceased, de bonis non & cum testamento annexo.

24. Thomas Simons, Caveat. I do hereby enter a Caveat against any person taking out Letters of Administration on the Estate & Effects of Thomas Simons, late of Capt. Hawkins, Company of Artillery Stationed at Fort Moultrie, deceased, until I am heard before the Ordinary. Robert Simons of Charlotte Court House, No. Car.

29. Citation granted to Martha Knox of Charleston, Widow to administer on, the Estate & Effects of Matthew Knox, late of Charleston, Crier of the Court of Common Pleas, General Session, deceased, as next of Kin.

30. Citation granted Jane Wilson of Charleston, Widow, to administer on the Estate & Effects of Samuel Wilson, late of Capt. King's Company of 18 Regt. of Infantry at Fort Johnson, deceased, as next of Kin.

31. Caveat - Joseph Maxey. I do hereby enter a Caveat against any person taking out letters of Administration on the Estate & Effects of Joseph Maxey, late of [St.] John's Parish, Overseer, deceased, until I am heard before the Ordinary. Signed: Isaac Fickling.

Citation granted to Isaac Fickling of St. Andrew's Parish, Overseer, to administer on the Estate & Effects of Joseph Maxey, late of John's Island, Overseer, deceased, as next of Kin.

[Page 85]

1815 January 2. Qualified James Grady of Charleston, Grocer, admor of the Estate & Effects of James Colvin, late of Charleston, Mariner, deceased.

Proved the last Will & testament of Matthew Fleming, late of Charleston, Grocer, deceased, by the testimony of Richard McCormick, one of the subscribing Witnesses thereto:

4. Proved the last Will & testament of Peter Guerry, late of St. James' Parish, Santee, Schoolmaster, deceased, by the testimony of Daniel Darby, one of the subscribing witnesses thereto: at the same time qualified James Edward German, executor named therein.

5. Proved the last Will & testament of Thomas Blackmon, late of St. James' Parish, Goose Creek, planter, deceased, by the testimony of John Willson, one of the subscribing witnesses thereto: at the same time qualified Thomas Blackmon, executor named therein.

Approved the last Will & testament of William Henry Roper, late of Charleston Mariner, deceased, by the testimony of John S. Rose, a subscribing Witness thereto: at the same time qualified John Thomas Smart[?], named executor therein.

Citation granted to John Morrison of Charleston, Boarding House Keeper, to administer on the Estate & Effects of John Bateze, late of Charleston, mariner, deceased, as principal Creditor.

Read the Petition of the Revd. Dr. Simon Felix Gallagher, praying to be appointed Guardian to Jim, a free mulatto boy of about five years of age mentioned in the last Will & Testament of Joseph Brown, late of Charleston, Grocer deceased. Ordered accord'y.

6. Proved the last Will & testament of John White, late of Charleston, Mariner, deceased, by the testimony of William Porter and subscribing witness thereto; at the same time qualified Mary Smith, executrix named therein.

7. Citation granted to William Wood of Charleston, Rigger, to administer on the Estate & Effects of Jacob Buchanan, late of Charleston, Gunsmith, deceased, as principal Creditor.

9. Citation granted to Sarah Sampson of Charleston, Widow, to administer on the Estate & Effects of Henry Fennick, late of Charleston, Mariner, deceased, as principal Creditor.

[Page 86]

1815 Jany. 9. Proved the last Will & Testament of Ann Woodmancy, late of Charleston, Widow, deceased, by the testimony of John Dixon, one of the subscribing witnesses thereto: at the same time qualified Catherine Seavery, executrix named therein.

Proved the last Will & testament of Alexander Quinn, late of Charleston, Mariner, deceased, by the testimony of William Porter, the subscribing witness thereto: at the same time James Grady, executor therein named.

9. Qualified Martha Knox of Charleston, Widow, admix of the Estate & Effects of Matthew Knox, late of Charleston, Cryer of the Court of Common Pleas & Gen. Sessions, deceased.

10. Qualified John Gadsden, an executor named in the last Will & testament of Mary Edwards, late of Charleston, Spinster, deceased.

Proved the last Will and testament of Robert Dewar, late of Charleston, Esquire, deceased, by the testimony of Henry H. Bacot, one of the subscribing witnesses thereto; at the same time qualified Thomas Wright Bacot, executor named therein.

Proved the last Will & testament of Alexander McMorton, late of Wadmalaw planter, deceased, by the testimony of Charles G. Capers, the subscribing witness named thereto:

13. Citation to William Adams of Capt. Donoho's Company of Artillery to administer on the Estate & Effects of Elisha Hancock of the same Company, deceased, as principal Creditor.

Qualified John Morrison of Charleston, Boarding House Keeper, administrator of the Estate & Effects of John Bateze, late of Charleston, mariner, deceased.

Qualified William Woods of Charleston, Rigger, administer of Estate & Effects of Jacob Buchanan late of Charleston, Gunsmith, deceased..

Citation granted to Mary Smith of Charleston, Widow, to administer on the Estate & Effects of Scipeo Smith, late of Charleston, a free Black hand and mariner, deceased, as principal Creditor.

14. Citation granted to Martha Fairley, Charleston, Widow, to administer on the estate & Effects of Hana Fairley, late of Charleston, Cabinet Maker, as the next of Kin.

Citation granted to Michael Watson Perry of Capt. Balter's Company of Inf., to administer on the Estate & Effects of John Cole late of Capt. Taylor's Company of Infantry, deceased, as next friend. see 10 Dec. 1814. the 1st Cit. lost.

[Page 87]

1815 January 16. Proved the last Will and testament of Willard Fultz, late of St. John's Parish, Berkeley, Planter, deceased, by the testimony of Benjamin

Scott, one of the subscribing witnesses thereto, at the same time Deammah Fultz, executrix, named therein.

17. Citation granted to Ann Hurst of Charleston, Widow, to administer on the Estate & Effects of John Hurst, late a Sutler attached to Garrison of Fort Moultrie, dec., as next of Kin.

20. Proved the last Will and testament of Ann E. Dennison late of Charleston, deceased, by the testimony of John E. Shirmer, one of the subscribing witnesses thereto, also three separate Codicils of the testimony of Charles H. Turner, one of the subscribing witnesses to each of them.

Qualified Martha Fairley of Charleston, Widow, Administratrix of the Estate & Effects of Hance Fairley, late of Charleston, Cabinetmaker, deceased.

Qualified Jane Wilson of Newberry District, Widow, Administratrix of the Estate & Effects of Samuel Wilson, late of Capt. King's Company of Infantry, deceased.

Qualified William Adams of Capt. Donoho's Company of Artillery, administrator of the Estate & Effects of Elisha Hancock, late of same Company, deceased.

Qualified Michael Watson Perry of Capt. Butler's Company of Infantry, administrator of the Estate & Effects of John Cole, late of Capt. Robinson's Company of Infantry, deceased.

Citation granted to William Crafts of Charleston, Merchant, to administer on the Estate & Effects of Thomas Loughton Smith, late of Charleston, Esquire, deceased, de bonis non and cum testamento annexo, as next friend.

Citation granted to Davis Stallings of Capt. Donoho's Company of Artillery, to administer on the Estate & Effects of Wiley Stallings, late of the same Company, deceased.

21. Qualified James Dennison and James Mitchell, named executors in the last Will and Testament of Ann Elizabeth Dennison, late of Charleston, deceased.

23. Citation granted to Sarah Sampson of Charleston, Widow, to administer on the Estate & Effects of John Anderson, otherwise called Johannes Johannissan, late of Charleston, Mariner, deceased, as principal Creditor.

[Page 88]

1815 January 24. Proved the last Will & testament of Robert Smith, late of Charleston, mariner (in the schooner Alligator), deceased, by the testimony of H. Magruder and John Robinson, two of the subscribing witnesses thereto; at the same time qualified James Gillespie, executor, therein named.

Qualified Clinton Gregier, Administrator of the Estate & Effects of Samuel Gold, late a Mariner and carpenter's mate in the service of the United States, deceased.

Citation Granted to Bridget Jones of Charleston, Widow, to administer on the Estate & Effects of John Page, late of Charleston, mariner, deceased.

25. Citation granted to Elizabeth Robinson of Wadmalaw, Widow, to administer on the Estate & Effects of Thomas John Robinson, late of same place, Overseer, deceased, as next of Kin.

Citation granted to John Jeffords of Christ Church Parish, planter, to administer on the Estate & Effects of Daniel Jeffords, late of same place, Carpenter, deceased, as next of Kin.

27. Qualified Sarah Sampson of Charleston, Widow, to administer on Estate & Effects of Henry Fennick, late of Charleston, mariner, decd.

Qualified Mary Smith of Charleston, Widow, to administer on Estate & Effects of Scipio Smith (a free black man), mariner, dec.

Qualified Davis Stallings of Capt. Donoho's Company of Artillery, admor of the Estate & Effects of Wiley Stallings, late of same Company, deceased.

Citation granted to William Sandiford of Capt. Donoho's Company of Artillery, to administer on the Estate & Effects of Edward Wiley, late of same Company, dec.

Citation granted to William Sandiford of Capt. Donoho's Company of Artillery, to administer on the Estate & Effects of Charles Manning, late of the same Company, dec.

Citation granted to Jesse Herring of Capt. Donoho's Company of Artillery to administer on the Estate & Effects of John McCurdy, late of the same Company, decd.

28. Citation granted to Joseph Sibley of Charleston, Store keeper, to administer on the Estate & Effects of Samuel Williams, late of Capt. Hamelton's Company of Infantry, decd., as principal Creditor.

[Page 89]

1815 February 1st. Qualified Isaac Fickling of St. Andrew's Parish, Overseer, admor of the Estate & Effects of Joseph Maxey, late of John's Island, Overseer, decd.

2. Citation granted to Marie Gabrielle Jeane Imbert, of Charleston, Widow to administer on the Estate & Effects of Charles Louis Imbert, late of same place, Mariner, decd., as next of Kin.

3. Qualified Ann Hunt of Sullivan's Island Widow, admix of the Estate & Effects of John Hunt, late a Sutler attached to the Garrison at Fort Moultrie, deceased.

Qualified Joseph Sibley of Charleston, Store Keeper admor of the Estate & Effects of Samuel Williams, late of Capt. Hamilton's Company of Infantry 18th. Regt., dec.

Qualified Bridget Jones of Charleston, Widow, Admix of the Estate & Effects of John Page. late of Charleston, Mariner, decd.

Qualified John Jeffords of Christ Church Parish. planter, Admor of the Estate & Effects of Daniel Jeffords, late of the same place, Carpenter, dec.

Proved the last Will and testament of William Russel, late of Charleston, Merchant, deceased, by the testimony of James S. Neilson, Esq., one of the subscribing witnesses thereto: and also the Codicil to the said Will by the oath of the same Gentleman he being one of the subscribing Witnesses thereto.

At the same time qualified Anthony McGriffie, alias Anthony McGuffie, an executor named therein.

7. Citation granted to Robert Lassiter, Sulter, attached to the troops at Castle Pinckney, to administer on the Estate & Effects of Nathaniel Gibson, a private in Capt. Hawkins' Company of Artillery, as principal Creditor.

Qualified Elizabeth Robinson of Wadmalaw Island, Widow, admix of the Estate & Effects of Thomas John Robinson, late of same place, Overseer, deceased.

Proved the last Will & testament of Arnoldus Vanderhorst of Charleston, planter, deceased, by the testimony of John Clifford You, one of the subscribing witnesses thereof.

[Page 90]

1815 February 10. Citation granted to Elizabeth Bunch of Charleston, Widow, to administer on the Estate & Effects of Timothy Bunch, late of same place, Butcher, deceased, as next of Kin.

Qualified John Stanyarne Vanderhorst and Elias Vanderhorst, executors, named in the last Will & testament of Arnoldus Vanderhorst, late of Charleston, Planter, Deceased.

11. Proved the last Will & testament of Sarah Prior, late of St. John's Parish, Berkeley, Widow, deceased, by the testimony of Revd. John Jacob Tschiedy, one of the subscribing witnesses thereto.

Qualified Marie Gabrielle Jeane Imbert of Charleston, Widow, admix of the Estate & Effects of Charles Louis Imbert, late of Charleston, mariner, deceased.

Qualified Sarah Sampson of Charleston, Widow, admix of Estate & Effects of John Anderson, otherwise called Johannes Johannesson, late of Charleston, Mariner, deceased.

Proved the last Will & testament of Hary Grant, late of Charleston, deceased, by the testimony of Samuel E. Axson, one of the subscribing witnesses thereto and also a letter parporting to be instructions to his executors by the testimony of Thomas W. Price, also qualified Thomas William Price an executor named therein.

17. Qualified Robert Lassiter, Sullter [sic] at Castle Pinckney, admor of the Estate of Nathaniel Gibson, late of Capt. Hawkins' Company of Artillery dec.

Qualified William Sandiford of Capt. Donoho's Company of Artillery, admor of the Estate & Effects of Edward Wiley, late of the same Company, dec.

Qualified the said William Sandiford of Capt. Donoho's Company of Artillery, admor of Estate & Effects of Charles Manning of the same Company, dec.

Qualified Jake Huring of Capt. Donoho's Company of Artillery, admor of the Estate & Effects of John McCurdy of the same Company, dec.

22. Citation granted to Elizabeth Brailsford of Charleston, Widow, to administer on the Estate & Effects of John Brailsford, late of same place, Planter, dec., as next of Kin.

[Page 91]

1815 February 24. Proved the last Will and Testament of Elizabeth Beckman, late of Charleston Widow, deceased, by the testimony of Charles Fraser and William Johnson, two of the subscribing witnesses thereto: also a Codicil to the same by the testimony of the s'd W. Johnson, a subscribing witness; at the same time qualified Beckman McCall, executor therein named.

Citation granted to Henry Philip Wesner of Charleston, Wharfinger, to administer on the Estate & Effects of John George Brindley, late of the Same place, Overseer, deceased, as next friend.

Qualified Henry Fickling of John's Island, Planter, admor of the Estate & Effects of Osborn Nicholls, late of Wadmalaw, Shipwright, deceased.

[in margin] Febry. 27. Proved the last Will & testament of Patrick Cormish Kelly, late of Charles[ton] Schoolmaster, dec., by the testimony of M. O. Donovan, one of the subscribing witnesses thereto.

28. Citation granted to John Swiley of Kershaw District, to administer on the Estate & Effects of David Swiley, late of Capt. Fessner's Company of Infantry.

March 2. Qualified Elizabeth Bunch of Charleston, Widow, admix of the Estate & Effects of Timothy Bunch, late of Charleston, Butcher, deceased.

Citation granted to Matthew O'Driscoll of St. Bartholomew's Parish, to administer on the Estate & Effects of Paul Hory Dudley, late of same place, planter, deceased, as next friend.

Qualified William Windham Trapier of Georgetown, So. Ca,. admor de Bonis non of Peter Roberts late of St. Stephens' Parish, planter, dec.

3. Proved the last Will & testament of William Martin, late of Capt. Donoho's Corps. of Artillers, deceased, by the testimony of Benjamin Prince, one of the subscribing Witnesses thereto:

at the same [time] Citation granted to James Martin of the same Corps, to administer on the Estate & Effects of the said William Martin, dec., as next of Kin with his Will annexed there being no executor named in the said Will.

Citation granted to Ann Dyson, Widow, to administer on the Estate & Effects of Thomas Dyson, late of St. John's, Berkeley, fanner, dec., as next of Kin with the Will annexed.

Citation granted to Robert Lassiter, a sulter (sic). to the Garrison of Castle Pinckney, to administer on the Estate & Effects of Obidiah Rutland, late of Capt. Hawkins' Corps of Artillery, deceased, as principal Creditor.

[Page 92]

1815 March 8. Qualified John Swilley of Kershaw District, planter, admor of the Estate & Effects of Daniel Swilley, late of Capt. Fenner's Company of Infantry, dec.

Citation granted to Richard Baker North, of Charleston, Factor, to administrator on the Estate Effects of Tucker North, late of the same place, Esquire, deceased, as next of Kin.

Citation granted to John Laurens North, Esquire, to administer on the Estate & Effects of Glen Drayton, late a Lieut. in the Navy of the United States, dec., as next friend.

Citation Special granted Marie Elliott, a legatee named in a certain paper purporting to be the last Will & testament of William Austin to cite William Austin, of Charleston, Schoolmaster, to show cause why the said Will should be not received to be Proved & to appear on tomorrow the 9 inst. at 11 O'clock.

William Austin Case - In the Court of Ordinary 9 March.

Mr. Craft in behalf of Marie Elliott appeared and moved that Sam. W. Miller, one of the Subscribing witnesses of the Will should be sworn and examined: Mr. Miller was then sworn & proved the Will in the usual manner. Stating that he saw the testator, William Austin sign & seal the same as his Will & testament that he together with David G. Denson and Peter X Lafar signed their names as witnesses at the request of the testator in his presence & in the presence of each other: Mr. Peter X Lafar who was examined on the 15 Sept. 1814 declared to the same effect: Mr. Lafar being in ill health his evidence was taken by consent at that time, and he has since died. Mr. Craft then moved that a citation should issue citing William Austin to support his Caveat or show cause why the will should not be proved; when Mr. Grimke appeared in behalf of Austin & engaged to be prepared on Wednesday next at 11 o'clock to which time the Court was adjourned.

9. Qualified William Bahob Craig of Capt. Donoho's Company of Artillery, admor of the Estate & Effects of James Cooper, late of same Company, deceased.

10. Citation granted to Elizabeth Malpass of St. James' Parish, Santee, Widow, to administer on the Estate & Effects of Lewis Malpass, late of same place, planter, decd., as next of Kin.

11. [in margin] March 11. Citation granted to John Hicks of Capt. King's Company of Infantry, to administer on the Estate & Effects of William Watson Brown of the same Company, deceased, as principal Credit.

[Page 93]

1815 March 10. Qualified James Martin, admor with Will annexed of William Martin, late of Capt. Donoho's Company of Artillery, deceased.

15. Citation granted to Margaret Lawton of James Island to administer on the Estate & Effects of Hearne Freer, late of same place, planter, deceased, as next of Kin.

17. Qualified Richard Baker North of Charleston, Factor, to administer on the Estate & Effects of Tucker North late of Charleston, Esquire, deceased.

Qualified John Laurens North of Pendleton district, Esquire, admor of the Estate & Effects of Glen Drayton, late a lieutenant in the Navy of the United States, deceased

Citation granted to Frederick Gallagher of Charleston, Grocer, to administer on the. Estate & Effects of James Cotterel, late of same place, mariner, deceased, as next friend.

Citation granted to Elizabeth Furman of St. James' Goose Greek, to administer on the Estate & Effects of Josiah Furman, late of Capt. Hawkins' Company of Artillery, decd., as next of Kin.

[in margin] 18 March. Qualified Elizabeth Brailsford of Charleston, Widow, admix of the Estate & Effects of John Brailsford, late of same place, planter, decd.

27. Qualified Frederick Gallagher of Charleston, Grocer, administrator of the Estate & Effects of James Cotterel, late of Charleston, mariner, deceased.

Citation granted to John Allen Talley of Capt. Donoho's Corps of Artillery to administer on the Estate & Effects of Abraham Taylor, late of the same Company, deceased, as principal Creditor.

Citation to the said John Allen Talley to administer on the Estate & Effects of William Perry, late of the same place, decd., as principal Creditor.

Citation granted to Wm. Hickling of Chester District, farmer, to admor on the Est'a. & Effects of Robert Potts, late of _____ deceased, as next of Kin.

28. Proved the last Will & testament of George Mathewes, late of Charleston, Esquire, decd., by the testimony of Dr. Alex'r Baron, one of the subscribing witnesses thereto.

[Page 94]

1815 March 29. Citation granted to William Owen of St. John's Parish, Berkeley, planter, to administer on the Estate & Effects of Silas Simmons Owen, late of same place, Schoolmaster, decd., as next of Kin.

Citation granted to Elizabeth Ann Nichoels of Charleston, Widow, to administer the Estate & Effects of Henry Nichoels late of the same place, Planter, deceased, as next of Kin.

30. Citation granted to Thomas Young Smith and Morton Wilks Smith of Charleston, Planters, to administer on the Estate Effects of Jane Smith, late of same place, Widow, deceased.

Qualified Jeremiah Faust of Charleston, Grocer, admor of the Estate & Effects of Josiah Furman, late of Capt. Hawkins' Company of Artillery, deceased, in the room of Elizabeth Furman of St. James' Parish, Goose Creek, Widow, who on the 17 inst. obtained Citation, she being the mother of the dec. the said Elizabeth Furman having in person appeared in Court and requested the same.

31. Citation granted to Abraham Hood of St. Stephen's Parish, farmer, to administer on the Estate & Effects of Shadrack Williams, late of same place, farmer, deceased, as next friend.

Qualified Margaret Lawton of James' Island, admix of the Estate & Effects of Hearne Feer, late of same place, planter, deceased.

March 31. Robert Pottes' Case. William Hickling who had obtained a Citation to administer on the Estate & Effects of Robert Pottes, or Potts, appeared in Court with securities and after he had been qualified he produced a paper purporting to be the last Will & testament of the said Robert Pottes; which being proved to the satisfaction of the Ordinary, the same having been in his possession but not knowing the nature of the business he did not exhibit to the Ordinary: therefore

Proved the last Will & testament of Robert Pottes, late private in Robert M. Giles' Company of Artillery, deceased, by the testimony of John McDaniel, one of the subscribing witnesses thereto, at the same time qualified William Hickling, executor.

[Page 95]

1815 April 4. Qualified Elizabeth Malpass of St. James' Parish, Santee, widow, Admix of the Estate & Effects of Lewis Malpass late of same place, planter, dec.

[in margin] April 7 Qualified Wilkes Smith of Charleston, planter, admor of the Estate & Effects of Jane Smith, late of same place, Widow, deceased.

7. Qualified Charles G. Coslet and Edmund M. Phelon executors named in the last Will and testament of Patrick Cormick Kelly, late of Charleston, Schoolmaster, deceased.

Proved the last Will & testament of Francis Louis Noah Roux, late of Charleston, Merchant, deceased, by the testimony of William C. Wiggins and also the Codicil attached thereto by the same witness he being a subscribing witness to both instruments of writing: at the same time qualified Dr. Peter Joseph Moses and Lewis Roux, executors therein named.

Proved the last Will & testament of William Conyers, late of Charleston, mariner, deceased, by the testimony of David Adams, one of the subscribing witnesses thereto: at the same qualified Lydia Conyers executrix named therein.

Qualified Thomas Young Smith, admor of Jane Smith, late of Charleston, Widow, dec.

Citation to William Devlin of Capt. William Taylor's Company of Infantry to administer on the Estate & Effects of Henry Major, late of Capt. Blount's Company of Infantry, decd., as principal Creditor.

Citation granted to said W. Devlin to administer on Estate of Robert Gibbons, late of Capt. H. P. Taylor's Company of Infantry.

Citation granted said W. Devlin to administer on the Estate & Effects of John Dirquil, late of Capt. Dick's Company of Infantry, deceased, as principal Creditor.

Citation granted to P. W. Devlin to admor on the Estate & Effects of John Lang, late of Lieut. King's Company of Infantry, dec. as principal Creditor.

Citation granted to said W. Devlin to admor on the Estate & Effects of Henry James, late of Capt. James Hamilton's Company, deceased, as principal Creditor.

Citation granted to John Everingham of Charleston, Merchant, to administer on the Estate & Effects of Peter Sicard, late of Charleston, mariner, deceased, as principal Creditor.

[Page 96]

1815 April 14. Citation granted to Wm. Devlin of Capt. H. P. Taylor's Comp: of Infantry to adm on the Estate & Effects of Samuel Timmons, late of Capt. Dick's Comp: of [Infantry], deceased, as principal Creditor.

Citation granted to William T. Botang of Charleston, Mariner, to administer on the Estate & Effects of Isaac Griffin, late of Charleston Mariner, dec. as principal Creditor.

Qualified Elizabeth Ann Nicholes of Charleston Widow admix of the Estate & Effects of Henry Nicholes, late of same place, Planter, deceased.

18. Citation granted Henry Killingsworth of Capt. Blunt's Comp: of Infantry to administer on the Estate & Effects of Jesse Lenier, late of same Comp: deceased, as principal Creditor.

Citation granted to Bryant Shot of Capt. Blunt's Comp: of Infantry to administer on the Estate & Effects of Arthur Nowels, late of same Comp: decd. as principal Creditor.

John Campbell's Case. This day appeared in Court John Magrath of Charleston, Merchant, in pursuance of a Special Citation at the instance of John Gordon, one of his sureties in the admor of John Campbell's Estate, and offered other sureties in the Room of the said John Gordon who prayed to be relieved.

21. Citation granted to Elizabeth Malpass of ____ to adm: on the Estate & Effects of Joel Malpass, late of ____ planter, dec. as next of Kin.

[in margin] 25 April 1815. Citation granted to Ann Smith of Charleston to administer on the Estate & Effects of Hannah Christiana Walters, late of Charleston, Spinster, decd., as next friend.

25. Caveat entered by Thomas Towle against proving any Will of John Neder, late of Charleston mariner, decd.

26. Qualified William Botang of Charleston, Mariner, admor of the Estate & Effects of Isaac Griffin, late of same place, Mariner, decd.

28. Qualified Robert Simons of Mecklenburg County, North Caro., admor of the Estate & Effects of Thomas Simons, late of Capt. Hawkins' Company of Artillery, decd.

Qualified Abraham Hood of St. Stephen's Parish, Farmer, admor of the Estate & Effects of Shadrach Williams, late of same place, decd.

[Page 97]

1815 April 28. Qualified John Everingham of Charleston, Merchant, admor of the Estate & Effects of Peter Sicard, late of same place, Mariner, deceased.

28. Citation granted to Robert Griggs of Capt. Hawkins' Company of Artillery to administer on the Estate & Effects of Jonathan Tanner late of the same Company, decd. as principal Creditor.

Citation granted to Robert Griggs of Capt. Hawkins Company of Artillery to administer on the Estate & Effects of William Lingo, late of the same Company, decd., as principal Creditor.

Special Citation granted to Jane Nolen to cite Richard Henry Gradrick [Gradick], admor of Christian Gradrick [Gradick] to show cause why he should not make a true and faithful acct: before me to appear on Wednesday the third day of May next. At 11 o'clock in the forenoon.

Caveat entered by Tho. Towle against any Will or Wills, Letters of administration or otherwise of John Medie, late of Charleston, Mariner, decd. being proved or granted.

29. The above Caveat withdrawn and another entered by Eliza Meder, to the same affect.

May 2nd. Proved the last Will & Testament of Nicol Bryce, late of Charleston, Merchant, by the testimony of Alex'r Kirk, one of the subscribing witnesses thereto: also a Codicil to the said Will by the same witness being also a subscribing witness thereto: at the same time qualified James Scot, executor named therein.

4. Citation granted to Patrick Connele Plunkett of Charleston, Grocer to administer on the Estate & Effects of Thomas Lynch, late of Charleston, Bricklayer, decd, as next friend.

Citation granted to Samuel Verree of Charleston, Goldsmith, to administer on the Estate & Effects of Joseph Verree, Senior, late of Charleston, Carpenter, decd., as next of Kin so far as they were left unadministered by Mary Virree, executrix, decd.

Qualified William Cattell of St. Andrew's Parish, planter, admor of Hannah Christianna Walton, late of Charleston Spinster, decd., as next of Kin. Mrs. Ann Smith who had Obtained a Citation having declined in his favor.

[Page 98]

1815 May 9. Qualified Robert Griggs of Capt. Hawkins' Company of Artillery, admor of the Estate & Effects of Jonathan Tanner, late of same Company, decd.

Qualified the said Robert Griggs, admor of the Estate & Effects of William Lingo, late of the same Company, decd.

Qualified Israel Moses of Charleston, Cooper, admor of the Estate & effects of Sarah Moses, late of Charleston Widow, decd.

10. Caveat entered by M. King as Proctor for P. McDermott against admor on the Estate of Thomas Lynch, late of Charleston, Bricklayer, being granted until he is heard before the Ordinary.

11. Citation granted to Rubin Grady of Capt. Hawkins' Company of Artillery to administer on the Estate & Effects of Thomas Bampfield, late of same Corps, deceased, as principal Creditor and next friend.

Citation special granted to William Allen Deas in behalf of the heirs of Rebecca Keley, a free colored woman, to cite John Hinces of St. James, Parish Goose Creek to make and render an account of his admor to appear on Thursday the twenty fifth day of May instant at Eleven O'clock in the forenoon.

12. Proved the last Will & testament of David Ramsey, late of Charleston, Physician, deceased, by the testimony of Hext McCall, Esquire, there being no subscribing witnesses thereto: At the same time qualified Robert Y. Hayne, executor, named therein.

Proved the last Will & testament of Joseph Augustus DeViller, late of Charleston, Book Seller, deceased, by the testimony of John B. White, Esquire, one of the subscribing witnesses thereto: at the same time qualified Jacob F. Mintzing and Henry Siffley, Executors named therein.

Qualified William Owen of St. James' Parish, planter, admor of the Estate & Effects of Silas Simmons Owen, late of St. John's Parish, Berkeley, Schoolmaster, deceased.

[Page 99]

1815 May 16. Citation granted to Douglass Patterson of Capt. Hawkins' Corps of Artillery, to administer on the Estate & Effects of Matthew Watson, late of the same company, deceased, as principal Creditor.

Citation granted to Richard Jones, Head of Capt. Hawkins' Company of Artillery to administer on the Estate & Effects of Alsey Burges, late of the same Company, decd., as principal Creditor.

17. Proved the last Will & testament of Stephen Shrewsbury, late of Charleston, Esquire, deceased, by the testimony of James Futerell, one of the subscribing witnesses thereto: at the same time qualified Francis Dickinson, executor thereto named.

Citation granted to Robert Lehre Key of Charleston, Taylor, to administer on the Estate & Effects of Elizabeth Key, late of St. Stephen's Parish, widow, deceased, as next of Kin.

18. Proved the last Will & testament of James Blair, late of Charleston, Vendue Master, decd., by the testimony of Henry Alexander DeSaussure, Esq., one of the subscribing witnesses thereto:

19. Qualified Robert Anderson, an executor named in the last Will & testament of James Blair, late of Charleston, Vendue Master, deceased. At the same time of qualifying Mr. Anderson requested that he might have three months to make his Election whether he should take upon himself the burthen and execution of the last Will and testament of Margaret Warner Maine, late of Charleston, Widow, decd., the said James Blair having been the sole Executor thereof.

Qualified Bryant Shots of Capt. Blount's Company of Infantry, Admor of the Estate & Effects of Arthur Vowels, late of the same Company, decd.

Qualified Rubin Grady of Capt. Hawkins' Corps of Artillery, admor of the Estate & Effects of Thomas Bampfield late of the same Company, decd.

Citation granted Isaac Wood of Capt. Hawkins' Company of Artillery to administer on the Estate & Effects of James Darnell, late of the same Company, decd., as next friend.

[Page 100]

1815 May 22. Citation granted to Isaac Sketelstrass of Capt. Blount's Company of Infantry to administer on the Estate & Effects of Isaac Rousen, Joseph Spruel and William Sketelstrass, all of Capt. Blount's Company aforesaid, decd., as next of Kin.

24. Citation granted to Denson Pilkenton of Capt. Hawkins' Company of Artillery to administer on the Estate & effects of Ezekiel Futch, late of Capt. Hawkins', Corps of Artillery, decd., as principal Creditor.

23. Qualified Patrick McDermot of Charleston, Carpenter, Admor of the Estate & Effects of Thomas Lynch, Bricklayer, deceased.

[in margin] 25 May. Citation granted to William Medlin of Capt. Hawkins' Company of Artillery, to administer on the Estate & Effects of James Brown, late of same Company, decd., as principal Creditor.

26. Qualified Joseph Palmer of St. John's Parish, Berkeley, planter, admor of the Estate & Effects of George Porcher, late of same place, planter, decd.

Qualified Douglass Patterson of Capt. Hawkins' Company of Artillery, admor of the Estate & Effects of Matthew Watson, late of the same Company, deceased.

[in margin] May 26. Qualified Richard Jones, Head of Capt. Hawkins' Company of Artillery, admor of the Estate & Effects of Alva Burges of the same Company, decd.

30. Qualified Catherine Lee Edwards, late Catherine Lee Banks, as executrix named in the last Will & testament of Charles Banks, late of Charleston, Merchant, deceased.

Citation granted to John McDaniel of a Corps of Artillery late Capt. R. M. Gilles to administer on the Estate & Effects of James Whitehead, late of same Corps, deceased, as principal Creditor.

Qualified Isaac Wood of Capt. Hawkins' Company of Artillery, admor of the Estate & Effects of James Darnell, late of same Corps, decd.

Citation to Cader Parker of Capt. Hawkins' Company of Artillery to administer on the Estate & Effects of William Church, late of the same Company, decd., as principal Creditor.

21. Proved the last Will & testament of Susanna Eady, late of St. James Parish, Berkley, Widow, deceased, by the testimony of Nathaniel Marion, one of the subscribing witnesses thereto.

Qualified John Allen Talley of Capt. Donoho's Company of Artillery, admor of the Estate & Effects [of] William. Perry, late of same Corps, deceased.

Qualified John Allen Talley, admor of Abraham Taylor, decd., of the same Corps.

[Page 101]

1815 June 1. Special. Citation granted to James Sparrow and John Strohecker, securities to Richard Henry Gradrick [Gradick], admor of Christian Gradick, late of Charleston, Butcher, decd., to cite the admor to show cause, why such order and decree should not be made as to grant the securities relief.

2d. Qualified John McDaniel of the Corps of Artillery, late Capt. R. M. Giles, admor James Whitehead, decd., of the same corps.

Proved the last Will and testament of Benoit Vieusse, late of Charleston, Confectioner, deceased, by the testimony of E. Polk, one of the subscribing Witnesses thereto: at the same [time] Francoise Duero Vieusse, executrix, therein named.

Qualified Denson Pilkenton of Capt. Hawkins' Company of Artillery, admor of the Estate & Effects of Ezekiel Futch, late of the same corps, decd.

Citation granted to William Jennings, late of Capt. Clinton's Company of Infantry to Admor on the several[?] Estate of John Jurneken and Peter Linquist, both of them late of the same Company, deceased, as principal Creditor.

[in margin] June 3d. Qualified Ann Legge of Charleston, Widow, admix de bonis non cum testamento annexo of Sophia Packrow, late of St. Bartholomew's Parish, Widow, decd.

3d. Qualified Isaac Sketalstrass of Capt. Blount's Company of Infantry, admor of the Estate & Effects of Joseph Spruce, late of same corps, decd.

Proved the last Will and testament of Joseph Finck, late of Charleston, Merchant, deceased, by the testimony of James Mackie of Charleston, Esquire, there being no security witness thereto: At the same time the said James

Mackie renounced his Executorship and reported Letters of Administration, ad colligendum bona defuneti which was accordingly granted.

Qualified Daniel Ravenel, an executor named in the Will of Daniel Ravenel, late of Charleston, planter, deceased.

6. Citation granted to Jedidiah Whitney, Sutler, at Fort Moultrie to administer on the Estate & Effects of Lewis Williams, late of Capt. H. P. Taylor Company of Infantry, deceased, as principal Creditor.

9. Citation granted to _____ to administer on the Estate & Effects of Sion King, late of ___.

[Page 102]

1815 June 9. Qualified Henry Philip Wesner of Charleston, Wharfinger, admor of the Estate & Effects of John George Brindley, late of St. James' Santee, Overseer, deceased.

Qualified John R. Mathewes and executor named in the last Will and testament of George Mathewes, late of Charleston, Vendue Master, deceased.

Citation granted to David Wood of Capt. Blount's Company of Infantry, to administer on the Estate & Effects of Enoch Ferby of the same Company, deceased, as principal Creditor.

Citation to David Wood, to administer on the Estate & Effects of Benjamin Lewis Balance Cox, late of Capt. Blount's Com: of infantry, deceased.

Citation granted to William Brims of Capt. Tindal's Comp of Infantry to administer on the Estate & Effects of Jesse McGoine, late of the same corps, decd., as next of Kin.

Citation granted to Robert Bond of Capt. Blount's, Company, of Inf. to administer on the Estate & Effects of William Timmons, late of same Corps, decd., as Principal Creditor.

Qualified William Jennings of late Capt. Clinton's Company of Infantry, admor of John Jurniken, late of same Corps of Infantry, decd.

Qualified the sd. William Jennings, admor of Peter Linquist, late of Capt. H. P. Taylor's Company of Infantry, decd.

10. Proved the last Will and Testament of Daniel E. Graham late of Capt. Wages, Company of Infantry, and by the testimony of W. Musgrove, a subr. wit.

Citation granted to Joshua Hammonds of the same Corps to administer on the Estate & Effects of the sd. Daniel E. Graham as next friend, with the Will annexed.

Qualified Willis Medlin of Capt. Hawkins' Company of Artillery, admor of the Estate & Effects of James Brown, late of same Company, deceased.

12. Citation granted to Samuel Jones of Capt. Blount's Comp of Inf, to administer on the Estate & Effects of James Moon, late of the same Company, decd., as principal Creditor.

Qualified Benjamin Burgh Smith of Charleston, Attorney at Law, admor or, the Estate & Effects of Hugh Rutledge, late of Charleston, Esquire, deceased.

[Page 103]

1815 June 13. Qualified Cader Parker of Capt. Hawkins' Corps of Artillery, admor of the Estate & Effects of William Church, late of the same Corps, decd.

15. Qualified Robert Lehre Key, admor of the Estate & Effects of Elizabeth Key admor of the Estate & Effects of Elizabeth. Key, late of Charleston, Widow, deceased.

16. Qualified David Wood of Capt. Blount's Corps of Infantry admor of the Estate & Effects of Benjamin Lewis Balance Cox, late of the same Company, deceased.

Qualified the said David Wood, admor of the Estate & Effects of Enoch Forbes, late of the same Comp: deceased.

Citation granted to Francis Kinloch, Esquire, of Charleston, to administer on the Estate & Effects of Abraham Wharton, late of Christ Church Parish, Millwright, deceased, as next friend.

Citation granted to Benjamin Blount of Capt. Blount's comp of Infantry to administer on the Estate & Effects of Charles George Lafar, late of the same corps, deceased, as principal Creditor.

Citation granted to David Wood of Capt. Blount's Corps of Artillery to administer on the Estate & Effects of Yarborough Taylor, late of same Company deceased, as next friend.

Citation granted to Isaac Sitterson of Capt. Blount's or Tindal's Company of Infantry to administer on the Estate & Effects of Thomas Clifton, late of the same Company, deceased, as principal Creditor.

Citation granted to William Jackson of Capt. Tindal's Company of Infantry to administer on the Estate & Effects of William Pegram, late of Capt. Robinson's Company of ____, decd., as principal Creditor.

Citation granted to Richard Palmour of Capt. Blount's Company of Infantry to administer on Estate & Effects of Elijah Gatlin, late of the same Comp: deceased, as principal Creditor.

17. Citation granted to Joseph Snyder of Capt. Tisdal's Company of Infantry to administer on the Estate & Effects of Cyrus R. Hearne, late of Capt. H. F. Taylor's Comp. of Infantry, decd., as Principal Creditor.

Citation granted to Margaret Munro of Charleston, Widow, to administer on the Estate & Effects of Robert Munro, late of Charleston, Cooper, decd., as next of Kin.

[Page 104]

1815 June 21. Citation granted to Benjamin B. Blount of Capt. Blount's Company of Infantry to administer on the Estate & Effects of William Souder late of the same Corps, decd., as principal Creditor.

Citation granted to Benjamin B. Blount to administer on the Estate & Effects of John Wheeler, late of the same Company, deceased, as principal Creditor.

22. Qualified Isaac Sitterson of Capt. Tisdal's Company of Infantry, to administer on the Estate & Effects of Thomas Clifton, late of Capt. Blount's Company of Infantry, decd.

23. Qualified Margaret Munro of Charleston, Widow, admix of the Estate & Effects of Robert Munro, late of Charleston, Cooper, deceased. see page 104.

22. Granted to Susanna Boyd, late of Admor ad colligendum bona defuneti of William Boyd, late of Charleston, Merchant, deceased.

22. [in margin] Qualified John Vingard, exor named in the last Will & Test. of Paul Pritchard Senr., late of Daniel's Island, Shipwright, decd.

26. Qualified David Wood of Capt. Tisdal's Company of Infantry, admor of the Estate & Effects of Yarborough Taylor, late of Capt. Blount's Company of Infantry, decd., also see page 104 [in Original Book].

27. Qualified Daniel Magrath of Charleston, Gentleman, admor of Estate & Effects of Humphrey Magrath, late a purser in the Navy of the United States, deceased.

Citation granted to Thomas Hanahan of Charleston, Mariner, to administer on the Estate & Effects of James Conner, late of Charleston, Minister of the Gospel, deceased, as next friend

Citation granted to John Brown of Capt. H. P. Taylor's Com. of Inft. to administer on the Estate & Effects of James Bean, late of same Company, deceased, as principal Creditor.

Citation granted to John Brown of Capt. H. P. Taylor's Company of Infantry to administer on the Estate & Effects of Paul Smith, late of Capt. Hamilton's Company of Infantry, decd., as principal Creditor.

28. Qualified Samuel Jones of Capt. Tisdal's Company of Infty., admor of the Estate & Effects of James Moon, late of Capt. Blount's Company of Infantry, decd.

Qualified Robert Bond of Capt. Tisdal's Company of Infantry, admor of the Est. & Effects of William Timmons, late of Capt. Blount's Company of Infantry, decd. [see also 102 in original book].

[Page 105]

1815 June 30. Qualified Felix Bruneau Warley, executor named in the last Will & testament of Felix Warley, late of Charleston, Planter, deceased.

Citation granted Patrick Duncan of Charleston, Esquire, to administer on the Estate & Effects of Andrew Hannah, late of Charleston, Merchant, deceased, as principal Creditor.

Qualified Benj. Blount of Capt. Blount's Company of Infantry, admor of the Estate & Effects of Charles George Lafar, late of the same Company, deceased. See P. 102 & 105 [of original book].

Qualified Benjamin B. Blount admor of the Estate & Effects of Elijah Gatlin, late of the same Corps, decd. P. 103 & 105 [of original book].

Qualified John Brown of Capt. H. F. Taylor's Company of Infantry, admor of the Estate & Effects [of] James Bean of the same Company, decd.

July 3d. Citation granted to David Porter of Capt. King's Company of Infy. to administer on the Estate and Effects of John Cain, late of the same Company, deceased, as next of Kin.

Citation granted to Anthony Newton of Charleston, Butcher, to administer on the Estate & Effects of John Gill, late of Charleston, Stable Keeper, deceased, as next of Kin. p. 106.

July 6. Citation granted to Jacob Duryea of Charleston, Shop Keeper, to administer on the Estate & Effects of Ebenezer Smith, late of Charleston, Mariner, deceased, as next of friend.

7. Qualified Patrick Duncan of Charleston, Esquire, Admor of the Estate & Effects of Andrew Hannah, late of Charleston, Merchant, deceased. See above.

Qualified James Nicholson of Charleston, Attorney at Law, and executor named in the last Will and testament of David M. Credie, late of Charleston, Merchant, deceased.

8. Proved the last Will and testament of Samuel Barksdale Jones, late of Charleston, Esquire, decd., by the testimony of Frederick Beard, one of the subscribing witnesses thereto: at the same time qualified Mary Jones, Executrix.

12. Citation granted to Daniel Davis of Charleston, Butcher, to administer on the Estate & Effects of William G. Sturges, late of Capt. Taylor's Corps of Infantry, decd., as next friend. P. 107

[Page 106]

1815 July 14. Qualified Anthony Newton of Charleston, Butcher, admor of the Estate & Effects of John Gill, late of Charleston Stable Keeper, deceased.

Citation to John Franklin of late Capt. Dick's Comp'y of Infantry to administer on the Estate & Effects of George Bowlan Caldwell, late of the same Company, decd., as next friend. P. 106, 107 [in original book].

Qualified John Hicks of Capt. King's Company of Infantry to admor of the Estate & Effects of William Watson Brown, late of the same Company, decd.

Qualified Samuel Verree of Charleston, Goldsmith, admor Cum testamento annexo of Joseph Verree, Senr., of Charleston, Carpenter, deceased. 106 [in original book].

Qualified David Porter of Capt. King's Company of Infantry, admor of the Estate & Effects of John Cain, late of the Same Company, decd. P. 106 [in original book].

18. Citation granted to George Daniel Row, Steward attached to the General Hospital Department, to administer on the Estate & Effects of Richard Worthy, late of Capt. King's Company of Infantry, decd., as next friend.

19. Qualified Thomas Napier on an attached translation of the last Will & testament of John Fraser, late of Great Britain, Merchant, deceased.

Qualified Jacob Duryea, of Charleston, Shop keeper, admor of the Estate & Effects of Ebenezer Smith, late of Charleston, Mariner, deceased. 105, 106

20. Citation granted to William Brinn of Capt. Blount's Company of Infantry to administer on the Estate & Effects of Henry Mason, late of the same Comp, decd., as next of Kin.

21. Qualified David Wenchele of Capt. Tindal's or Blount's Company of Infantry, admor of the Estate & Effects of Chevalin Dermus, of late Capt. Hamilton's now Taylor's Comp of Infantry, decd.

Qualified Benjamin B. Blount of Capt. Blount's Company of Infantry., admor of the Estate & Effects of William Souder, late of the same Company, decd. p. 106

[Page 107]

1815 July 21. Qualified Benjr. B. Blount of Capt. Blount's Company of Infantry, admor of the Estate & Effects of John Wheeler, late of the same Company, deceased. P. 104

Qualified John Franklin, of late Capt. Dick's Company of Infantry, admor of the Estate & Effects of George Boulan Caldwell, late of the same Company, decd.

Qualified Daniel Davis of Charleston, Butcher, admor of the Estate & Effects of William G. Sturges, late of Capt. Taylor's Comp of Infantry, decd.

24. In the Court of Ordinary. William Rouse and Anthony Newton appeared in Court and stated that there had been found a paper purporting to be the last Will and testament of John Gill, late of Charleston, Stable Keeper, decd., and moved that the same should be received to be proved: Wherefore proved the last Will and testament of the same John Gill, deceased, by the testimony of James Nicholson, Esquire, one of the subscribing witnesses thereto: at the same time qualified William Rouse and Anthony Newton, executors named therein:

25. Citation granted to John Jones and Christian Schneider, both of Charleston, Grocers, to administer on the Estate & Effects of John Wilte, late of Charleston, Grocer, deceased.

26. Citation granted to John Baxter of Lt. Sharp's Artillery to administer on the Estate & Effects of James McHanney, late of same Company, decd., as principal Creditor.

27. Citation granted to Roger Pinckney of St. Thomas' Parish, planter, to administer on the Estate & Effects of Francis Dallas, late of same place, planter, decd., de bonis non et cum testamento annexo.

Citation granted to Ann Torrey of Charleston, Widow, to administer on the Estate & Effects of William Torrey, late of Charleston, Mariner, decd., as next of Kin.

28. Qualified George Daniel Row, a Steward attached to the General Hospital Department, admor of the Estate & Effects of Richard Worthy, late of Capt. King's Company of Infantry. P. 107

Citation granted to John Snell of St. James' Parish, Goose Creek, farmer, to administer on the Estate & Effects of Frederick Snell, late of same place, farmer, deceased, as next of Kin. see 108

[Page 108]

1815 July 29. Proved the last Will & testament of David Chalmers, late of St. Andrew's Parish, planter, deceased, by the testimony of Thomas Tocole, one of the subscribing witnesses thereto.

August 4. Qualified John Snell of St. James' Parish, Goose Creek, farmer, admor of the Estate & Effects of Frederick Snell of same place, farmer, decd.

Qualified William Brinn of Capt. Blount's Comp: of Infantry, admor of the Est. & Effects of Henry Mason, late of the same Corps, deceased.

Qualified John Jones and Christian Schneider of Charleston, Grocers, admors of the Estate & Effects of John Hitte, late of the same place, Grocer, decd.

Citation granted Jones Watson, Sutler, to the 18th Regt. to administer on the Estate & Effects of Durk Well, late of Capt. Dick's Company, decd., as principal Creditor.

Qualified Roger Pinckney of St. Thomas' Parish, planter, decd., admor of Francis Dallas, late of same place, planter, dec., de bonis non & cum testamento annexo.

Christian Gradick's Case. In the Court of Ordinary. August 9th 1810 John Strohecker and James Sparrow who obtained a Special Citation to cite Richard Henry Gradick, admor of Christian Gradick to appear on Tuesday the eighth instant to show cause why they should not be relieved from their securityship and in Court and it appearing that the said admor had been regularly personally summoned, neglected to appear and show any cause whereupon they moved that John Strohecker should be approved admor: upon which qualified John Strohecker of Charleston, Blacksmith, admor of the Estate & Effects of Christian Gradick, late of Charleston, Butcher, decd.

11. Qualified Jones Watson, Sutler, to the 18 Regt. admor of the Estate & Effects of Durk Well, late of Capt. Dick's Company of infantry, decd.

Qualified John Brown of Capt. H. P. Taylor's Company of Infantry, admor of the Estate & Effects of Jacob Smith, late of Capt. Hamilton's [Company] of infantry.

[Page 109]

Aug. 12. Proved the last Will & Testament of James Bartlet, late of Charleston, Mariner, deceased, by the testimony of Thomas G. Saburn, one of the subscribing witnesses thereto: at the same time qualified William Banks, executor, therein named.

15. Qualified Washington Potter of Charleston, Merchant, admor of the Estate & Effects of Ann Pillans, late of same place, Widow, decd.

Citation granted to Andrew McCallister of Lieut. Sharp's Command of Artillery to administer on the Estate & Effects of Benj. McKinney, late of the same Corps, decd., as principal Creditor & next friend.

18. Qualified Ann Torrey of Charleston, Widow, admix of the Estate & Effects of William Torrey, late of Charleston, Mariner, decd.

19. Citation granted to William Hayward of Charleston, Boarding House Keeper to administer on the Estate & Effects of William King, late of same place, Mariner, decd.

21. Proved the last Will and testament of James Grady, late of Charleston, Grocer, deceased, by the testimony of John Dunn, one of the subscribing witnesses thereto: at the same time qualified Catherine Grady, executrix.

25. Qualified Andrew McCallister of Lieut. Sharp's Command of Artillery, admor of the Estate & Effects of Berry McKinney, late of same Corps, decd.

Proved the last Will and testament of John Christian Classon, late of Charleston, Butcher, deceased, by the testimony [of] J. C. Vogler, one of the subscribing witnesses to the same: also qualified George Vonganer, executor named therein.

28. Qualified William Hayward of Charleston, Boarding House Keeper, admor of the Estate & Effects of William King, late of Charleston, Mariner, decd.

31. Citation granted to Robert Jackson of Charleston, Carpenter, to administer on the Estate & Effects of Mary Bross, late of Charleston, Widow, decd. as principal Creditor.

[Page 110]

1815 September 1st. Citation granted to William Morgan Scott of Charleston, Esquire, to administer on the Estate & Effects of John Boyd, late of Charleston, Merchant, deceased, as Principal Creditor.

7. Citation granted to Mary Colley Dupont of Charleston, Widow, to administer on the Estate & Effects of John DuPont, late of same place, Planter, deceased as next of Kin.

8. Qualified William Morgan Scott of Charleston, Esquire, administer of the Estate & Effects of John Boyd, late of same place, Merchant, decd.

Citation granted Lawrence Ryan, Esquire, to administer on the Estate & Effects of James Ryan, late of Charleston, Esquire, decd.

Citation granted to Henry Jernigan of Capt. Hawkins' Company of Artillery to administer on the Estate & Effects of Hilan McCoy, late of Lieut. Turpin's Command of Cavalry, decd.

12. Qualified Robert Jackson of Charleston, Carpenter, administer of Estate & Effects of Mary Bloss, late of Charleston, Widow, deceased.

15. Citation granted to Daniel Joy of Christ Church Parish, planter, to administer on the Estate & Effects of Joseph Dorrill, late of Christ Church Parish, Planter, deceased, as principal Creditor.

Samuel Billing's Case. Elizabeth Simmons (late Billing) appeared in Court in compliance with a special Citation which had been granted yesterday to Betje Henrickson to cite her to procure other Security, which having produced she entered into a new Bond.

16. Proved the last Will and testament of Mary Catherine Haiser[?], late of Charleston, Widow, deceased, by the testimony of George Shively, one of the subscribing witnesses thereto: at the same [time] qualified John Henry Margart executor therein named.

Citation granted to John Frazer of Christ Church Parish, Planter, to administer on the Estate & Effects of William Basden, late of St. Thomas', Parish, Cordwainer, decd.

[Page 111]

1815 September 15. Citation granted to Samuel Patterson of Charleston, Merchant, to administer on the Estate & Effects of John Smith, late a Capt. in the United States Navy, decd., as next of Kin.

18. Proved the last Will & testament of the Revd. Joseph Warren, late Rector of St. Thomas' Parish, decd., by the testimony of Lewis Ogier, one of the subscribing witnesses thereto.

19. Citation (special) granted to Richd. McCormick, one of the sureties of Mary Lindsay, admix of Robert Lindsay, late of Charleston, Carpenter, decd., to cite her to show cause why she should render an acct. and abide such order and decree as unto grant to said surety, to appear on Wednesday next at 11 o'clock in the forenoon. The 21st inst.

20. Citation granted to Thomas Fitzgerald Quin to administer on the Estate & Effects of Thomas Hutchinson, late of Brevet Major Bird's Company of Infantry, decd., as principal Creditor.

Citation granted to John Henry Margart of Charleston, Blacksmith, to administer on Estate & Effects of Charles Christian Philips, late of Charleston, Butcher, deceased, as next friend.

Robert Lindsay's Case. Mrs. Mary Lindsay appeared in Court and stated that she had obedience to the Citation issued on the seventeenth inst. appeared to ask for further time to render her account that she was under the impression that Mr. McCormick would have done so for her and was therefore altogether unprepared at present & prayed to be allowed until Thursday next the 27 inst. which was accordingly granted.

21. William Bold enters a Caveat against John Rhodes or any other person qualifying on the Estate of John Bold Senr., late of Charleston, decd., until he is heard before the Ordinary.

22. Citation granted Joseph Samuel Chapman, Grocer, and Joseph Parsons, Esquire, of Charleston, to administer on the estate & Effects of William Rose, late of John's Island, planter, decd.

[Page 112]

1815 September 22. Proved the last Will and Testament of John Blome, late of Charleston, Physician, decd., by the testimony [of] J. B. Benoist, one of the subscribing witnesses thereto: and at the same time qualified Cesar Blome, executor. N.B. The Will was exhibited in the French Language with a translation attested by the executor.

Qualified Samuel Patterson of Charleston, Merchant, administer of the Estate & Effects of John Smith, late a Captain in the Navy of the United States, deceased.

21. Qualified Joseph Taylor, executor, named in the last Will & testament of Joseph Warren of St. Thomas Parish, Minister of the Gospel, decd.

Qualified John Fraser of Christ Church Parish, admor of the Estate & Effects of William Basden, late of St. Thomas' Parish, Cordwainer, deceased.

25. Qualified Lawrence Ryan, admor of James Ryan, late of Charleston, Esquire, decd.

26. Qualified Thomas Hanahan of Charleston, Mariner, Admor of the Estate & Effects of James Conor, late of Charleston, Minister of the Gospel, decd.

Read the Petition of Elizabeth Walton, late Elizabeth Johnston, praying that she be appointed Guardian of her Children by her former husband, Alexander Johnston, decd., late of Charleston, Printer, decd., to wit Peter Shand Johnston, Margaret Gensel Johnston, Louisa Lane Johnston, and Eliza Johnston, minors.

Nathan Legare's Case. Mrs. Mary Legare and Dr. Anthony Vander Horst Toomer, former Admor & Admix of Nathan Legare, late of Christ Church Parish, planter, decd., In Court. Dr. Toomer having rendered his account & expressed his wish to surrender the Admon, into the hands of the Widow, whereupon qualified Mary Legare administratrix of the Estate & Effects of Nathan Legare, late of Christ Church Parish, planter, decd.

[Page 113]

1815 September 29. Citation granted to Anne Delanoy of Charleston, Widow, to administer on the Estate & Effects of Dennis Alexander Delanoy, late of Charleston, Storekeeper, decd., as next of Kin.

Qualified Thomas Fitzgerald Quin Admor of the Estate & Effects of Thomas Hutchinson, late of Bervet Major Bird's Company of Infantry, decd.

Qualified John Henry Margart of Charleston, Blacksmith, Admor of the Estate & Effects of Charles Christian Philips, late of Charleston, Butcher, decd.

Citation granted John Fraiser of late Capt. Donoho's Corps of Artillery to administer on the Estate & Effects of Ranson Fraiser, late of Lieut. Sharp's Command of Artillery, decd. as the next of Kin.

30. Citation granted Samuel Alexander of Charleston, Mariner, to administer on the Estate & Effects of Zebulon Miller, late of the same place, Mariner, deceased.

Citation granted to Charles Rutledge of Charleston, Physician, to administer on the Estate & Effects of Frances Button, late of Charleston, Spinster, decd., as principal Creditor.

October 2d. Proved the last Will and testament of Susanna Nelson, late of Charleston, Widow, deceased, by the testimony of James McCall, one of the subscribing witnesses thereto: at the same time qualified James Oliver, Executor, named therein.

Proved the last Will and testament of George Reilly, late of Charleston, Tavern Keeper, deceased, by the testimony of William Porter, one of the subscribing witnesses thereto: at the same time qualified June Rielly, executrix, named therein.

Citation granted to Benjamin B. Blount of Capt. Blount's Company of Infantry to administer on the Estate & Effects of Zachariah Ferrill, late of same Comp: decd., as principal Creditor.

3. Zechariah French of Rhode Island, Mariner, enters a Caveat against any persons whatever taking out letters of Admor on the Estate & Effects of Zebulon Miller, late of Charleston, Mariner, decd., until he is heard before the Ordinary.

4. Zachariah French withdraws the foregoing Caveat.

[Page 114]

1815 October 6. Qualified Anne Delanoy of Charleston, Widow, Admix of the Estate & Effects of Dennis Alexander Delaney, late of Charleston, Storekeeper, decd.

Qualified Samuel Alexander of Charleston, Mariner, admor of the Estate & Effects of Zebulon Miller, late of Charleston, a Mariner, decd.

Qualified John Fraiser of Late Capt. Donoho's Corps of Artillery, admor of the Estate & Effects of Ransom Fraiser, late of Lieut. Sharp's Command of Artillery, decd.

7. Qualified Dr. Charles Rutledge, admor of the Estate & Effects of Frances Hutton, late of Charleston, Spinster, decd.

Citation granted Joseph Parsons of Charleston, Esquire, to administer on the Estate & Effects of Ann Humphrys, late of John's Island, Widow, decd. as next friend de bonis non & cum test: annexo.

Citation to Joseph Parishs of Charleston, Esquire, to administer the Estate & Effects of Thomas Humphrys, late of John's Island, planter, decd., as next friend de bonis non & cum testemento annexo.

Proved the last Will & testament of John Shepperd, late of Charleston, a free black man, by the testimony of Charles Holmes, one of the subscribing witnesses to the same.

9. Citation granted to Christopher Jenkins of St. John's Parish, Colleton District, to administer on the Estate & Effects of Mary Toomer, late of Sumter District, Widow, deceased.

12. Citation granted Catherine Grady of Charleston, Widow, to administer on the Estate & Effects of Uriel King, late of same place, Mariner, decd., as principal Creditor.

Citation granted to Margaret Peters of Charleston, Widow, to administer on the Estate & Effects of John Peters, late of Charleston, Mariner, decd., as next of Kin.

13. Qualified Joseph Parsons of Charleston, Esquire, admor of the Estate & Effects of William Rose, late of John's Island, Planter, decd.

Qualified said Joseph Parsons, admor of the Estate & Effects of Thomas Humphrys, late of John's Island, planter, decd., so far as they were left unadministered by Ann Humphrys, executris, decd., & with her Will attached.

[Page 115]

1815 Oct. 13. Qualified Joseph Parsons aforesaid, admor of the Estate & Effects of Ann Humphrys, late of. John's Island, Widow, decd., de bonis non & cum testamento annexo.

18. Qualified Frederick S. Roux, executor, named in the last Will & testament of Francis Louis Noah Roux, late of Charleston, Merchant, decd.

20. Qualified Joseph Jenkins of St. John's Colleton, planter, administrator of the Estate & Effects of Mary Toomer, late of Sumter District, Widow, decd.

Qualified Margaret Peters of Charleston, Widow, admix of the Estate & Effects of John Peters, late of Charleston, Mariner, deceased.

Qualified Catherine Grady of Charleston, Widow, admix of the Estate & Effects of Uriel King, late of Charleston, Mariner, decd.

William Rose's Case. Mary Browning and William Browning appeared in Court and moved that the letters of administration granted to Joseph Parsons on Friday last should be revoked and granted to her as Widow of the deceased, William Rose concurrently as Estate was prepared to cite the said Joseph Parsons who appeared while the Ordinary was in the act of issuing it: and Mary Browning having produced securities, the said Joseph Parsons surrendered his administration. Whereupon qualified Mary Browning, admix of the said William Rose, late of John's Island, decd.

21. Qualified Mary Motte of Charleston, Widow, admix de non bonis & cum testamento annexo of Charlotte Izard, late of Charleston, Widow, decd.

25. Citation granted to Eliza Folle of Charleston, Widow, to administer on the Estate & Effects of William Russell, late of the 18th. Regt. of Infantry, Musician, deceased, as next of Kin.

27. Citation granted to Peter Javain of Charleston, Grocer, to administer on the Estate & Effects of John Francis Chion, late of same place, Grocer, deceased, as next friend.

Nov. 1. Citation granted Richard Furman of John's Island, planter, to administer on the Estate & Effects of John Seabrook, late of same place, planter, deceased, as principal Creditor & heir at Law.

[Page 116]

1815 November 2. Citation granted to Michael Magrath of Charl'n, Merchant, to administer on the Estate & effects of John Lawson, late of Georgetown, Mariner, deceased, as next friend.

3d. Proved the last Will and testament of Philip Henry Munch, late of Charleston, Grocer, deceased, by the testimony of John S. Courtnay, one of the subscribing witnesses thereto: at the same time filed the Renunciation of Louis Monnar and John F. Culter, named executors who renounced their executorship in writing, and

Citation granted to Dorothy Eleanor Munch of Char. Widow, to administer on the said estate with the Will annexed as next of Kin.

1815 November 6. Citation granted to Ann Holmes of James' Island, Widow, to administer on the Estate & Effects of Daniel Holmes, late of same place, Planter, deceased, as next of Kin.

10. Citation granted to Lewis Henry Christian Schutt of Charleston Merchant, to administer on the Estate & Effects of Margaret Dorothy Schutt, late of Charleston, Widow, deceased, as next of Kin.

Citation granted to Maria Jacques and James Richardson of Charleston Mariner to administer on the Estate & Effects of John Parks, late of Charleston, Shoemaker, deceased, as principal Creditors.

[in margin]. 13 December. Cita. granted to John Elijah Rivers to administer on the Est. & Effects of Elizabeth Holmes, late of James' Island, Spinster, decd., as next friend.

16. I do hereby enter a Caveat against Richard Freeman or any other person taking out letters of Admon. on the Estate & Effects of John Seabrook, late of John's Island planter, deceased, until I am heard before the Ordinary. J. B. White Proctor Pro. Joseph S. Seabrook.

The above Caveat withdrawn by Mr. White in person on the 23 Nov'r 1815.

20. Qualified the Revd. Thomas H. Price, admor of the Estate & Effects of Daniel Holmes, late of James' Island, deceased, Planter.

N.B. Mrs. Ann Holmes in whose name the Citation was obtained declined by letter taking out the admor but requested that the Rev. Mr. Price should be appointed. See letter filed with Citation.

Proved the last Will & testament of Jane Barton, late of St. John's Parish, Berkeley, Spinster, deceased, by the testimony of Peter Gaillard Senr., one of the subscribing witnesses to the same: at the same time qualified Samuel Dwight, executor, named therein.

[Page 117]

1815 November 20. Citation granted to Emily Louisa Couturier, Widow and Elias Couturier, planter, of St. John's Parish, Berkeley, to administer on the Estate & Effects of Joseph Couturier of the same place, planter, deceased, as next of Kin.

Citation granted to Samuel William Bates of Lieut. Sharp's detachment of Artillery to administer on the Estate & Effects of John O'Neal, late of Capt. Shot's Company of Artillery, decd., as principal Creditor.

21. Proved the last Will and testament of Rebecca Motte, late of Charleston, Widow, deceased, by the testimony of Isaac Motte, Dart Esq., one of the subscribing witnesses to the same: also the Codicil thereto by the same testimony, and qualified the honorable Thomas Pinckney, executor, named therein.

22. Citation granted to Jane Scouler of Charleston Widow, to administer on the Estate & Effects of Jasper Scouler, late of St. Stephen's Parish, House Carpenter, deceased as next of Kin de bonis non.

23. Qualified Richard Freeman of John's Island, Planter, Admor of the Estate Effects of John Seabrook, late of same place, planter, deceased.

24. Citation granted to Ashbourn Davis of Capt. Spot's Crops of Artillery to administer on the Estate & Effects of Thomas Price, late of the same Corps, deceased, as principal Creditor.

Jeremiah Ives enters a Caveat against Ashman Davis or any other person whatever taking out letters of Admor on the Estate & Effects of Thomas Price, Late of Capt. Spott's corps of Artillery, deceased, until he is heard before the Ordinary.

Qualified Lewis Henry Christian Schutt of Charleston, Merchant, admor of the Estate & Effects of Margaret Dorothy Schutt, late of the same place, Widow, deceased.

Proved (on the 23rd instant) the last Will & testament of John Owen, late of Charleston, Factor, deceased, by the testimony of Jams Bampfield, one of the subscribing witnesses to the same.

[Page 118]

1815 December 1. Citation granted to Mary Blum of Charleston Neck, widow, to administer on the Estate & Effects of Andrew Blum, late of the same place, Butcher, deceased, as next of Kin.

Caveat. Martha Findley of St. James' Parish, Widow, enters a Caveat against Maria Jacques & James Richardson or any other person taking out letters of admor on the estate & effects of John Parks, late of Charleston, Shoemaker, deceased until she is heard before the Ordinary.

2d. Qualified Henry Bryce an Executor named in the last Will & testament [of] Nicol Bryce, late of Charleston, Merch'n, deceased.

6th. Qualified Henry Jernigan of late Capt. Hawkins' Company of Artillery, admor of the Estate & Effects of Hilan McCoy, late of Lieut. Turpin's Command of Calvery, deceased.

8. Qualified Henry H. Bacot and Morton Waring executors named in the last Will & testament of John Owen, late of Charleston, Factor, deceased.

Qualified Mary Blum of Charleston Neck, Widow, admix of the Estate & Effects of Andrew Blum of same place, butcher, deceased.

Proved the last Will and testament of William Faulling, late of St. James, Goose Creek, planter, deceased, by the testimony of Lewis Singletary, one of the subscribing witnesses to the same, at the same time qualified Thomas Faulling, sole executor therein named.

Qualified Samuel William Bates of Lieut. Sharp's Command of Artillery, admor of the Estate & Effects of John O'Neal, late of Capt. Spot's Corps of Artillery, deceased.

Qualified Jeremiah Ives of Charleston, Merchant, admor of the Estate Effects of Thomas Price, late of Capt. Spot's Corps of Artillery, decd. N.B. Ashbourn Davis who obtained the Citation admitted that Jeremiah Ives was the Greatest Creditor and suffered the admon after some litigation to be granted to him.

12. Citation granted to Anna Hutchinson of Charleston Widow, to administer on the Estate & Effects of Leger Hutchinson, late of Charleston, planter, decd., as next of Kin.

[Page 119]

1815 December 12. Citation granted to Jane of Charleston, Widow, to administer on the Estate & Effects [of] Jasper Scouler, late of St. Stephen's Parish, House Carpenter, decd., as next of Kin so far as they were left unadministered by Thomas Scouler, admor, decd.

N.B. The former Citation granted on the 22d Nov. last was lost. Citation Special was granted to John Parker, one of the sureties for Elizabeth Malpass, admx. of Lewis Malpass, late of St. James Parish Santee, planter, decd., to cite her to appear on Thursday the 21 day of Dec. inst., to acct. & show cause why such decree thereto not be made as will grant relief to the Petitioner.

14. Citation granted to Clinton Crugier of Charleston Boarding House Keeper, to administer on the Estate & Effects of James Traves, late of Charleston, Mariner, decd., as principal Creditor and next friend.

Citation granted to Clinton Crugier to administer on the Estate & Effects of James Blake, late of Charleston, mariner, decd. as Principal Creditor & next friend.

Citation granted Simon Jude Chancognie of Charleston, Merchant, to administer on the Estate & Effects of John Levraux, late of Corail in the Island St. Domingo, deceased, as next friend.

15. Qualified Martha Findley of St. James' Parish Santee, Widow, admix of Estate & Effects of Henry Findley, late of same place, planter, deceased.

Read the petition of Martha Findley praying to be appointed guardian of the personal Estate of Sarah Parks, an infant daughter of John Parks, late of Charleston Shoemaker, deceased; which was accordingly granted.

Qualified Martha Findley, admix of the Estate & Effects of John Parks as Guardian to Sarah Parks aforesaid.

Qualified Eliza Folle of Charleston, Widow, admix. of the Estate & Effects of William Russell, late a musician attached to the 18th. Regt. of United States Infantry, deceased.

[Page 120]

1815 December 19. Proved the last Will & testament of Mary Esther Marion, late of Saint John's Parish, Berkeley, deceased, by the testimony of Alexander

Hamilton, one of The subscribing witnesses thereto: at the same time qualified Keating Lewis Simons, executor named therein.

Proved the last Will & testament of Zebulon Miller, late of Charleston, Mariner, deceased, by the testimony of Jonathan Brown. At the same [time] qualified Samuel Gale, executor therein named: N.B. Samuel Alexander who had obtained Letters of Administration surrendered the same.

20. Citation granted to Richard Cunningham of Charleston, Planter, to administer on the Estate & Effects of John Cunningham, late of the same place, Esquire, deceased, as next of Kin.

Citation granted to William Donaldson of Charleston, Bookseller, to administer on the Estate & Effects of John Smiton, late of North Britain, Musician, deceased, as next friend.

Citation granted, said Wm. Donaldson, to administer on the Estate & Effects of Charles Smiton, late of North Britain, Hatter, decd., as next Friend.

Citation to said Wm. Donaldson to administer on the Estate & Effects of Brunson Smiton, late of Charleston, Silkdyer, decd., as next friend, with his Will annexed, so, far as they were left unadministered by James Allison, executor, decd., during the absence of William Bell who is out of the limits of this State.

22. Citation granted to _____ to administer on the Estate & Effects, of Linquist Magness, late of Charleston, Mariner, decd., as principal Creditor.

Qualified John Elijah Rivers of James' Island, Planter, to admor with the Will annexed of Elizabeth Holmes, late of the same place, decd.

Qualified Simon Jude Chancognie of Charleston, Mert., admor of the Estate & Effects of John Levraux of the town of Corail, Island of St. Domingo, decd.

[Page 121]

1815 Decr. 22. Qualified Samuel Dorrill of Christ Church Parish, planter, to administer on the Estate & Effects of Joseph Dorrill, late of same place Planter, decd.

23. Qualified Ann Nathaniel Hutchinson of Charleston, Widow, admix of the Estate & Effects of Leger Hutchinson, late of the same place, planter, decd.

27. Citation Special granted to John Johnson of Charleston, Carpenter, one of the sureties of Elizabeth Simmons, late Billing, to show cause why he should be relieved to his securityship to appear on Friday next the 29th. inst. at 11 o'clock in the forenoon.

29. Qualified William Donaldson of Charleston, Bookseller, admor of the Estate & Effects of John Smiton, late of North Britain, Musician, decd.

Qualified said W. Donaldson, admor of Charles Smiton of North Britain, Hatter, decd.

Qualified said W. Donaldson, admor of Bryson Smiton, late of Charleston, Silk-Dyer, deceased, with his Will annexed so as his goods & Chattels were left unadministered by James Allison, executor, decd., & during the absence of William Bell.

30. Citation granted to Elizabeth Sweasey of Charleston, to administer on the Estate & Effects of Benjamin Sweasey, late of same place, Mariner, decd.

Samuel Billing's Case. Mrs. Elizabeth Simmons (late Billing) app'd in Court and offered other Security agreeably to the Citation.

[Page 122]

1816 January 4. Qualified Jane Scouler of Charleston, Widow, admix of the Estate & Effects of Jasper Scouler, late of St. Stephen's Parish, House Carpenter, deceased.

5. Citation granted to Stephen Burbridge [sic] of St. James' Parish Goose Creek, planter, to administer on the Estate & Effects of Richard Burbridge [sic] late of same place, planter decd., as next of kin.

Proved the last Will & testament of Elizabeth Bradley, Widow, late of Charleston, deceased, by the testimony of William Crafts Junr., one of the subscribing witnesses, at the same [time] Sarah Cornelia Teboat, executrix, named therein also proved the Codicil to the said Will by the testimony of the same gentleman

6. Citation granted to Charles Francis Lee, of Charleston, Saddler and Harness maker, to administer on the Estate & Effects of Alexander Lee, late of the same place, Mariner, decd., as next of Kin.

8. Qualified Richard Cunningham of Charleston, Planter, to administer on the Estate & Effects of John Cunningham, late of Charleston, Esquire, deceased.

10. Qualified The Revd. Thomas H. Price of James' Island, admor of the Estate & Effects of Elizabeth Holmes, late of the same place, Spinster, deceased, John Elijah Rivers who had administered on the 22d. Dec. last came into Court and Surrendered his Letters of Administration.

12. Qualified Emily Louise Couturier, Widow, and Elias Couturier, Planter, both of St. John's Parish, Berkeley, admix and Admor of Joseph Couturier late of same place, deceased.

Citation Special Granted to Sylvanus Keith, Mert., to cite Major General Fishburne, executor, named in the last Will & testament of Benjamin Snipes, late of Charleston, Factor, decd., to render an acct. & Inventory of said Estate to appear on the day of.

Citation granted to Isabella Stout formerly of Nassau in the Bahamas & now of Charleston, Widow, to administer on the Estate & Effects of Ann Peat, late of same place, decd., as next of Kin.

[Page 123]

1816 January 12. Citation granted to Mary Spencer of Charleston, Widow, to administer on the Estate & Effects of Joseph Vesey Spencer, late of the same place, Mariner, deceased.

12. Qualified Stephen Burbage of St. James' Parish, Goose Creek, planter, admor of the Estate & Effects of Richard Burbage, late of same place, Planter, decd.

Qualified Charles Francis Lee of Charleston, Saddler, to admor on the Estate & Effects of Alexander Lee, late of same place, Mariner, deceased.

13. Citation granted to John Morison of Charleston, Storekeeper, to administer on the Estate of John Slickman, late of same place, Mariner, decd., as principal Creditor.

Citation granted to Wm. Cunningham of Lieut. Brown's Artillery to administer on the Estate & Effects of Thomas Landreth, late of the same company, decd., as principal Creditor.

17. Samuel W. Bates of Lieut. Sharp's Artillery enters a Caveat against William Cunningham or any other person taking out Letters of Admor on the Estate & Effects of Thomas Landreth, late of the same Company, decd., until he is heard before the Ordinary.

19. Citation granted to Henry Stocker of Charleston, Boat Builder, to administer, on the Estate & Effects of James McBain, late of Charleston, Sail Maker, decd., as next friend.

Qualified Isabella Stout of Nassau, Bahamas, admix of the Estate & Effects of Ann Peat of the same place, Widow, decd.

Qualified Mary Spencer of Charleston, Widow, admix of the Estate of Joseph Vesey Spencer, late of Charleston, Mariner, deceased.

Qualified John Morrison Junr., of Charleston, Storekeeper, admor of the Estate & Effects of John Slickman, late of Charleston, Mariner, decd.

Proved the last Will & testament of Deborah Scanlin, otherwise called Deborah Hartman, late of Charleston, Spinster, by the testimony of Elizabeth Frost, one of the subscribing witnesses to the same.

19. Proved the last Will and testament of Anna Maris Hoyland, late of Charleston, Widow, deceased, by the testimony of Eliza Campbell, one of the Subscribing witnesses thereto.

[Page 124]

1816. Citation granted to Eleanor Sarah Bonneau of Chasn. Widow, to administer on the Estate & Effects of Deborah Scanlin, otherwise called Deborah Hartman, late of Charleston Spinster, decd., as next friend with the Will annexed.

Proved the last Will & testament of John Mercier, late of Charleston, Mariner, deceased, by the testimony of Peter Cuttino, one of the subscribing witnesses thereto.

23. Citation granted to John Elijah Rivers of James' Island, Planter, to administer on the Estate & Effects of William Rivers, late of the same place, planter, decd. as next of Kin with his Will annexed.

24. Citation granted to Marie Francoise Wiss of Charleston, Widow, to administer on the Estate & Effects of John Peter Wiss, late of Charleston, Taylor, decd., as next of Kin.

26. Qualified Henry Stocker of Charleston, Boat Builder, admor of the Estate & Effects of James McBain, late of Chas., Sail-maker, decd.

Caveat entries by Langdon Cheves, Esquire, in behalf of Henry Canaday and Martha Sams Canaday and William Hanahan Junior, against probate of any last Will & testament of William Hanahan, the Elder, late of Edisto Island, planter, decd., until he is heard before the Ordinary.

29. Citation granted to Charles White of St. Stephen's Parish, farmer, to administer on the Estate & Effects of James Wright, late of the same place, farmer, deceased, the said Charles White having intermarried with the Widow of the deceased, as next friend.

February 1. Citation granted to Kezia Jane Rich of St. James' Parish Santee, to administer on the Estate & Effects of Christopher Rich, late of same place, Planter, decd. as next of Kin.

2. Qualified Marie Francoise Wiss of Charleston, Widow, admix of the Estate & Effects of John Peter Wiss, late of Charleston, Taylor, deceased.

[Page 125]

1816 February 2d. Qualified Samuel William Bates of Lieut. Sharp's Detachment of Artillery, admor of the Estate & Effects of Thomas Landreth, late of Lieut. Sharp's detachn. of Artillery, deceased.

Qualified John Elijah Rivers of James, Island, planter, admor de bonis non & cum testamento annexo of William Rivers, late of same place, planter decd.

3d. Qualified Margaret Mercier, Executrix named in the last Will & testament of John Mercier, late of Charleston, Mariner, deceased.

5. Citation granted to Peter Varner to administer on the Estate & Effects of Peter Varner, planter, late of St. James' Parish Goose Creek, deceased, as next of Kin.

6. William Hort, one of the executors named in the last Will & Test: of John Francis Chion, late of Charleston, Grocer, deceased, came into Court renounced his Executorship.

7. Proved the last Will & testament of John Francis Chion, late of Charleston, Grocer, deceased, by the testimony of David Haig, one of the subscribing witnesses thereto: and the several Codicils thereto by the test: of Lewis Roux.

8. Citation Special granted to Joseph Parsons to cite James Legare, Esq., an Executor named in the last Will and test: of Benjn. Humphreys to show cause why he does not qualify or renounce to appear on the day of next.

Citation Special granted to William Allen Deas to cite John Hinds of St. James' Parish Goose Creek to acct. for the Estate of Rebecca Kaley, decd., or show cause why the admor granted to him should not be revoked & granted to the said W. A. Deas, Esq.

Citation Special granted to ___ Fuller to cite William Bellinger to qualify on, or show cause why he should renounce his executorship on the Will of Zaccheus Fuller, decd., late of St. Andrew's Parish, planter, decd.

9. William Bellinger an Executor named in the last Will & testament of Zaccheus Fuller, late of St. Andrew's Parish, planter, decd. came into Court & renounced his Executorship on the said Will and Citation granted to ___ ___ to administer on the same.

10. Citation granted to James Mitchell of Charleston, House Carpenter, to administer on the Estate & Effects of George Harvey Bedon, late of Chas., Mariner, decd., as next friend.

Qualified Robert Maxwell, an executor named in the last Will & testament of Elizabeth Christian, late of Charleston Widow, decd.

[Page 126]

1816 February 16. Citation granted to Sarah S. Peirce of Boston, State of Massachusetts, Widow, to administer on the Estate & Effects of Henrietta B. Vibut Alice Somerset, late of Charleston, Spinster, decd., as next of Kin.

Proved the last Will & testament of Sam Savage, a free black man of Charleston, decd., by the testimony of B. S. Grimke, a subscribing witness thereto: See 23d. February following.

Qualified James Mitchell of Charleston, House Carpenter, admor of the Estate & Effects of George Hardy Bedon, late of Charleston, Mariner, decd.

23. Qualified Richard Shea of Charleston, Board House Keeper Administrator of the Estate & Effects of Magness Linguist, late of Charleston, Mariner, decd.

Qualified Sarah B. Peirce of Boston, Massachusetts, Widow, admix of the Estate & Effects of Henrietta B. Vibut Somerset, late of Charleston, Spinster, late of Charleston, Spinster, decd.

Citation granted to Francis Fickling of Barnwell District, planter, to administer on the Estate & Effects of Henry Fickling, late of John's Island, planter, deceased, as next of Kin.

William Hort, Thomas Jones & Thomas Blackwood, severally renounced their executorship on the last Will & testament of John Francis Chion, late of Charleston, Grocer, decd.

Citation granted to George Ginty[?] of Charleston, Gentleman, to administer on the Estate & Effects of Philip Hawkins of Charleston, Merchant, deceased, with the will annexed so far as they were left unadministered by John Lewis Gervais and John Owens, executors, deceased, as principal Creditors.

Citation granted to Jane Muir of Charleston, Widow, to administer on the Estate & Effects of William Muir, late of Charleston, Merchant, deceased as next of Kin.

Sam Savage's Case. Thomas Raine with George W. Cross, his Proctor, came into Court and moved that a certain paper, purporting to be the last Will & testament of Samuel Savage, a free black man decd., which had been presented for Probate on the 16th. Inst. should not be proved: but that an instrument of writing which was now produced in which was said Raine was named Executor should be received to be proved. It appeared

[Page 127]

in evidence that Samuel Savage had regularly made his Will dated on the 25th. Nov. 1814, and named Thomas Raine his sole executor and had placed it in his possession for safe keeping, and that Savage being very sick not long before his death sent to Raine for the Will: that during the time he had it, there were some words stricken out by running a pen through them which rendered that clause of the Will without any meaning at all, and other words inserted at the foot of the Will just above the signatures; for which circumstances no person could account, two of the subscribing witnesses who were examined and Raine himself who wrote the will in saying that the words through which the pen was run & the inserted were not done at the time of the execution of the Will, the paper objected to was written by young Mr. B. S. Grimke by the request of Sam Savage, but he was so ill he could not execute it although it was read to him, and he approved of it, no Executor was named in it and there appeared nothing in it which contravened or altered or added to the Will regularly executed: the Ordinary therefore confirmed the Will in which Raine was nominated executor, therefore

March 1st. Proved the last Will & test. of Samuel Savage, late of Charleston, a free black man, by the testimony of George Smith and Stephen Chastrier, two of the subscribing witnesses thereto: at the same qualified Thomas Raine executor named therein.

23rd. Feby. Qualified Eleanor Sarah Bonneau of Charleston, Widow. admix of the Estate & Effects of Deborah Scanlin, alias Deborah Hartman, late of Charleston, Spinster, deceased.

28. Proved the last Will and testament of Sarah Faesch, late of Charleston, Widow, deceased, by the testimony of Henry Muckenfuss, one of the subscribing witnesses: also a Codicil to the same by the testimony of the same person; and the second Codicil to the same by the testimony of Isaac Griggs, Esq., a subscribing witness to the same, at the same qualified Charles Prince and Harriet Frances Faesch, executor and executrix therein named.

Citation granted to Eleanor Carr of Christ Church Parish, Widow, to administer on the Estate & Effects of Christian Carr of the same place, planter, decd., as next of Kin.

Proved the last Will & test: of William Blacklock, late of Charleston, Merchant, decd., by the testimony of J. D. Sommers, one of the subscribing witnesses thereto: at the same time qualified William Robertson, executor named therein.

[Page 128]

1816 March 1st. Qualified Peter Varner of St. James Parish Goose Creek, planter, admor of the Estate & Effects of Peter Varner, late of the same place, deceased.

Qualified Jane Muir of Charleston, Widow, Admix of the Estate & Effects of William Muir, late of, same place, Merchant, deceased.

Qualified Francis Fickling of Barnwell District, planter, admor of the Estate & Effects of Henry Fickling, late of John's Island, planter, deceased.

5. Proved the last Will & testament of Martin Daniel Blanck, late of Charleston, Mariner, deceased, by the testimony of Louis Roux, one of the Subscribing Witnesses thereto: at the same [time] qualified Mary Blanck, executrix therein named.

7. Citation granted to Bartholomew Gaillard of St. John's Parish Berkeley, Planter to administer on the Estate, & Effects of Peter Gaillard, Junior (son of Theodore), late of the same place, planter, deceased as next of Kin.

9. Citation granted to Richard Wall of Charleston, Grocer, to administer on the Estates & Effects of Michael Toole, late of same, place, Taylor, deceased.

12. Citation granted to Eadon Thrower of St. John's Parish, Berkeley, planter, to administer on the Estate & Effects of Baxter Thrower of the same place, planter, deceased, as next of Kin.

50 Qualified Bartholomew Gaillard of St. John's Parish, Berkeley, planter, admor of the Estate & Effects of Peter Gaillard, Junior (son of Theodore), late of same Parish, planter, deceased.

Citation granted to Nathaniel McCants of St. John's Parish, Berkeley, planter, to administer on the Estate & Effects of James McCants, late of same parish, planter, decd., as next of Kin.

Citation granted to Hugh Monies of Charleston, Merchant, to administer on the Estate & Effects of John Monies, late of Charleston, Merchant, deceased, as next of Kin.

Citation granted to Commodore Hugh George Campbell of Charleston, to administer on the Estate & Effects of Mary Ann Campbell, late of same place, Spinster, decd., as next of Kin.

[Page 129]

1816 March 16. Citation granted to Mark Williams of John's Island, planter, to administer on the Estate & Effects of Benjamin Cochran, late of same place, Overseer, decd., as next friend.

18. Special Citation granted to John Ray and Susanna Jane Hay, his wife, legatees under the Will of William Sparkman to cite Ann Sparkman, executrix, to appear on the 17th instant to show Cause [why] she has not rendered an Inventory & acct. of said estate.

19th. Citation granted to Peter Johnson & Ann his wife, late Ann Corkell, to administer on the Estate & Effects of Charles Stevens, late of Charleston, Mariner, decd., as principal Creditor.

22d. Proved the last Will and testament of Judith Tobias, late of Charl., Widow, deceased, by the testimony of Elias Levy, one of the subscribing witnesses thereto: at the same time qualified Abraham Tobias, executor, named therein.

Citation granted to Mary Smith of Charleston, Widow, to administer on the Estate & Effects of John Miller, late of Charleston, Mariner, deceased, as principal Creditor.

Citation granted to John Magrath of Charleston, Merchant, to administer on the Estate & Effects of Mary Gordon, late of Charleston, Widow, deceased, as next of Kin.

Citation granted to Sarah Ann Legare of Charleston, Spinster, to administer on the Estate & Effects of Thomas Savage Legare, late of Charleston, deceased.

Citation granted to John Andrew Graeser of Charleston, Merchant, to administer on the Estate & Effects of Arnold Duckwitz, late of Bremen, Merchant, decd., as next friend.

25. Qualified (on the 11th of March 1816) Elizabeth Malpass of St. James' Parish, Santee, Widow, admix of the Estate & Effects of Joel Malpass, late of same place, planter, decd.

Proved the last Will and testament of Eleanor Marshall of Charleston, Widow, deceased, by the testimony of William Roach, [one] of the Subscribing witnesses thereto: at the same [time] qualified Sarah Young, late Sarah Marshall and Jane Leach, executrices named in the said Will.

27. Proved the last Will and testament of Catherine Gruber, late of Charleston, Widow, decd., by the testimony of John Jones, one of the subscribing

witnesses thereto at the same time qualified Charles Gruber executor named therein.

[Page 130]

1816 March 28. Recorded the last Will & testament [of] David Willes, late of Medford, in the County of Middlesex & Commonwealth of Massachusetts, Mariner, decd., at the request of John Whiting of Charleston, Turner[?].

Qualified William Mason Smith, an executor named in the last Will and testament of Elizabeth Beckman, late of Charleston, Widow, decd.

Caveat. Patrick Kavanagh of New York enters a Caveat against any person taking out Letters of Admor on the Estate & Effects of _____ Reed, of the same place, decd., until he is heard before the Ordinary.

29. Qualified John Magrath of Charleston, Merchant, admor of the Estate & Effects of Mary Gordon, late of Charleston, Widow, decd.

29. Citation granted to Benjn. Lupe of Charleston. Merchant, to administer on the Estate & Effects of John Dunn, late of Charleston, Merchant, decd., as next friend.

30. Qualified Sarah Ann Legare of Charleston, Spinster, admix of the Estate & Effects of Thomas Savage Legare, Mariner. decd.

April 1. Qualified Nathaniel McCants of St. John's Berkeley admor of the Estate & Effects of James McCants, late of same place, Overseer, decd.

Qualified Pete Johnson & Ann his Wife admor & admix of Charles Stevens, late of Charleston, Mariner, decd.

5. Citation granted to Mary Eliza Maull of Charl., Widow, to administer on tie Estate & Effects of David Maull, late of Charleston, Taylor, decd., as next of Kin.

Citation granted Elizabeth Robinson of Charleston to administer on the Estate & Effects of Zephaniah Howland, late of Ireland, Mariner, deceased, as next of Kin.

Citation granted to Elizabeth Robinson of Charleston, to administer on the Estate & Effects of William Clay, late of Cowes in the Isle of Wight, Mariner, decd., as principal Creditor. Vide two following entries.

[Page 131]

1816 Ap. 5. Citation granted to Rufus Severance of Charleston, Merchant Clerk, to administer on the Estate & Effects of George Taylor, otherwise called William Clay, late of Cowes of the Isle of Wight, Mariner deceased, as next friend.

Citation granted to Rufus Severance of Charleston, Merchant Clerk, to administer on the Estate & Effects of Richard Edwards, otherwise called Zephaniah Howland, late of Ireland, Mariner, deceased, as next friend.

Qualified Hugh Monies of Charleston, Merchant, admor of the Estate Effects of John Monies, late of Charl., Merchant, decd.

8. Caveat. Isham Britt of St. Paul's Parish enters a Caveat against the probate of the Will of Miles Britt.

10. Qualified Thomas Young Smith, an executor named in the last Will and testament of Thomas Smith, late of St. Paul's Parish, Planter, deceased

William Hanahan's Case. Ordinary 11th April 1816. Langdon Cheves, Esq. appeared in Court and submitted a letter received from Col. Simons, which stated that he was unable to attend to the Hearing of this Case today in consequence of the illness of one of his Children at Georgetown and Samuel Hanahan being also present it was mutually agreed that the Case should lay over until further order.

Citation granted to Elias Whilden of Christ Church Parish, planter, to administer on the Estate & Effects of James Eden, late of same place, Planter, deceased, as principal Creditor.

12. Citation granted to William Broadfoot of Charleston, Merchant, to administer on the Estate & Effects of William Boyd, late of Charleston, Merchant, deceased, as principal Creditor and next of Kin.

Qualified John Cassford Ker of Charleston, Merchant, admor of the Estate & effects of John Dunn, late of same place, Merchant, deceased. Benjamin Lupe who obtained a Citation on the 29th ulto. having relinquished in favor of Mr. Ker. See Letter annexed to Citation.

[Page 132]

1816 April 12. Qualified Mary Eliza Maull of Charleston, Widow, admix of The Estate & Effects of David Maull, late of the same place, Taylor, deceased.

13. Qualified Rufus Severance of Charleston, Merchant Clerk, Admor of the Estate & Effects of Richard Edwards, alias Zephaniah Howland, late of Ireland, Mariner, deceased.

Qualified the said Rufus Severance, admor of the Estate & Effects of George Taylor, alias William Clay, late of Cowes in the Isle of Wight, mariner, deceased.

Proved the last Will and testament of Antoine Plumet, late of Charleston, Storekeeper, deceased, by the testimony of Philip Muck, one of the subscribing witnesses to the same; at the same Time qualified Lewis DeVillers, executor named therein: N. B. The original Will was exhibited in the French Language with a translation thereof attested by James S. Neilsen, Esq.

16. Proved the last Will & testament of Francis Coran, late of Charleston, Factor, deceased, by the testimony of John Ker, one of the subscribing witnesses thereto.

18. Qualified John Andrew Graeser of Charleston, Merchant, Admor of the Estate & Effects of Arnold Duckwitz, late of Bremen, Merchant, deceased.

19. Edward Mortimer in Behalf of John Eden enters a Caveat against any person taking out letters of administration on the Estate & Effects of James Eden, late of Christ Church Parish planter, deceased.

Citation granted to William Ashley of Fairfield District, planter, to administer on the Estate & Effects of Jonas Bearn, late of Charleston, Planter, deceased, as next friend.

Qualified Willia Broadfoot of Charleston, Merchant, admor of the Estate & Effects of William Boyd, late of Charleston, Merchant, deceased.

Qualified Eadon Thrower of St. John's Parish, Berkeley, planter, admor of the Estate & Effects of Baxter Thrower of the same place, planter, deceased.

Citation granted to John Strobel of Charleston to administer on the Estate & Effects of Jonas Beard, late of same place, planter, decd., as next of Kin. N.B. This Citation substituted in lieu of one granted on the 19 inst. to Wm. Ashley.

[Page 133]

1816 April 24. Citation granted to Arnold Harvey of St. James' Parish Goose Creek, planter, to administer on the Estate & Effects of Henry Barber of St. John's Parish, Colleton, planter, decd., as next friend.

Citation granted to Ann Benoist of St. John's Parish, Berkeley, Widow, to administer on the Estate & Effects of Philip Benoist, late of same place, planter, decd., as next of Kin.

25. Qualified Charlot Coram, executrix named in the last Will & testament of Francis Coram, late of Charleston, Factor, decd.

26. Edward Mortimer withdraws his Caveat in behalf of John Eden against any person taking letters of Admor on the Estate & Effects of James Eden, late of Christ Church Parish, planter. decd.

Citation granted to Ann Hutchinson of Charleston, Widow, to administer on the Estate & Effects of Hugh Hutchinson, late of Charleston, Mariner, decd., as next of Kin. with his Will annexed.

29. Citation granted to Sarah Allman of Christ Church Parish, Widow, to administer on the Estate & Effects of John Allman of said place, planter, deceased, as next of Kin.

20. Proved the last Will and testament of Elizabeth Hollingsbee, late of James Island, Widow, deceased by the testimony of _____.

May 3d. Qualified Arnold Harvey of St. James' Parish, planter, admor of the Estate & Effects of Henry Barber, late of St. James' Parish Goose Creek, formerly of St. John's Parish, Colleton, planter, decd.

6. Proved the last Will and testament of Peter Smith, late of St. Andrews Parish, planter, deceased, by the testimony of James Mair, one of the subscribing witnesses thereto: by Virtue of a Dedimus to Thomas Ham, Esq.

7. Citation granted to Sabina Hall of Charleston, Widow, to administer on the Estate & Effects of James Mitchell, late of Charl., Factor, deceased, with his Will annexed, de bonis non cum testamento ann., as next friend.

Citation granted to Solomon Middleton of Charleston, tailor, to administer on the Estate & Effects of John Marshall Junior, late of Charleston, Gentleman, deceased, as principal Creditor.

[Page 134]

1816 May 10th. Mary Gordon's Case. Agreeably to a Citation issued John Magrath who had obtained letters of admor on the 29th day of March last, appeared in Court & Col. Simons with John Gordon: Col. Simons moved that the admor granted to John Magrath should be revoked in as much as John Gordon was entitled to the same and was proceeding to substantiate his Case, when Mr. Magrath yielded the Admon stating that he had been informed that he could obtain his rights as well without retaining the admon.

17. Citation granted Samuel Hartwell Lothrop of Charleston, Merct., to administer on the Estate & Effects of Seth Lothrop, late of Charleston Merchant, deceased, as next of Kin.

20. Proved the last Will and testament of John Mauger, late of Charleston, Merchant, deceased, by the testimony of Thomas Higham, one of the

subscribing to the same: at the same time qualified Harriet Mauger, executrix, therein named.

21. Qualified Sarah Allman of Christ Church Parish, Widow, admix of the Estate &. Effects of John Allman, late of same place, planter, deceased.

Citation granted Alexander L. McGregor of St. James' Parish Santee, to administer on the Estate & Effects of Alexander McGregor, late of same place, deceased, as next of Kin, de non bonis.

22. Qualified Sabina Hall of Charleston, Widow, admix of James Mitchell, late of Charleston, Factor, deceased, de bonis non cum testamento annexo.

24. Edmund Mead Phelon an executor named in the last Will & testament of Thomas Flyn, late of Charleston, Grocer, deceased, renounced his executorship: and

Citation granted Washington Potter of Charleston Merchant, to administer on the Estate & Effects of the said Thomas Flyn, deceased, as principal Creditor.

Proved the last Will & testament of said Thomas Flyn by the testimony of Thomas B. Wall, a subscribing witness thereto.

[Page 135]

1816 May 24. Citation granted to Jeremiah Russell of Lieut. John Irvin's Corps of Artillery, to administer on the Estate & Effects of Hartwell Russell, late of Capt. Stephen R. Proctor's Corps of Artillery, deceased, as next of Kin.

Qualified George Ginty of Charleston, Merchant, admor of the Estate & Effects of Philip Hawkins, late of Charleston, Merchant, decd., de bonis non & cum testamento annexo.

Thos. F. Quin enters a Caveat agt. letters [of] admor being granted on the Estate & Effects of Thomas Flyn, late of Charleston, Grocer, decd., until he is heard that.

Proved the last Will and Testament of Jean Baptiste Benoist, late of Charleston, decd., by the testimony of Peter DesPortes, one of the subscribing witnesses thereto: at the same time qualified Sophia Burnet Benoist, executrix named therein by virtue of a Dedimus before Thomas Ham, Esq.

31. Citation granted to John Henry Wilson of Charleston, Esquire, to administer on the Estate & Effects of Charles Freer late of John's Island, planter, deceased, as next of Kin, the said John Henry Wilson having intermarried with a daughter of the deceased, so far as the Goods were left unadministered by Mary Freer and William Blacklock, Exix & Exor, deceased, with his will annexed.

Special Citation granted to the said Wilson to cite Thomas Hanscome and James Legare, executors named in the Will of the said Charles Freer, decd., to appear on Monday the third of June at 11 o'clock to qualify or show cause why admon should not be granted to said Wilson.

June 3. Proved the last Will & Testament of James Wright Cotten, late of St. James' Parish Santee, deceased, by the testimony of Samuel Hyam, one of the subscribing witnesses thereto. At the same time qualified Christiana Cotten, exix, named therein.

1. Citation granted to Thomas Fitzgerald Quin of Charleston, Grocer, to administer on the Estate & Effects of John Tommy, late of Charleston, House Carpenter, deceased, so far as they were left unadministered by Thomas Flyn, admor, deceased.

[Page 136]

1816 June 1. Qualified Samuel Hartwell Lathrop of Charleston, Merchant, admor of Estate & Effects of Seth Lathrop, late of Charleston, Merchant, deceased.

Citation granted to William Hedderly of Charleston, House Bell Hanger, to administer on the Estate & Effects of William Twaits, late of Charleston, Comedian, deceased, as next friend.

3. James Legare and Thomas Hanscome, Executors named in the last Will & testament of Charles Freer, late of John's Island, decd., appeared agreeably to Citation & renounced there executorships.

Qualified Jonathan Eady, executor named in the last Will & Testament of Susannah Eady, late of St. John's Parish Berk'y, Widow, decd.

4. Qualified Mary Smith of Charleston, Widow, admix of the Estate & Effects of John Miller, late of Charleston, Mariner, decd.

Approved the last Will and testament of Katherine Fuller, late of St. Andrew's Parish, Widow, decd., by the testimony of James Potter, one of the subscribing witnesses to the same, at the same time qualified Benjamin Fuller, executor therein named.

5. Proved the last Will & testament of Robert Rowand, late of Charleston, Gentleman, by the testimony of Thomas Ogier, one of the subscribing witnesses thereto, also the Codicil to the said Will by the testimony of Solomon Legare, one of the subscribing witnesses thereto and, a Second Codicil by the testimony of E. M. Phelon, one of the subscribing witnesses thereto: at the same time Qualified Charles Elliott Rowand, executor named therein.

6. Qualified Ann Smith, an executrix named in the last Will & testament of Peter Smith, late of St. Andrew's Parish, planter, deceased.

Qualified Jeremiah Russell of Capt. John Irvin's Company of Artillery, admor of the Estate & Effects of Hartwell Russell, late of Capt. Stephen R. Proctor's Corps of Artillery, decd.

7. Qualified Thomas Fitzgerald Quin, of Charleston, Grocer, to administer on the Estate & Effects of John Tommy, late of Charleston, Carpenter, decd.

[Page 137]

1816 June 7. Qualified John Henry Wilson of Charleston, Esquire, admor of the Estate & Effects of Charles Freer late of John's Island, planter, decd., so far as they were left unadministered by the executors, decd., with his Will Annexed.

Citation granted to Robert Turner Roberts of St. Thomas' Parish, planter, to administer on the Estate & Effects of Henry Liebehantz, late of same place, Planter. decd., as next of Kin.

8. Qualified Joseph Curtes, Executor named in the last Will & test. of Sarah Prior, late of St. John's parish Berk., decd.

10. Qualified Alexander Legare McGregor admor de bonis non of Alexander McGregor, late of St. James Parish, Santee, planter, decd.

13. Special Citation granted to cite Enos Easterling, a subscribing witness to the Will of Miles Bull to appear on the 11 July next, and to Isham Bull to appear on the same day and support his Caveat.

14. Citation granted to Sarah Peronneau Legare of Charleston, Widow, to administer on the Estate & Effects of Joseph Daniel Legare, late of Charleston, physician, decd., as next of Kin.

Qualified William Hedderly, House bell hanger, admor of the Estate & Effects of Wm. Twaits, late of Charleston, Comedian, deceased.

19. Qualified Hugh George Campbell of Charleston, Commodore in the United States Navy, admor of the Estate & Effects of Mary Ann Campbell, late of Charleston, Spinster, deceased.

20. Citation granted to Catherine Patton Benoist of Charleston, Widow, to administer on the Estate & Effects of Daniel Boinest, Bricklayer, decd., as next of Kin.

21. Qualified Sarah Peronneau Legare of Charleston Widow, to administer on the Estate & Effects of Joseph Daniel Legare, late of Charleston, physician, decd.

28. Qualified Catherine Patton Benoist of Charleston, Widow, admix of the Estate & Effects of Daniel Benoist, late of same place, bricklayer, deceased.

Qualified Robert Turner Roberts of St. Thomas' Parish planter admor of the Estate & Effects of Henry Liebehantz, late of same place, decd.

[Page 138]

1816 July 1. Citation granted to Cochran McClure of Charleston, Merchant, to administer on the Estate & Effects of William McClure, late of same place, Merchant, deceased, as next of Kin de bonis non & cum testamento annexo.

2. Citation granted Richard Reynolds of St. Helena's [Parish], Beaufort District, planter to administer on the Estate & Effects of Jonathan Reynolds late of Wadmalaw Island, deceased, as next of Kin.

5. Citation granted to Cochran McClure of Charleston, Merchant to administer on the Estate & Effects of Alexander McClure, late of Charleston. Merchant decd., as next of Kin and principal Creditor.

Citation granted to Cochran McClure aforesaid to administer on the Estate Effects of John McClure, late of same place, Merchant, decd., as next of Kin and principal Creditor.

Citation granted to John Cordes Prioleau of Charleston, Factor, to administer on the Estate & Effects of Elizabeth Prioleau, late of Charleston, Spinster, deceased, as next of Kin.

7. Special Citation granted to George Henry Eden to cite Elias Whilden of Christ Church parish, planter, to appear on the eighteenth inst. to show cause why the letters of admor on the Estate & Effects of James Eden, late of same parish, planter, decd., should not be revoked and granted to the said George Henry Eden as next of Kin.

11. Proved the last Will & testament of Miles Britt, late of St. John's Parish, Farmer, deceased, by the testimony of Enos Easterling and James Bunch, the two subscribing witnesses thereto, at the same time qualified Mary Britt, executrix therein named. N.B. Isham Britt appeared in Court and withdrew the Caveat which he had entered against the Probate of the said Will.

Proved the last Will and testament of Sarah Hill Lining, late of Charleston, Spinster, deceased, by the testimony of Solomon Legare, one of the subscribing witnesses thereto: at the same time Polly Lining, executrix named therein.

Proved the last Will & testament of John Lining, late of Charleston, Esquire deceased, by the testimony of Solomon Legare as one of the subscribing Witnesses thereto: at the same time qualified Polly Lining, executrix.

[Page 139]

1816 July 12. Qualified Cochran McClure of Charleston, Merchant, admor of the Estate & Effects of John McClure, late of Charleston, Merchant, deceased.

Qualified the said Cochran McClure, admor of the Estate & Effects of Alexander McClure, late of Charleston, Merchant, decd.

Qualified John Cordes Prioleau of Charleston, Factor, admor of the Estate Effects of Elizabeth Prioleau, late of Charleston, Spinster, deceased.

16. Citation granted to John Whiting of Charleston, Turner, to administer on the Estate & Effects of James Johnston, late of Charleston, Mariner, deceased, as principal Creditor.

18. Citation granted to Honoria Fitzpatrick of Charleston, Widow, to administer on Estate & Effects of Peter Fitzpatrick, late of Charleston, Taylor, decd., as next of Kin.

James Eden's Case. This day appeared Elias Whilden with Mitchell King, Esq., his Proctor, in appliance with a Citation, and George Henry Eden with his Proctor, Wm. Price, & J. D. Heath, Esq. Mr. King opened the Case by stating that the Ordinary having made his election, he did not conceive it proper that he should revoke the admon and particularly so as George Henry Eden was a stranger and it was believed that no pretension whatever to the claim of relationship which he made in the eye of law as he was under the impression that George Eden, the father of the present claimant was never married to his mother and was therefore not entitled to the regard of the Court, and as he had not appeared before the admon was granted after due publication of the Citation it must be considered as a waver of the right: Mr. Heath on the other hand contended that as Geor: H'y Eden lived out of the District and was out of the State at the time, his appearing to the Citation was impossible and ought not to effect his right, that the asking for a revocation of admon on the grounds he assumed was usual and had been repeatedly done and he held that the act of assembly was imperative on the subject whatever the next of Kin applied and submitted the point to the Ordinary's decision.

[Page 140]

The Ordinary was clearly of opinion that he had a right to revoke the Admon and that George H. Eden ought to be heard and suffered to produce evidence of his being entitled to the admor as next of Kin. Whereupon the following persons were sworn and examined.

Mrs. Elizabeth Gouldsmith Sworn. That George Henry Eden is the son of witness and that George Eden was his father: that she often heard George Eden mention James Eden, his Brother, father of the deceased James Eden, that there were five brothers George, Andrew, Joshua and James whom she knew and Jerry whom she did not know. George Eden had a Sister named Elizabeth she died while the British were in Charleston, and believes she was never married.

Martha Hill swore She knew George Eden and knew Mrs. Gouldsmith when she was his wife: knew Mrs. Gouldsmith when she was the Widow Edwards & when Geo: Eden was courting her: this was at St. Helena's Island. Knew Geo: Eden & Mrs. Eden as man & wife When Geo: Henry Eden was born. She knew that Isaac Edwards, the first husband, was dead long before Geo: Eden courted Mrs. Edwards and knew when Geo: H. Eden was born. She often heard George Eden speak of his brothers James, Jerry, Andrew and Joshua as his brothers. It was a common report at St. Helena's that Geo: Eden had got married to the Widow Edwards in Charleston. It was a fact well known to every body. Mrs. Edwards was of a respectable family and not likely to disgrace it by living with a man unmarried: could not have lived in a state of adultery in St. Helena, with out its being known: there are a number of respectable people on the Island and were visited which would not have been the case if they were not married. Heard Geo: Eden speak of his brother James Eden as playing well on the Violin at his father's house: Geo: Eden was a Taylor and mended her father's billiard table cloth: Never heard Geo: Eden speak of his nephew James Eden. She knew Widow Edwards thirty years ago about a year after she knew Geo. Eden and widow Edwards there was a report circulated that the were married about 27 years ago she was the child Geo: H. Eden and his mother who was always called Mrs. Eden when she left the Island.

[Page 141]

Dr. James E. B. Findley was sworn & stated that he practiced on St. Helena In 1788, '89 & 90. knew Mrs. Gouldsmith then, who had with her Geo: H. Eden the reputed son of Geo: Eden her former husband, Geo: H'y Eden was always considered as the lawful son of Geo: Eden. It was commonly reported that Geo: Henry Eden had an uncle in Christ Church Parish whose heir he would be. Knew Mrs. Goldsmith in 1789. Never knew her as Mrs. Eden. Dr. Findley on referring to his books of account found a charge against Mr. Goldsmith, the husband of Mrs. Goldsmith who is the mother of Geo: H'y Eden, dated 12 May 1789.

Mr. Peter Samuel Perry sworn: that he knew Geo: Eden who was a tailor and made his Clothes and knew Mrs. Goldsmith as his wife then and that they would not have been received in Company if they were not married, they visited at his mother's house, to his own knowledge Mr. & Mrs. Eden were received and visited by respectable people on the Island, which would not have been the Case if they were not married. They left the Island in 1782, Mr.

Goldsmith returned with Mrs. Goldsmith in 1787 to the Island land; has heard Joshua Eden inquire after Geo Henry Eden and acknowledge him as his lawful nephew. It was a current report that Geo: H. Eden was a nephew of James Eden who was brother of George Eden and would inherit his property. Knew George Eden & Mrs. Eden as man & wife about 1775. Geo: Henry Eden went apprentice to his father in law, Mr. Goldsmith about two or three years after their return to St. Helena. Witness does not recollect Geo: H. Eden as an infant: witness is about 50 years old. Has heard from his father & mother that Mrs. Goldsmith was Mrs. Edwards.

Martha Hill called again. Stated that Mr. & Mrs. Eden were married in her father's House. Mrs. Elizabeth Gouldsmith called a second time. Knew James Eden, brother of her husband and has heard him say that he wished to carry home Geo: H. Eden to see his cousin James: It was a common report that James Eden Junior was the Son of James Eden, brother of George Eden. Witness often heard her husband speak of his brother James and of his children, and among them of this James. Has heard her husband speak of his nephew James, son of James Eden: Heard her husband say that James himself were the only brothers who had children; often heard that her Son Geo: H. Eden would be the Heir to his cousin

[Page 142]

James' Property. Witness was in New Providence when her husband Geo: Eden died. He died of a fever. Geo. Eden was about 7 years of age at that time: had two children between the birth of Geo: H. Eden and the death of her husband. George was born on St. Helena, thinks she is about 57 years of age. Her first husband Isaac Edwards was killed by the British at Savannah. She was four month's gone with child when Mr. Edwards was killed: it was a year and a half after he went away that he was killed: married Mr. Geo: Eden about three years after Mr. Edwards death: was married by Parson Bird to Mr. Eden. After marrying Mr. Eden went to St. Helena she thinks she stayed there about three years. Mr. Eden died at Nassau, New Providence: they lived one year in Charleston before they went to [St.] Augustine, where they stayed three years and then went to N. Providence where Geo: Eden died. Was married to Mr. Goldsmith in [New] Providence. Saw Mr. James Eden at Joshua Eden's in Charleston where Joshua died: after witness moved from the Island she saw James Eden at Joshua's in Charleston about 1782. James Eden visited her in Guignard Street: never brought his son James: her own Son George was then born which was why she left Charleston for St. Augustine which was in 1782. Her daughter by Eden died in Charleston. Geo: was born before this girl: she was 4 months old when she died and died some time before she left Charleston. Richard Royas Knew five brothers James Eden, had tushes (and was called Tush Eden), George, Jerry, Joshua and Andrew. Joshua a Chairmaker with Straw bottoms, does not know what trade Geo: was of: there were two tailors: Does not [know] what trade James or Tush Eden knew, James Eden the intestate was the son of Tush Eden, Geo: Eden & Tush were brothers: always understood, or Tush Eden, George, Jerry & Andrew and Joshua brothers: general reputation that they were brothers. Never heard that George Eden was married: witness lived in Christ Church in 1782. Had not seen for some time before the war began: never heard James Eden intestate say to whom his property would go: does not

[Page 143]

know Geo: Eden's family, does not know when Tush Eden died. Family Bible produced entries Corresponding with Mrs. Gouldsmith's evidence, but appears to have been made after occurrence happened from her recollection of facts, Mrs. Mr. Daniel Joy: Knew the intestate as well as he knew himself, it was reported he was the son of James called Tush Eden. Knew Joshua and Jerry; always understood Tush Eden was the brother of Joshua and Jerry did not know George or Andrew; never heard anything of George; thinks Tush Eden died before the War. Intestate was a married man in 1781. James Eden the intestate never had any children. John Dorrill knew the Grandfather, and father and intestate James Eden called Tush Eden was the father of the intestate. The brothers were Joshua, James, George, Andrew, Wm. died long ago, Jerry, one daughter, Elizabeth does not know when she died. Tush Eden died before the commencement of the Revolutionary War 76. Tush Eden had four children all died without issue before him except James: the intestate's wife died before him and he died without issue: the last time he saw George Eden he left him in town when the British had possession of the place: never heard that George Eden was married, heard that George went away with the British and never heard of him since: never heard of Geor: H. Eden being son of George nor did he know to the contrary: Geo: was a sort of a tailor, but never saw him work: knew Joshua, but cannot recollect when he died. None of the brothers, but Tush Eden left children that he knew of: thinks there is a strong family likeness as in Geo: H, Eden and knew the man said to be his father as well as he knew himself and thinks there is a likeness between them. After hearing this testimony Mr. Whilden the present admor being satisfied of the claim surrendered the admon and accordingly Qualified George Henry Eden of St. Helena Island, Beaufort District, administrator of the Goods and Effects of James Eden, late of Christ Church Parish, planter deceased, this 31 July 1816.

[Page 144]

1816 August 1. Proved the last Will and testament of James Douglas, late of Charleston, Turner, deceased, by testimony of John Innes, one of the subscribing witnesses thereto: at the same time qualified Mitchell King, Robert Walker, John Boutiton[?] and George Leghorn, executors therein named.

2. Qualified Eliza Wotton of Charleston, Administratrix of the Estate & Effects of Jacob Labough, late of Charleston, mariner, deceased.

3. Qualified Newman Renshew of Charleston, Merchant, administrator of Sarah Halfield with her Will annexed, late of Charleston, Widow, decd.

5. Proved the last Will and testament of George Cross, Mariner, deceased, by the testimony of John F. Trezevant, one of the subscribing witnesses to the same: at the same time qualified George Warren Cross, executor therein named.

[There is no page numbered 145.]

[Page 146]

In the Court of Ordinary Charleston District, September 7, 1819. In the Case of William S. Kelly, deceased.

White & Delesseline, Simons & Waring, Proctors for Roderick Le Roux in person.

Anthony Roderick of Charleston, Grocer, obtained a Citation on the 3d of September 1819 to administer on the Estate and Effects of William S. Kelly of Charleston, State Constable, deceased, as next friend. On the 4th Inst. a Caveat was entered against letters of administration on the Estate of said Kelly by Lewis Roux, Esquire, who claimed the same as next friend and on the 7th September another Caveat was entered by Letcha Miller against admon being granted to any other person, the said Miller claiming as principal Creditor. On the 8th a third Caveat was entered by W. P. Dove, Captain of the City Guard, of which Corps Kelly was a private. On the 14 September the Case came to a hearing when to the surprise of the Ordinary, Mr. Roderick appeared to claim as a Creditor as well as next friend; at the granting of the Citation Mr. Roderick was expressly asked if he had any claim against the Estate of Kelly, then replied had not, but was his particular friend. The circumstances of the Case were in substance as follows: Several Witnesses were sworn and examined in behalf of Roderick, who declared that the deceased and Roderick were both members of the City guard, and they heard Roderick ask Kelly to go and see him and that generally the deceased and Roderick appeared to be esteemed[?]. An account amounting to $165 principally for money lent was presented upon which his claim as Creditor was founded & there were charges also in this account for groceries &c furnished but not regularly entered; the account was attested. In behalf of Mr. Louis Roux, several witnesses were sworn & examined who proved that when Kelly was sick about 6 months ago he expressly sent for Mr. Roux and in their presence requested Mr. Roux to take charge of his papers and said that he wished to make Mr. Roux his executor, he also gave his trunk & papers into the care of Mr. Roux. Mrs. Tisha Miller a Creditor and Capt. Dove

[Page 147]

relinquished their claims in favor of Mr. Roux. Decision. The Ordinary felt little difficulty in making up his mind in this case, conceiving it one in which it was left by the Act altogether in his discretion to elect the person best fitted for the duties of Admor: as however this discretion ought not to be executed in an arbitrary or capricious manner, he felt himself bound to state the motive which activated his decision. It was contended by the council for Roderick, that as he obtained the Citation that the maxim of law "Prior tempore potior est in Jure" should prevail in his favor; the Ordinary disclaimed such a construction to defeat the very object of a Citation which is summon all persons interested to appear at a certain tine to make known their claims and as encouraging applications for Citation as in the indecorous as in human frequently before any search has been made for a Will and sometimes before the deceased is deposited in his grave. It was also contended that the Act of the Legislature regulating the manner of granting admon makes it obligatory on the Ordinary to give preference to Creditors over other persons: In perusing that clause of the Act it appears to me, that so long as Kindred are interested it is obligatory on the Ordinary to observe the preference therein prescribed: but as soon as the grades of Kindred are past the Act drops the emphatic words "default of" and says "in default of such" remaining Kindred to the greatest creditor or creditors, or to such other persons as the Count shall appoint. The Act does not say in default of creditor then to such other persons the Court shall appoint and for obvious reasons as the Creditors claim may be of equivocal nature or disputed or he may be otherwise an improper person and it is chiefly in favor of the blood and to prevent disputes among relatives that the Act has so carefully marked the preference in the former part of the Clause. To apply the circumstances of the present Case Mr. Roderick on obtaining the Citation was

[Page 148]

distinctly informed that the Ordinary would generally prefer a substantial creditor in granting admor: he replied he had no claim but wished the admor as a friend and although he attended several times during the week expressly on this business he never intimated that he had any claim against Kelly's Estate: Mr. Roux's claim as next friend was in the opinion of the Ordinary paramount to Roderick's. Mr. Roux as a Magistrate patronized Kelly as a Constable from the time of his arrival in this State until his death, under these impressions the Ordinary conceived Mr. Roux as the person to be appointed and accordingly decreed in his favor.

In the Case of George Miles, deceased. In the Court of Ordinary Nov. 15, 1819. Crafts & Eckard & Furman, Proctors for the Widow
Toomer for Quin.

Mary Miles, Widow of George Miles, deceased vs Thomas Fitzgerald Quin. Motion to revoke administrations.

The Statement of Mary Miles, a colored woman, was taken by consent subject to all legal objections. She declared that she was the wife of George Miles, that her husband left Charleston on the 14th August 1819, he went fishing and has never been heard of from that time to this: one Wilson went with him in the same boat & she understood he returned and said that Miles and himself were cast away and landed on Bull's Island and were together two days. Certificate of Marriage between George Miles and Mary Riley, now Mary Miles, dated 28 April 1818 by the Revd. Dr. C. E. Gadsden: William McIntosh sworn. Witness stated that on the 28th Sept. 1819 Mr. Quin asked him to step into the lobby of the Sheriff's Office and asked deponent where Mary Miles lived, he went with Quin to her House: Quin asked her for George Miles, and said that

[Page 149]

there were conjectures respecting his being lost. Quin asked her who were to pay the debts supposing Miles to be dead. She told him he had better take the management of the Estate and pay the debts and should there be any surplus to pay it over to her. Quin had papers in his hand at that time witness saw no papers offered to Mary Miles to sign, not a word said about signing papers. Witness produced a Memorandum in writing that he had made to keep conversation in his recollection, was in the habit of making them entered in his memorandum and copied the one presented yesterday: the council for Mary Miles called for the production of this Book, Mr. McIntosh was directed by the Court to fetch it and almost immediately returned saying that he had forgot that he had been some time ago and this Book was lost (yet he had just declared that he copied the memorandum from that Book yesterday). Mr. Thomas sworn. Witness stated that George Miles and Wilson went out in Deponent's boat: it was a small boat sloop rigged, the Boat was found sunk in the sand at the North East corner of Bull's Island: Miles was not seen with her: from all information he has, he thinks Miles must be dead. The Affidavit of Quin (who was confined to his bed by Gout), was read by consent subject to exception in which he declared in substance that Mary Miles had consented that he should take the Administration. It was at first contended that it was not certain that Miles was dead, but the fact was afterwards admitted. Decree. In the consideration of the case the manifest in consistency and contradictions, in the evidence of Mr. McIntosh must induce the Court to give but little attention to it. Quin's affidavit, although it might perhaps admitted under some circumstances, being in his cause, it ought to be received with great caution if admitted at all: granted however that the consent of Mary Miles was fully proved, yet it appears only to have been a Verbal permission, and surely with a view that Quin administer for her advantage: if however, upon having a further knowledge of Mr. Quin's Character, she has reason apprehend that her interest would

[Page 150]

not be promoted by his agency and upon her coming personally into Court to claim the administration the Court will not reject her petition under the circumstances of the case, and bind her by a more parole assent. It has been contended that the Administration having been granted in due form to Quin, cannot be revoked now without fraud or a surprise proved. The doctrine may be applicable where the rights of the parties to the administration are equal but surely will not apply where this contest is between a stranger as Creditor and the next of Kin. Here the widow is entitled "in exclusion to all other persons." In this case I feel myself bound to revoke the administration granted to Mr. Quin and do hereby decree and grant the administration to Mary Miles.

In the case of Robert Haig, deceased. January 7th 1820. There were three papers exhibited. The first marked A is a Will dated 1810 regularly Signed, Sealed & published and witnessed by three witnesses. This Will is admitted to have been duly executed. The second paper marked B is a memorandum in the hand writing of the deceased, it is not Signed, sealed nor dated nor has it the name of the deceased expressed throughout the whole of it. The third paper marked C is a Will dated 1813 prepared for execution and supposed to have been drawn from the memorandum B, it is not in the hand writing of the deceased nor is it signed by him. The following parol testimony was produced in support of the two last papers. Mr. Thomas Logan swore that in the year 1815 he thinks the month of May the deceased showed the witness the paper B in his own hand writing and said it was a memorandum by which he intended to make a Will. Mr. James Evens one of the executors named in the papers B. & C. renounced his executorship in order that his testimony may be received. He swore that he was with the deceased the day before he died and that the deceased produced

[Page 151]

the Will of 1813 paper C, but he was very unwell and would postpone it until the next day; decd. to witness that he meant to destroy the Will of 1810, paper A; Witness read the whole of the paper C and the memorandum on the back of it and that was the Will the testator said he meant to execute. Decree. My mind has been very doubtful how to form an opinion in this case: at first I was strongly in favor of the Will of 1810 in consequence of its being duly executed, that I was induced to think that the paper B could not be set up, but upon mature reflection and in hearing the testimony in favor of that paper I think entitled to more consideration. The Will of 1810 was duly executed but it is to be observed conveys nothing but personal property and that so formal a revocation is not necessary as when real estate is divided. The Paper B would certainly been sufficient to convey personal property. If the Will of 1810 did not exist: now it remains to consider whether paper B is sufficient testament to supercede that: It is unquestionably very informal not having the name of the deceased throughout the whole of it nor his subscription to it yet, it is in his own handwriting and contains testamentary words & dispositions and has Executors duly appointed. It is proved by the testimony of Mr. Logan that it is of subsequent Date to the Will of 1810 as the deceased showed it to him in 1815 as a memorandum by which he intended to make a Will not the authorities show that testament not signed or witnesses provided in the hand writing of the decd. are sufficient to convey personal property, and paper B being written since 1810 or to supercede paper A. The paper C which by the testimony of Mr. Evens was the Will the decd. meant to sign not being in his hand writing and not executed by him cannot be set up; it is however substantially the same as paper B. I must confess I feel my self much embarrassed with regard to this decision, but as the law does not make it necessary that testaments to convey Personal Estate should be sealed and witnessed. It. is to be presumed that at such a testament of later date ought

[Page 152]

to supercede one of prior date although _____ regularly executed under the circumstances _____ the evidence. I am of the opinion that the equity and substantiated justice of the case are in favor of the paper B and therefore pronounced for it as being the latest testament made.

Mar. 13, 1820. Granted a Special Citation to William Wightman, Administrator de bonis non of Ann Paul Emanuel Sigesman de Montemorency, Luxembough, late of Paris, Gentleman, decd., to cite John Brown Cutting formerly Administrator de bonis non of the said Estate, personally to be and to appear before me in the Court of Ordinary to be held at Charleston on Friday the twenty-first day of April at eleven in the forenoon to show cause if any he have, why he would not render before me a true and faithful account of his admon of said Estate. The said Citation was returned duly certified as personally served on the 12 April 1820. See original citation No. 4.

In the Matter of George Rivers' Will. Pettigreu for the Will. King Contra. In the Court of Ordinary, Charleston District. September 17th 1823.

Mrs. Martha Rivers propounded into Court to Probate a paper written in pencil proporting to be the last Will of George Rivers, late of St. Paul's Parish, deceased. It was written on the inner side of a letter addressed by Benjamin Reynolds to the deceased. The Pencil writing was proved to be his handwriting. It was admitted that a Will in pencil was in itself Valid, but it was opposed on two grounds. 1st. that the testator was not of sane mind at the time of the execution: 2nd. that it was merely deliberative and not designed as a Will. On the first point a mass of Testimony was produced to impeach the sanity of the deceased. This is contained in the testimony of Mrs. McCants,

[Page 153]

Benjamin Reynolds and Mallory Rivers and a letter from Mrs. Rivers to Mrs. McCants was produced. The extent of the testimony was to this effect: That the deceased was for some years previous to his death in a most miserable and unhappy state of mind, that they at times thought him deranged and that this miserable state of feeling and derangement continued to the time of his death. The evidence to rebut this charge of insanity contained in the testimony of Messrs. Taylor, Smith, Dr. Lynah and Dr. Ramsay and Mr. Thompson. They state generally that while it was manifest, that he labored under the most distressful feelings so as to render his life comfortless and miserable in the extreme, yet that the deceased never exhibited any loss of his reasoning faculties that he would describe his suffering to be most dreadful and distracting, but that he could restrain himself in company and did reason on his situation justly, and lament bitterly his deplorable situation: that he conducted his business usually himself and generally with propriety. Dr. King who was summoned by defendant, after a minute and elaborate examination in which he describes at great length the symptom of the disorder under which the deceased labored, comes to the conclusion upon being asked the question whether in the acceptance of the disorder the deceased could make a Will: he replied that he did not think him at such time capable of making a Will as some nobleman did of seventy five sheets, but that at he could make such a Will as that before the Court. Dr. Ramsay also in his examination went into a long and critical investigation of his disease in which he stated that the disorder with which Mr. Rivers was afflicted, when in its greatest effects he took of the nature of madness or rather his delirium, but that there were many grades of this disease which did not amount to prostration of mind: on being asked if the deceased was always rational in what he did so far as his situation permitted him to do any thing, he answered I believe

[Page 154]

I think he was always sensible of what was right or wrong during those paroxysms in the height of which I conceive he would have expressed his disapprobation, if any one had proposed to him to do what was normally wrong or against his interest. Dr. Lynah was also examined and the tenor of his evidence was that however uncomfortable & depressed Mr. Rivers was that he never in any one instance in his intercourse with a neighbor, saw him manifest anything like unsoundness of mind, and that his house he believes, was perhaps the last the deceased was in before his death. Mr. Thomas Smith was the nearest neighbor of the deceased and as intimate with him as any person, states that Mr. Rivers at some time he does not exactly recollect whether before or after the date of Mr. Reynolds letter upon which the Will was written, request him to draw a Will for him that he replied to Mr. Rivers had done so to have drawn his Will: that Mr. Rivers was subject to deep fits or paroxysms of Melancholy when alone, but that he would control his feelings and behave with propriety in company: Mr. Smith states the manner in which the Will was found. Mr. Josiah Taylor in his testimony states that he often saw Mr. Rivers in the course of the year of 1822, and never saw him other than in his right sense, thinks he was sound of mind to make a Will he came to town, settled his accounts and acted rationally: Mr. Thompson, the manager of Mr. Rivers was examined fully before the Court: the substance of his testimony is that he was long in the service of Mr. Rivers, that he never saw anything in him like insanity: That he was subject to fits of Melancholy:

[Page 155]

in those fits he never did strange or wild acts, but would lament his uncomfortable situation then in the most of these fits he always considered him a rational man, and never scrupled to follow his directions: his situation made him incapable of enjoying his life but never to his knowledge caused him to act irrationally: In receiving the testimony of Mr. McCants, Mr. Reynolds and Mr. Mallory Rivers it may be observed that often they speak of his being deranged yet when called to state the acts by which they infer this derangement they do not mention any thing which indicates insanity, but the amount of it was that he was miserable, unhappy, distressed with his disorder, depressed in his Spirits, undecided in some of his orders that he mistook objects in the road and missed his way: that may show abstraction and distress of mind, but nothing like a want of the reasoning faculty. Besides it may be further observed that every one of them have had transactions with him in which they must have considered him a rational man except it be Mallory Rivers. In reviewing the testimony the Ordinary can draw no conclusion but that while Mr. Rivers' station was truly to be deplored he exhibited no acts which would in law amount to insanity. Indeed the contents of the paper bears satisfactory evidence that it must have been written when he was of sane mind. The second question is of more difficult solution. It appears that the paper is written in pencil in the inner side of a letter from Benjamin Reynolds to the deceased. This letter appears to have been found in a trunk in the possession of Mrs. Rivers: the letter on which it is written is dated 15 March 1822 and Mr. Rivers' death occurred about the 9th of June 1822 so that the Will must have been made by Mr. Rivers at some time within those periods There is nothing before the Court that can determine more precisely the time of its execution. The difficulty is the case is to determine whether the deceased intended this paper to operate as his

[Page 156]

Will: as the Ordinary will _____ on the motives have influenced his mind in the decision of the Case. The contents of the paper are as follows; after my just debts are paid I give to my beloved wife Martha Rivers the use of all my property, the plantation I now reside on and the negroes with the increase of my plantation during her nat. life, at her death to be equally divided among my Grand children, the property I got by my marriage to her to will and dispose as she may think proper, George Rivers. It may be perceived in perusing this will that the whole of his property is disposed of, that the words are clearly testamentary, that it is perfectly consistent from the beginning to the end in short it appears complete in all dispositions, the only thing against it is the conclusion which arises from its being in pencil that he may have intended it as deliberative, but this may be rebutted when it is considered how complete it is in all its parts, embracing the whole of his Estate and leaving nothing further to be done unless it was that he may have wished to transcribe it in ink and perhaps have the paper couched in better language, bit it would have been substantially the same Will and this strictly was not necessary as it has the legal requisites in its present form, for it is admitted that a Will in pencil is as valid as a Will in Ink, provided the testator meant it to operate, now when it is considered that he had in some measure advanced his Son and his Son had also acquired something by marriage and that he was already in a State of Competency, to say the least of it, and when we also advert to the great affections which he manifested to his wife and that

[Page 157]

she brought him considerable property on his marriage with her that he may have been desirous to give it an enlarged expression of his affection to her while he conceived that in providing for the grandchildren he did substantially assist his son in a mode congenial to his own feeling and when we called to mind his anxious desire expressed to Mr. Reynolds to make a Will and his request to Mr. Smith to assist in that way we must draw the conclusion how much importance he attached to it and to infer that he did intend that Will to stand rather than die Intestate: but whatever his motives were in making the Will in the manner he did, I am inclined to thank that the contents of that paper contained his final disposition on that subject. I must therefore decree for the Will (continued p. 162)

James Mead's Case. In the Court of Ordinary, Charleston Dist. September 1, 1819. In the case of James Mead, deceased. Prioleau in behalf of Thomas F. Quin in support of the will. Bennett & Hunt for James White and Edward Dowling Contra. A more painful subject for investigation has never been presented to my consideration since I have been acting as a judge of the Court, nor any that would produce more serious sequences in the result to the Character of the individual principally interested that the one before me. A paper purporting to be the last Will of James Mead, decd., had been presented for Probate and a caveat entered under the suspicion of forgery not indeed expressly avowed by the strongest implications I have patiently investigated the testimony offered on both sides and attentively considered the arguments of the Council with an ernest desire to obtain the most satisfactory information and draw the truth out with as much certainty as the

[Page 158]

circumstances of the case would admit. In behalf of the will Several witnesses were examined to prove the Signature of the two subscribing witnesses who were both dead. Since the execution of the Will which is dated the 9 April 1806, also to prove the signature of the testator. This Testimony would have been Sufficient to have established the will for personalities in the usual course of probate: but the contending party has raised a mass of testimony with a view to defeat the effect of the evidence offered in favor of the Will. The evidence in favor of the Will may be summed up [in] the testimony which came from Mr. Young, Mr. Folker, Mr. McIntosh and Eliza: all of whom declare the signature of John O'Kelly to the Will of 1806 to be in their opinion the signature of John O'Kelly the first subscribing witness to the Will: They speak as positively as prudent men ought upon such a subject, the only witness that favors John Gready's signature, the other subscribing witness to this Will is Mr. Thomas Thaeum his half brother who says he is as positive on the point as reason will let him go. The testator Mead's signature is proved by

Mr. Lynah who believes that it is his; thinks he knew it well; and thinks he knows it from the character of the writing and particularly from the formation of the capitol "Jas." These are the material witnesses for the Will. In opposition to the Will Mr. Patrick Healy, Mr. Drummond, Mr. Galloway, W. McGann and Mr. Pitsch have all declared their opinions that it is not O'Kelly's signature. Some giving one reason and some another for their belief; some asserting that O'Kelly always wrote pretty much alike, while others thought he wrote differently, they all however concur in thinking it is not O'Kelly's signature. Mr. Corker was called to disprove Gready's signature and said he did not think it was his, but he did not recollect certainly seeing him write but once. To disprove the signature of Mead's to the Will were brought forward Mr. Galloway, Capt. Porton, Mr. Sullivan,

[Page 159]

Mr. J. H. Mitchell, Mr. McDonald, all of whom concur thinking it was not Mead's signature. Some speak very positively on the subject, others less so. In the Course of the examination of all these witnesses: various specimens of the signature of John O'Kelly and James Mead were introduced, and a comparison of hand writings made by the witnesses: those called to support the Will generally thought there was a resemblance to the signatures on the Will to the specimens produced both of John O'Kelly's and Mead's signatures were differently written at different times. Much comment was made on the appearance of the paper and Ink, of which the Will was composed some alleging that there was a freshness in its appearance and others thought its complication would warrant a belief that it was 10 or 13 years old. Such was the nature of the testimony offered to the Court, and amidst these conflicting opinions and jarring conjectures with the weight of testimony in point of numbers rather against the Will, it was impossible to come to that satisfactory conclusion which in a case of this kind would be so desirable: when at this Stage of the case a species of evidence was discovered and introduced which threw great light on the subject: in my mind corroboration and strengthening all the evidence in the Will while it weakened that against the Will. This was a letter in the following words directed to Mr. Quin. "9th. April 1806 Mr. Quin our friend Mr. Mead is very poorly and requests me to send for you as he wishes to make his Will in your favor. "John O'Kelly." This letter, has been proved to be the hand writing of O'Kelly and as it bears irrefragable marks of age and exposure it cannot have been conjured up for the purpose: it bears date of the same day of the Will

[Page 160]

in a manner calls for the Will: it is strong evidence of the animus testandi or intention to make a Will originating from the testator; for by this letter O'Kelly is directed by Mead who is sick "to send for Quin" to have his Will made in Quin's favor: and the Will accordingly is made and O'Kelly is a subscribing witness together with Gready whose hand writing is proved by his brother: and if I have any skill in the comparison of Handwriting this

Signature is as near (if it be not the nearest) resemblance to O'Kelly's signature as witness in the Will of 1806 of any specimen of his handwriting which has been produced. The Comparison of Mead's handwriting to the receipt and order written about this time 1804 strikes me as the nearest resemblance to the signature of the Will of any other produced. This I am persuaded will appear on inspection to any unbiased mind the only remaining doubt then in mind is in respect to the hostility which existed against Quin and that under this impression he should have made him legatee: It appeared by Mr. Byrnes' testimony, that the difference between Mead and Quin arose about the time of the dissolution of the copartnership, which is ascertained to have taken place August 1804 and this conversation as Mr. Byrnes says between Mead and himself in less than one year after the dissolution of copartnership: this brings the difference up to August 1805 leaving the time between that period and the date of the Will April 1806 on the change in testators mind in favor of Quin: when or how this change was effected does not appear, but it must have been before the letter written by O'Kelly for that letter proves a reconciliation and several witnesses said they had afterwards seen Quin at Mead's: this is enough to ground the presumption when connected with the letter. I have not adverted particularly to Stoll's evidence against

[Page 161]

Quin because the course which the case has taken makes it unnecessary. Having come to a conclusion from a train of deductions warranted as I conceive by the evidence I have now only to state the effect of that conclusion which is that if there be no other Will of later date in Will of 1806 in law must be the last Will of Mead. The Will of 1816 I conceive is revoked by the testators own act, his tearing off the witnesses names in consequence of the death of one of the Legatees, and the other having abused his confidence it therefore follows that the revocation of 1816 sets as rather leaves in force the Will of 1806 and that by a strange fatality of things and the neglect of Mead to destroy Will of 1806 Quin may become possessed of the personal property. Such I conceive is the effect of the law and such the result of my investigation and I now pronounce and declare for the Will of 1806.

In the Case of Henry Bradly, deceased. In the Court of Ordinary, April 21, 1820. John White has been cited to show cause why letters of administration which he obtained on the Estate of Henry Bradley, deceased, should not be revoked and a paper purporting to be a testament of the said Henry Bradley, deceased should not be proved. Miss Deliesseline and Mitchell moved that the Admor might be discharged as the testiment was not proved in solemn form or Form of Law inasmuch as John Lochlear, one of the subscribing, witnesses had not been examined & was not now present to be examined: at a former Hearing John Locklear was present, but was not examined as Mr. Crafts was called into the Court of Equity and did not claim before the Hearing adjournment. It now remains to determine whether the testament ought to be dismissed for want of Proof: in this inquiry it will be proper to take a view of the different modes of proving a Testament: all the writers on the subject

[Page 162]

lay down that it is of two kinds, Viz:- the common or vulgar form and the solemn Form or Form of Law: this testament has received proof in the common form by the testimony of Jonathan Wright, one of the subscribing witnesses to the same, but could not be established until Citation had been issued to call in the administrator & next of Kin to name such objections as they might deem proper: they had now appeared by Council and demanded that the testament should be proved in form of Law in the strictest manner: Jonathan Wright is since dead and his hand writing can only be proved by the party objecting never having had an opportunity to examine him. John Locklear alone remains to be examined and every opportunity ought to be afforded to those interested in the event of Henry Bradley having died intestate before a Testament involving their rights should receive the sanction of the Court. The Testament therefore has not received that proof Which solemn Form or of Law points out which seems requires two witnesses when the testament is not in the handwriting nor signed by the testator himself.

In the Case of James Mead, deceased, in the Court of Ordinary, Charleston District. June 16, 1821. Prioleau for Quin. J. B. White for Wilkie.

The Case came before the Ordinary on a Citation issued to William Wilkie, Administrator, ad Colligendum of James Mead, decd., to show cause why the letters granted to him should not be revoked and the letters of Administration cum testamento be granted Thomas F. Quin, the legatee, named in the testament of the said James Mead, deceased. Mr. White objected to the revocation on the ground that Mr. Wilkie was absent being sick at Walterborough

[Page 163]

and could not attend stating that there was no reason to change the Administration as the appeal from the decision of the ordinary still pending and that Mr. Wilkie intended to carry it on in his own name. Mr. Prioleau in behalf of Quin stated he was principally interested if the testament was sustained and thought there would [be] no time lost in changing the administration as both the Sureties of Wilkie were insolvent: Stated that the case was stricken from the docket of the Court of Common Pleas.

Decree. The Ordinary was of opinion that there was no occasion for the presence of Mr. Wilkie: that he was no way interested in the case and was only as it were stake-holder for the parties: that since granting the Letters ad colligendum to Wilkie both of the Sureties had failed: that Quin was sole legatee in the testament which by the Ordinary's decision is thus far established: that the Appeal from this decision had never been brought before the Court of Common Pleas and as he understands it has been stricken from the docket: he would however leave the case open for the direction of that Court as it is understood that the appeal is to be carried on by some person. He would not therefore interfere further than to put Quin into the administration ad colligendum, as he was most interested if the testament should it be finally Sustained, which the Ordinary was bound to presume would be the case. It is therefore ordered that Thomas F. Quin be appointed Admor ad Colligendum of James Mead, decd., pandente Lite upon his giving sufficient security.

James Mead, deceased. In the Court of Ordinary, Charleston District. August 26, 1823. This case came before the Court on the application or a special Citation by John Scannel as next of Kin to James Mead, deceased, to cite Thomas Quin the legatee named in a certain paper purporting to be the

[Page 164]

Will of the said Mead to show cause why the said Will should not be proved in solemn Form. The case is moved in this country, but from all information on the subject which the Court could obtain: it appeared that the application ought to be granted: upon which evidence was adduced to prove the right of John Scannel to make this application which proved satisfactory to the Court: Mr. Quin then offered some witnesses to the Court in support of the Will upon whose testimony connected with what was before the Court on the first hearing, he rested his claims: not however without application for the postponement of the Case on the ground of the absence of these material witnesses: but the Ordinary being of the opinion that as this case had been before the Court so long pending, that he had used due diligence he may have availed himself of their testimony and therefore he refused the application. There are two Questions which call for the attention of the ordinary. 1st. is the Will genuine.

2. if genuine, then has it been revoked by the testators making a second Will which he afterwards cancelled. In regard to the first question it will be observed on reading the decree which I formerly made that I was perplexed with the contrarety of the testimony and seemed rather in time against the admission of the Will when a paper was produced was the evidence written by John O'Kelly addressed to Mr. Quin informing him that Mead was sick and wished to make a Will in his favor and requesting him to attend for that purpose: at that time forming conclusions in my mind that the paper bore all the appearance of authenticity, I considered it a very conclusive circumstance in favor of the Will

[Page 165]

being as it were the animus testande proceeding from the testator and therefore disposed to give greater weight to the testimony in favor of the Will and finally to decide for it, but in reviewing the testimony connected with some evidence which has since transpired and weighing generally the inability of the witnesses offered on both sides in the case and the aspect of the whole of the affair: I am disposed to give less consequence to that paper to say the least of it, it is now weakened particularly where it appears in evidence that the copartnership between Mead and Quin was dissolved in 1804 two years before the date of the Will and that Mead ever after a dissolution held Quin in abhorrence that although, when Quin was present, he treated him as he did others, yet when he was not present, he frequently expressed his aversion in strong terms, it seems difficult to draw any conclusion but that there must be something inexplicable attending the Will: so much so that I feel myself bound to revoke the probate I formerly granted, On the second question after deciding as above it would seem hardly necessary to say anything, but that the whole matter may be before the Court above and that the case may receive a final decision at once on both questions, should the Will be established there. I would observe that I did formerly decree incidentally that the second Will being cancelled by the testator the effect in law was the revival of the first: but it appears by the decision in the case of Taylor and Taylor that although the common law does presume the first Will to be restored to its active energy by the canceling of the second, yet tho it is a question of intention and may be controlled by other circumstances: if therefore such a construction is to prevail, admitting the Will to be genuine, a stronger circumstance could handily be adduced

[Page 166]

to evince the intention of Mead to die intestate, rather than the first Will should revive in favor of Quin than his uniform hostility to Quin from 1804 to the time of his death: In short there are circumstances in this case which lead me to doubt the genuineness of the and to conclude if genuine, that Mead would rather have died intestate, than that the Will should have revived in favor of Quin upon the whole however, this is a Case more calculated for the decision of a Jury and I feel a degree of relief in this consideration that it is likely to take that course. I must therefore dismiss the Will upon both points. continued p. 176

The Case of Lewis Sweten, deceased. In the Court of Ordinary. December 13, 1821.

In reviewing the testimony in this case it appears that two points of form for my investigation. The first is whether any undue influence has been exercised to induce Sweten to make this Will in Connelly's favor: The 2nd. whether the testator was of sane mind at the time of the execution thereof. With regard to the first it is alleged by the Actors in the case that the removal of Sweten in his infebled State from the house of Lockart to that of Connelly where he makes a Will in favor of the latter is a very strong circumstance to fix the suspicion and fraud of undue influence on Connelly towards the testator. Now to my mind the Evidence does not warrant such an inference for look at the testimony. 1st. of Miss Connelly who expressly states that her father was sent for by the Testator therefore the removal, it is to be presumed, takes place at the instance of Sweten: examine the testimony of Mr. Lockart: they say expressly that Sweten an hour or so after the departure of Connelly called Lockart and desires him not to be vexed with him but he had requested Connelly to promise[?]

[Page 167]

him a room at his house near the water side and gives his reasons for wishing the change that he thought the salt air agreed better with his health and also that he might see his people as they came or landed from James Island: he also told Lockart that his house was too noisy and he wanted a room to himself: the testimony of Mr. Bull proved that there was good grounds for such a wish as he tells the Court that the house of Lockart was very noisy and the haunt of Guard men besides Mr. Lockart states that she did not hear Connelly used persuasive language to induce Sweten to move: they were closeted by themselves and nobody heard what past and surely as Sweten sent for Connelly it may, to say the least of it, be as readily inferred that the request for the removal proceeded from the witnesses charge him directly with persuasion: The Court therefore will not attack so gross a suspicion on Connelly from such slight inferences as are drawn in this Case. The next Question is the great Point in this Case to wit:- the Sanity of the Testator. Mr. and Mrs. Lockart and Jackson all state that he was generally flighty, but the chief witness relied on the charge of insanity is Dr. Thomas G. Prioleau, he states that he was called in by Mrs. Lockart to Sweten who had dislocated his Shoulder that although he had a cough he did not think him very sick: this was the last of Jany. On the 2nd of Feby. he had considerable fever, cough and pain in his side: that he attended on Sunday morning at Lockart and to his surprise found that he had been moved to Connelly's. Mrs. Lockart said Sweter had been moved against her consent, that Dr. did not go to see Sweten again until next day when Connelly called him in. Went to Connelly's on Monday morning: at that time, had a cough, fever, and a degree of delirium: he answered to questions tolerably correctly but attended with delirium of fever. While at Lockart he was also under occasional delirium does not think that he was capable of thinking correctly on any subject while under the delirium but if directed to might express himself: that during the time he saw him he was not in

[Page 168]

a situation to make a Will: that from Saturday until he died thinks he would not have been: was surprised knowing his situation to hear that he had made a Will. On being cross examined the Dr. Stated that he did not see Sweter at all on Sunday and he does not know the state of his mind, but supposes if anything was suggested he would assent to it: his delirium was occasioned and increased with the fever: every question the Dr. asked him he answered rationally yet there was a flightiness perceptible. The first witness in support was Joseph Dougherty, a subscribing [witness] to the Will: he is perfectly satisfied that Sweten was in his senses at the execution of the Will: he raised himself in his bed put out his feet: on signing somebody observed had left out a letter e̱ in writing his name, he answered never mind that would do he usually wrote so: When the Will was executed he appeared to understand what he was doing: it was about 2 or 3 o'clock in the morning he did not speak to Sweten, but was long enough with him to be confident he was in his senses. Mr. Axson, the 2nd subscribing witness swears that he was called up by Connelly & Dougherty before daylight to make a Will for a man whom they supposed would die before morning: That he was conducted into Sweten's room, and Connelly told him here was a gentleman would do what he wanted: he then called for a table, pen and paper which was placed at the foot of the bed and every person left the room. Sweten told him he wanted him to make his Will: The room was narrow so that Mr. Axson could not approach him and he turned himself without assistance to the foot of the bed and dictated to him his Will and he was drawing it a negro wench who was there in the room made some remark about some negro he had named when he answered she was old and might go with the rest. The testator told Mr. Axson that the names of the negroes himself, Connelly never mentioned to him anything: all instructions

[Page 169]

came from Sweten. After drawing the Will he read it distinctly to him and the testator listened attentively and asked that would be the effect of the Will if he survived: he was told it would have no effect if he survived, Sweten then said he was satisfied. He took a large Bible and held it to him and he signed it Dougherty and myself witnessed it. Mr. Axson concluded by saying if he was capable of Judging Sweten, was perfectly in his senses. Mr. Bull, Miss Connelly, Dougherty and Mr. Axson all Concur in saying he was in his senses when they saw him which embrace the time from Sunday afternoon until after the execution of the Will: during all which time Dr. Prioleau did not see him however respectable therefore the testimony of Dr. Prioleau may be he did not see him at the execution, nor the day before and the concurrent testimony of four witnesses establishes the fact of his sanity at the time of the execution of the Will. I have therefore no hesitation in saying that altho the testator had been the subject of occasionally delirium yet the evidence sustains the fact that the testator was in his senses at the time of the execution. It is not for me to account for his leaving his daughter unprovided for, I can only decree according to the testimony before me and however I may regret the circumstances I can not undertake to disturb the probate of this Will.

Emanuel Levy's Case
Mordicai Levy   )
Rosina Levy   )
Elizabeth Levy   )   In the Court of Ordinary, Charleston District.

Whereas Mordicai Levy, Rosina Levy, and Elizabeth Levy by their next friend Chapman Levy on the ninth day of May last represented to me that they are the children of Emanuel Levy, deceased, and that the aforesaid Nathan Hart and Jacob Lazarus have not accounted to them for the assets of the deceased and prayed that the said Nathan and Jacob

[Page 170]

should render before me a just and true account of their administration, and there upon process issued to cite the said Nathan and Jacob, and also their sureties Levy Moses and Moses Davis to appear before on the twenty-fourth day of the same month of May which said process was returned by F. G. Deliesseline, Sheriff of Charleston District, but the said Jacob Lazarus on the twentieth of the same month of May came and objected to the service of the said process because the copy wherewith he was served was not a true copy and said he would attend at any time: whereupon I adjourned the hearing of the said cause until the sixth day of June instance whereof the said Nathan and Jacob have been duly informed and the same sixth day of June, the Defendants did not come and the further consideration of the matter was deferred to this day and now on this day viz: the 7th day of June, J. L. Pettigru, the Proctor of the said Chapman comes into Court and prays that the said Nathan and Jacob may account and the said Nathan and Jacob also came, and the said J. L. Pettigru produces Certain accounts signed by the said Nathan and Jacob showing a certain balance in their hands wherefore in consideration of the matter and after hearing was offered by Mr. Pettigru on the part of the Plaintiffs and Mr. Bennett on the part of the Defendants. I do order the said Jacob Lazarus to pay to the plaintiffs the sum of $7191.42 with Interest from the 1 January 1821 and I order the said Nathan Hart to pay to the Plaintiffs the Sum of $2473.29 with Interest from the 1 January 1822 and I do further order that the defendants do deliver to the complainants the Bonds, Notes and Surety for money contained in the annexed Schedule and the said Jacob Lazarus to be accountable for the same if not duly paid.

[Page 171]

Schedule A. 24 shares of Capital Stock in the Planters and Merchants Bank Bella Hart Bond principal $896[?] and Int. from December 1818. Moses Davis Bond $12,271.76 said to be in the hands of Complainant's Guardian Mr. Levy. Levy Moses Bond $4,000. Interest from 1 June 1819. 7th June 1822. James Mitchell

In the Case of John Philips White deceased. John H. Sargent, Assignee of Robert Blakely vs. Patrick Fox, Admo'r John Philips White, decd. In the Court of Ordinary. Charleston District.

I do hereby certify that A Citation to administer on the Estate and Effects of John Philips White, late of Charleston, Attorney At Law, deceased, was granted to Patrick Fox, as next friend and principal Creditor on the ninth day of July 1821 and that the same was returned duly certified by B. Fenwick, Officiating Clergyman at the Roman Catholic Church in the usual manner on the fifteenth of 1821: That no Caveat having been entered against the same, that Letters of Administration were granted to the said Patrick Fox on the twenty-sixth of July 1821. That on the thirteenth day of August 1821, a Notice of an Appeal from the decision of the Ordinary on the grounds therein stated (a copy whereof is hereunto annexed) was entered in the Court by John H. Sargent, Assignee of Robert Blakely, and that satisfactory evidence has been adduced to the Ordinary that Patrick Fox the Administrator has been duly notified of such appeal. Copy notice of Appeal. "The State of South Carolina, Charleston District. John H. Sargent, assignee, of Robert Blakely vs. Patrick Fox, Notice of Appeal to the Court of Common Pleas for the decision of the Ordinary of the said District as to his having granted Letters of Administration the said Patt Fox upon the Estate of John P. White. This appeal is made upon the following grounds, Viz:

[Page 172]

1. That the Citation in this case was not advertised a certain number of times and for a Certain length of time in the State Gazette or any other Public Newspaper, as by reason, justice and the Acts of the Genl. Assembly of the State and particularly that past the 8th March 1787 in such case made and provided, it ought to have been before granting the said Letters of Administration. 2. That the Security given by the said Fox is insufficient. 3. That he is not the principal Creditor. Signed: John H. Sargent."

August 13, 1821. In the Case of William Davis, deceased, the State of South Carolina, Charleston District.

Personally appeared Robert Sutton who being duly sworn on the Holy Evangelist Saith that about 7 or 8 days after the death of William Davis who fell over board of one of the Packets in this harbor and was drowned on the Second day of August last, this Deponent who had been residing in the house of the said William Davis before and after his death, was called upstairs by Elizabeth Courtney, who has taken out Letters of Administration on William Davis' Estate under the name of Elizabeth Davis and was then and there showed by the said Elizabeth the last Will and testament of the said William Davis. That this Deponent then read the whole of the said Will to the said Elizabeth which contained as the will recalled these Provisions vis: That one thousand dollars were to be raised from the Sales of his (testator's) Estate for the use of his son, gave to his son also a negro girl by the name of Rose, the rest of testator's Estate to the best of Deponent's knowledge was to be at the disposal of Elizabeth Courtney and that John Phillips and Geo. W. Cross were appointed Executors of the said Will. This deponent further swears that after he had finished reading the said Will he returned it to the said Elizabeth and he saw her deposit it in a desk near her bed and she observed to the Deponent that

[Page 173]

there were several other Wills in the said desk. This deponent further swears that the said Elizabeth denied to him for several days that any Will had been left by William Davis, but then she learned that no copy could be found in the office of Cross & Gray or elsewhere she then said that she would keep the Will shown to deponent out of sight: Lastly this deponent has heard bind has reason to believe that the said Elizabeth has married since the death of William Davis. Signed: Robert Sutton. Sworn to before me the 25 Sept. 1822. Robert B. Gilchrist, Q. U.

South Carolina By James D. Mitchell, Esquire, Ordinary. To Elizabeth Davis otherwise called Elizabeth Davis.

Whereas John Phillips hath represented to me that he hath reason to believe that you are in possession of the last Will and Testament of William Davis, late of Charleston, Grocer, deceased, Founded on the affidavit of Robert Sutton who solemnly deposes that he has seen the Will in your possession since the decease of the said William Davis and that the said John Phillips and George W. Cross were named executors therein as in and by the said affidavit duly filed in the Court will more fully appear. This case therefore are to cite and admonish you to produce into the Court of Ordinary to be held at Charleston on Friday next the twenty-seventh inst. at 11 o'clock in the forenoon the Will of the said William Davis in order that the same may be proved according to law and to surrender up the letters of administration which you obtained on the Estate and Effects of the said deceased. Hereof fail not at your peril, Given under my Hand and Seal this twenty-fifth day of Sept. 1822: and in the forty-seventh year of American Independence.

In the Court of Ordinary, September 27, 1822 Personally appeared before me Elizabeth Davis who being duly sworn on the Holy Evangelist of Almighty God maketh Oath she has not in her possession at this time nor that she ever had or seen to the best of her knowledge & belief the last Will

[Page 174]

and testament of William Davis, deceased. That she believed that such a Will was executed by the said William Davis, but she has not seen nor heard the conditions of the said Will read by any person and thereby believes the said Will was lost with the said William Davis and the affidavit of Robert Sutton stating that he read the said Will seven or eight days after his death is unfounded as the deponent solemnly avers that such a circumstance never took place. Elizabeth Davis X her mark. Sworn to before me this 27 September 1822. James D. Mitchell. Witness Wm. G. Armstrong.

Personally appeared before me Joseph Wamsley, who being duly Sworn on the Holy Evangelist of Almighty God maketh Oath that at the request of Elizabeth Davis he, together with her examined in a careful manner all the papers of the said William Davis about three days after the death of the said William Davis and that he found no paper whatever which was anything like a Will: that the object of his search was a Will and that he took up the papers one by, one and found no Will. Given under my hand this 27 day of Septr. 1822. James D. Mitchell, Ordinary, Joseph Wamsley. Witness Wm. M. G. Armstrong.

In the Court of Ordinary, Charleston District, January 13, 1823.

In the Case of Sarah Ann Nowell, dec'd, a feme covert, Kennedy & Pettigru for the Will, King contra. An instrument of writing purporting to be the Testament of Sarah Ann Nowell was produced into Court for Probate and an objection was made against its reception, on the ground that being the testament of a feme covert, it was not entitled to Probate. Mr. King in support of this objection cited Grimke's Public Law P. 139. "Provided now and all times that any Will or testament made or to be made by any Feme Covert, idiot,

[Page 175--follows page 191 on microfilm, which follows several pages after page 210]

or any persons of insane memory shall not be good or valid in law, any thing [below?] to the contrary notwithstanding." He also cited a decision in the Constitutional Court of Appeals in Equity in this State. Lowndes & Champion in support of his position and also the Case of Hood & Archer decided in our Constitutional Court in May 1821 upon which he relied as much in point. Messrs. Kennedy & Pettigru in behalf of the Will urged that the Statute from Grimke merely declaratory and ought not to operate strictly: that the decision of the Ecclesiastical Courts in England were part of the Common Law here that the decisions of the Court of Ordinary ought rather to conform thereto than to this decisions of our Courts of Equity, as the Appeals from this Court is to the Common Pleas, that the Ecclesiastical Courts in England have accorded to the feme Covert the jus desponendi of her separate Estate: that the Case of Hood & Archer did not apply in as much as in that Case the wife bequeathed her [choice?] in action: but in the Case before the Court there was a separate Estate disposed of and that therefore the Will ought to be admitted to Probate.

After reflecting on the Case and referring to the authorities cited the Ordinary feels himself bound to give a brief exposition of his reasons for his decision. The general principal that of any covert cannot make a Will is so plain, that such a Will would not be offered for Probate unless there were some Special matter to be urged to entitle it to administration. In this case it is contended that the property herein bequeathed is the exclusive separate estate of the wife: that by the English decisions which ought to be respected here, the Jus disponendi was incident thereto: but it does appear that the Court of Equity in this State rejects the principal, unless the power is particularly given by the instrument reciting the Estate: it must be observed that in the case, although the father's Will gives a separate Estate there is no clause

[Page 176]

vesting her with the power to dispose, therefore the Jus disponendi merges on the marriage in the usual manner in the marital right there was no Covenant or agreement entered into by the parties to give the power to the wife. On adverting to the case of Hood & Archer it will be noted with what force and tenacity the law raises a Presumption of Constraint: it goes the length to say that a Feme Covert cannot make a Will or testament even with the consent of her husband unless it be to his prejudice, in order to avoid the presumption of coercion or restraint: it expressly says that a bequest to the husband is void even done [with] his consent, being as it were, a gift to himself. Upon the whole I find no Case so much like the present as that of Hood & Archer, and the principals there laid down, and the language used, appears to me as designed as far as possible, to settle this important question. I feel myself therefore in a manner bound to adopt the course there pursued and to dismiss the said Instrument without Probate.

John Scannel vs Thomas F. Quin. In the case of James Mead. Charleston District, March 24, 1823.

Dr. England: It was a matter of public notoriety in County of Cork that he was coming to Charleston latter part of 1820, he was called in by a friend of his the parish priest of Clanarkelty Cork, who told him that a man of the name of Scannel had died in Charleston possesses of some property that Scannel's friends were living in his parish and that he knew them all on subject of relationship hearsay testimony not admissible, he gave him papers relative to Scannel's property to bring to this country: they were mislaid: he stated that if my thing could be done a relation of Scannel would come out to get it, when [he] came here he inquired and gave the papers to Col. Heath about four months ago: John Scannel came here and brought a letter to him from

[Page 177]

the Clergyman station this was the individual who was to claim Scannel's Estate introduced him as Nephew to Mead [who] knows nothing of Scannel or his relations: letter of the priest stated that the bearer was the Son of Scannel of Clonarkelty & nephew of Mead, papers brought by John Scannel proved to have been so brought and handwriting of an American consul proven marked by Ordinary, J. D. M. power of Attorney letter and duplicate of Will.

Donald Collins Sworn, Born town of Bantry county of Cork: knew John Scannel the younger well, the present person lived twenty-two miles from Bantry to Clonarkelly: witness was married in Clonarkelly and lived there for sixteen years: knew Scannel's family well, Father David Wells was parish priest of Clonarkelly (confirmed by Dr. English). John Scannel's father and John: knew the family well, had an uncle James Scannel whom witness saw in Ireland Clonarkelly, July or August 1816. He had come from this place to Dublin and had brought Cotton and thence to Clonarkilly: he called himself Captain Mead: he was known by people to be the brother of John Scannel, Mead at Clonarkilly staid next door to residence of witness when Capt. Mead returned to this country he brought out two nephews with him, a brother of John Scannel and a son of Jeremiah Scannel who is dead: he brought out a son of James White also, a boy of 10 or 11 years of age John Scannel Jr. has no brother or sister: John Scannel Senr. had a brother Jeremiah. Jeremiah had a son: does not know if any more or a daughter, he lived about 3 miles from Clonarkelly: old John is a laborer, a poor man, no particular trade he has a wife, no child there. James Mead was an elderly looking man, lantherned face, bowlegged, about John Scannel, Junr., size but not so stout a middle sized man he had plenty of money with him at Clonarkelty, Mead did not tell him he had brought cotton to Dublin, but he had it from others, he sent first for the father of John Scannel, Jr., he never told witness he had changed his name: he called himself Capt. Mead, but was known by the old people there to be James Scannel, he went to hear James Mead speak

[Page 178]

of America, John Scannel Senr. and Capt. Mead were together every day that he was in Clorankilty. Jeremiah Scannel died in Ireland he told Quin a few days since that he saw Scannel in Liverpool, he told Quin on time: Quin was asking him Questions and he was determined to tell him nothing satisfactory until he was called on regularly X X. This Conversation at Quin's House: this was done to put Quin off he knew he would be called on to tell the truth here, the latter end of December he first met Scannel here and spoke to him. Dr. England testified that on December he saw Collins and knowing him to be from Clorankilty and that Scannel was also, he thought he must know about Scannel's relations. Collins called again he never told Quin that if [he] would give Scannel a little money he would go away. Dr. England proved handwriting of Scott a witness to power of Attorney May 7, 1823.

James Mead Case continued. John Diamond sworn. About two weeks before Mead sailed for Ireland was Mead's store, Quin was there. Mead got up and related to Quin and witness how he had made his Will. Will was drawn by Mr. White a lawyer who lately died. Mead told him so after he had done. Quin got up and went away. Mead said did you observe how dejected that fellow looked when he heard I had my Will, understood from Mead in several conversations that he was not a friend of Quin that he suspected he would try to come in this way after his death. Witness saw a nephew of Mead's in this country at Mead's understood from Mead he was his sister's Son, never saw the nephew but twice: Heard Mead often say he had put other nephew to Capt. Anthony to learn to be a soap boiler, the nephew who was with Capt. Anthony returned after the other went away and died at Mead's X witness was never examined before

[Page 179]

in this case: meaning he never was allowed to testify on the matter which he was now testified to: Witness is an Irishman. Mead brought the two young men out when he returned from Ireland. Mead told him he had been in Ireland, Mead, a small man, round Shouldered, when Mead spoke to witness after Quin left him he understood to mean that he suspected Quin would force his Will or something of that kind one, two or three years before Mead's death. Mead not sick at the time. Mead's relations his parents came from Ireland does not know where Mead was born. Mead told him that his nephew who was with him had robbed him and gone off. J. C. Anthony swore he knew pretty intimately, knew for 10 or 12 years before his death between 60 or 70 years when he died. Mead told him he was a British subject, he had [been] born on board a British man of War, he got into French service after he was a man grown, was taken by the British and put into Dartmore prison whence he escaped, after he made his escape he changed his name to Mead, never told him particularly was witness recollects what was his previous name, the name of the nephew who lived with witness was Dennis Scannel, but he was nicknamed Donoho: this he was told that while the young man lived with witness, the names of both the nephews was Dennis. Mead told him that when he went to Ireland he sent for a brother of his who resided near Cork or Dublin, and he was sent for by a brother to bring out his nephews and would probably leave them his property, that after they were on board ship three days he told the lads he was that uncle. Mead was a man of pride, witness did not that he had concealed from his brother who he was but only from his nephews. Mead brought out two nephews, called at the Store whenever he was down town. Witness and Mead were brother Masons and had been at Sea, was pretty intimate with him: the nephew who was with witness died here; if the nephew who lived with witness was

[Page 180]

a brother of John Scannel they could not have resembled each other more. Heard Mead say that he and Quin had been partners, but he was very glad they had dissolved and that he had got clear of him, was frequently heard Mead express his dislike of Quin; he said he looked upon Quin as a very dangerous man: very far from being on terms with Quin in the latter part of his life, frequently said he considered him a dangerous man, should think that the signature to the cancelled Will was Mead's. looks as if he had taken pains with it, but if it was in 1816 was well as witness recollects that Mead went to Ireland: does not know of any change in his disposition towards Quin until his death: Quin came into the store: they were drinking and he offered Quin something: after he went out he expressed his satisfaction at having got rid of him X first knew Mead he thinks in 1804 or 1805. John Scannel, Jr., sworn witness father's name is John Scannel, sometimes it is nicknamed O'Donoho.

It is known to be nicknamed in the town knows from his father and from all the family that he had a brother named James: Witness knew his other uncle Jeremiah very well his father in Clonarkelty 21 irish from Cork Jeremiah lived about 2 miles or 1 7 ½ from Clonarkelty: witness grandfather's name was Dennis Scannel and Grandmother, Nancy Cotterall: his brother Dennis died here and is buried in Hasel Street, Jeremiah the uncle left a widow and two children Dennis and a daughter has seen Collins in Clonarkelty, but did not know him personally (duplicate of cancelled Will introduced.) Witness first saw it in Mark's Office in Cork: witness brought this paper and the power of Attorney to Charleston and gave them to Bishop England who gave to Mr. Stoney and that from Copy about 22 August 1822 never before was born in

[Page 181]

Clonarkilty lived there till about 10 years ago. Came to Clonarkilty once a year or two years and sometimes in 10 months whenever he could spare a month's pay: was not in. Ireland when James Mead came there. Collins worked with witness' cousin who is a Mason: Jeremiah Scannel died before James. Timothy Sullivan Sworn. Knew James Mead was perhaps for 18 years; very generally intimate with him: very angry feelings existed on the part of Mead towards Quin after the dissolution of partnership up to his death. Witness lived in the Neighborhood all the time. heard Mead frequently express dissatisfaction towards Quin as of he would place no confidence in him. Witness would only say he entertained a strong dislike, but a strong hatred towards Quin, believes that Quin would be the last man on earth to whom he would give his property, cancelled Will and copy proves the signature to the cancelled Will to be the handwriting of James Mead: proves the copy to be in Mead's handwriting. Mead brought out his two nephews: went over to Ireland immediately after the war, Mead told Witness he was an Irishman born in the neighborhood of Clonarkilty and had relatives there of the name of Scannel: Mead told him that from having been a prisoner and other things he had changed his name; told him that two young men were his nephews: Never heard Mead express any dissatisfaction towards the nephew who died here X said he changed in Consequence of having been a prisoner during the war: said his name was originally Scannel. Has seen Mead write the common accounts and entries for Shop business: witness is well acquainted with his handwriting; undertakes to swear positively, that the name in the copy of his handwriting and the balance he believes to be his handwriting: in witness presence he more frequently wrote Jas. Quin and Mead Was not long in partnership; he gave him to understand it was from same difference they had in the copartnership, Witness' intimacy with Mead commenced soon after the dissolution of copartnership. Mead told witness that Quin sometimes came there

[Page 182]

apparently in Friendship but he regarded it as duplicity, this not long before his death. Mrs. Speissegger Sworn. Knew Mead nearly 19 or 20 years lived in that neighborhood, Mead and Quin had no dealings after dissolution of

Partnership, there was falling out: Mead never would have anything to say to Quin after separation. Mead would sometimes cuss Quin in his way and say he would have nothing to do with him: Mead was never on friendly terms with Quin after dissolution. Mead told witness before he went to Ireland that he had made a Will: said he had left the mulatto woman and child free: Child's name Eliza: said some thing should go to the Church: the rest was to go to his family in Ireland. Mead frequently said he had relations in Ireland: spoke of them with regard. Witness attended Mead during his last sickness always said his property should go to Ireland. This he said in a former illness two months before his death, never saw Quin at the house during his illness. Mead always had a bad opinion of Quin. Mead introduced the two young men as his nephews X. Witness lived opposite to Mead. Mead said he had another nephew in Ireland. Patrick McGan sworn. Produces Several Signatures of O'Kelly.

Ordinary's Office, August 18, 1823. John L. Smith Sworn. Never saw Quin before. It was nine or 10 years ago he knew Mead, dealt with him. said Quin was his partner. Introduced him as such and as a man whom he much respected: has seen Mead's receipts frequently; believes the signature to the Will to be that of Mead. witness is eighty years old. Thomas Fell Sworn. Knew O'Kelly well, a Schoolmaster, was his scholar: boarded with him: Should not take the Signature to the Will to be the hand writing of John O'Kelly. John is something like, rest too light. Should not take the

[Page 183]

invitation to be his. Handwriting less like his hand writing than the other, Joseph Baker. Knew Mead dealt with him during the copartnership, with Quin in 1803 acknowledged Quin to be his partner long time ago, has seen Mead's handwriting to the best of his knowledge, the signature to the Will is Mead's: like receipts which he thinks, he left with his daughter who is on Sullivan's Island, never heard Mead say anything about Quin for or against him John H. Kahnly Sworn. Knew James Mead in 1801 2. 3. Knew his hand writing, has seen him write. Knew John O'Kelly was an usher: deputy to the amicable Society: knew Gready, his brother in law to Mr. Quin. Knew Grady's hand writing: was back and forward to Quin's witness can tell any man's hand writing if he has seen him write once, this signature of Mead's and O'Kelly's are genuine. John Gready is written by Gready. It is all the writing of Gready. Invitation is signed by O'Kelly; in 1803 Mead told him Quin was a young man for whom he had a great liking and that he Should have all he possessed.
J. J. Baker Sworn. Knows Daniel Collins met him on Sunday morning March or April in company with Scannel. Collins invited him to take drink, Scannel dissuaded Collins from going with witness who refused. Collins went with him. Collins told witness if he would go into Court and Swear for Scannel it should be worth a $100 to him: Witness indignant refused Collins said Scannel dissuaded him from going because he was in favor of Quin: Cannot Swear any way positively about O'Kelly's signature: there is some resemblance but he wrote so differently that he cannot swear an signature to invitation not so near

as the other: would not say that either is like his hand writing: John is more like, could not undertake to say that either signature was O'Kelly's: John Hendrick Sworn. Knew Collins a little, he and Scannel boarded with Witness: Collins is a

[Page 184]

very clever man. Collins had a quarrel with Scannel and he told witness just as he was coming away that Scannel. was nothing but an imposter. Heard Collins say he knew Scannel in Ireland and once that he did not know them. John B. Smoke Sworn. had seen Skenne at Quin's, Scannel asked if he had any money: Scannel told Quin that the law was so expensive and troublesome that if he would give him $100 he would be off, thinks Scannel said that Quin's claim was too strong for him this was in February. N. G. Cleary Sworn. Sullivan voted at the election for Sheriff and it was afterwards decided to be a bad vote because he was not a Citizen: does not know whether Sullivan was acquainted with the facts, that his vote was questioned; the contest was generally known. John H. Kahnly again at Quin's in February and saw Scannel in Archdale Street. Scannel he should try to get property. Scannel told him in Archdale St. he should gain the property. Scannel told him if he would go against Mr. Quin would pay him handsomely for it, they parted. Michael Graham Sworn. Knows Scannel asked witness if he knew his uncle, said his uncle changed his name: had no other discourse with him. Scannel said he had not brought papers with him to prove his relationship.

Decree. John Scannel vs Thomas F. Quin. In the Court of Ordinary, Charleston District. August 26, 1823

This case came before the Court on an application for a Special Citation by John Scannel as next of Kin to James Mead. decd., to cite Thomas F. Quin, legatee named in a certain Paper purporting to be the last Will of the said Mead to show cause why the said Will should not be proved in solemn Form. The case is moved in this country; but from all information on the subject which the Court could obtain it appeared that the application ought to be

[Page 185]

granted: upon which evidence was adduced to prove the right of John Scannel to make this application which proved satisfactory to the Court. Mr. Quin then offered some witnesses in support of the Will upon whose testimony connected with that before the Court on the first hearing he rested his claim not proven, without an application for the postponement of the Case on the ground of three material witnesses, but the Ordinary vs the Case had been before so long pending that had he used due diligence he may have availed him of their testimony and therefore refused the application. There are two questions which call for the attention of the Ordinary. 1st. is the Will genuine. 2. If genuine then has it been revoked by the testator making a second which he afterwards cancelled. In regard to the first Question, it will be observed on reading the decree that I was much perplexed (see 1 Sept. 1819) with the contrariety of the testimony and seemed rather inclined against the admission of the Will. When a paper was provided in evidence purporting to be an invitation written by John O'Kelly addressed to Mr. Quin informing him that Mead was sick and wished to make a Will in his favor and requesting him to attend for that purpose: at that time forming conclusion on my mind that that paper bore all the appearance of authenticity I considered it a conclusive circumstance in favor of the will being as it were the animus testandi proceeding for the testator and looks was therefore disposed to give weight to the testimony in favor of the Will, and finally to decide for it: but in reviewing the testimony connected with some evidence which has transpired and weighing generally the credibility of the witness is offered on both sides in the case and the aspect of the whole affair. I am disposed to give consequence to that paper which to say the least if it is now weakened particularly when it appears in evidence that

[Page 186]

the copartnership between Mead and Quin was dissolved in 1804, two years before date of the Will and that Mead ever after the dissolution held Quin in abhorrence, that although when Quin was present he treated him as he did others yet when he was not present he frequently expressed his aversion in strong terms, it seems difficult to draw any conclusion; but that there must be something inexplainable attending the Will: so much so that I feel myself bound to revoke the probate formerly granted. On the second question after deciding as above it would seem hardly necessary to say anything, but that the whole matter may be before the Court above and that the Case may receive a final decision at one on both questions. Should the Will be established then, I would observe that I did formerly decree, incidentally that the Second being cancelled by the testator. the effect in law was the revival of the first: but it appears by the decision in this Case of Taylor & Taylor that altho the common law does presume the first to be restored to its active energy by the canceling of the second, yet that is a question of intention and may be control by the other circumstances. If therefore such a construction is to prevail, admitting the Will to be genuine a stronger circumstance could hardly be adduced to evince the intentions of Mead to die Intestate, rather the first Will should revive in favor of Quin, to wit:- when his uniform hostility to Quin from 1804 to the time of his death. In short there are circumstances in the Case which lead me to doubt the genuineness of the Will and to conclude of genuine that Mead

[Page 187]

would rather have died Intestate than that the Will should have revised in favor of Quin: however, if this is a Case more calculated for the decision of a Jury and I feel a degree of relief and this consideration that it is to take that course. I must therefore dismiss the Will upon both points.

Sarah Good's Will. In the Court of Ordinary, Charleston District, June 25th 1824. In reviewing the testimony in this case, although the case appears some contradictions in the course, yet it appears to me perfectly reconcilable so as to avoid any unpleasant imputations on any of the witnesses, a circumstance which is particularly gratifying, as they are all of reputable characters in Society. It appears from the tenor of the testimony as it comes from the witnesses against the Will viz: Mrs. Lloyd, Miss Russell and Mrs. Clement, that the deceased was very much reduced by debility of body and of mind, so much so according to the opinion of some of them, as to induce them to think that she was not fit to make a Will and were surprised at being informed that she had done so: while on the other hand the witnesses of the Will speak confidently of the sanity of mind in the testatrix and particularly that the Misses Bacot states that they were with her on the Friday before the Sunday on which the Will was made and also with her on the Monday after its execution and the subscribing witnesses do declare that they were fully under the impression that she was in her mind at the time of the execution: and altho they concur that she appeared extremely weak and that they were but a very short time in the room with her: Yet they say distinctly that everything seemed to have been done without any apparent hurry and they left the room fully under the impression of her sanity. Now it may be plainly perceived

[Page 188]

that admitting that she was light headed and in a Stupor at times as the witnesses have testified: it does appear by the testimony of those on whom we are chiefly to rely for information: at the practical moment of Execution, that she did seem to them rational, her conduct appearing so to them, as she seemed to understand what she was about and consummating what had apparently been previously arranged with her counsel; being however so weak in body as not to be able to do anything without assistance; and I am not at all surprised at her conduct when I read the Wills by her made in 1814 and a codicil to it in 1819 in which she manumits her negroes. Her desire to effect which evidently reigns paramount in the mind; for it seems after the Law preventing manumission she made a will in 1823 in which she bequeaths the negroes to her friends: not satisfied with the will which it does not effect her reigning desire relative to those negroes, she appears to have obtained advice from Council to devise some mode by which this desirable object could at last be partially obtained, which seems to have produced the last Will: nor does she appear to me to have neglected or given cause of umbrage[?] to her friends, for she gives in a manner the whole residue of her Estate, real and personal, to be divided among them, I am therefore under the impression that the Will has been substantiated as well as could have been done under the existing circumstances of the case: and I can not perceive but that it may be in every respect as good Will, for it certainly has not violated the letter although it may have encroached on the spirit of the Law,

[Page numbered 188¼]

on that point however it remains for the Court above to finally decide and it is a source of relief to my mind that the parties if they feel themselves aggrieved by the decision may so readily obtain redress in another tribunal.

Mrs. Jane Rockwell admix de bonis non of Thomas Craig vs Alexander England and George Timmons, Securities for W. M. Meeds, first admor of Thomas Craig, decd. In the Court of Ordinary, Charleston District. September 17th 1824.

This case come before me upon the application of the Administratrix de bonis non to cite the securities of the first administrator to make this account and vouch the same and pay the balance to the present representative of the Estate. The Securities being summoned attended by their Proctor and after repeated adjournments to give them opportunity to produce further proof the examination was finally closed and I shall proceed to state the result at a minute examination of the items of the account.

1. The first item is a charge of $83 for boarding Mr. Craig. To support this debit against the Estate Mrs. Meeds was ordered a witness but I rejected her testimony on the ground that she could not be a witness on behalf of her husband's Estate or of his Securities, no voucher was produced nor any proof that the amount had ever been paid nor is there any evidence that such a debt was ever due by Craig. It was contended by the Proctor of the Sureties that Mrs. Meeds must be regarded as a sole trader in keeping the boarding house of as the agent of her husband, but the constitutional Court have decided in Patison vs Holland that the keeping of a boarding house is not that description of business which constitute a Sole dealer because it is not in the way of trade. I cannot therefore admit

[Page numbered 188½]

her as a witness in the supposition that she was a creditor of Craig. Nor can she be admitted on the ground that she was a agent of Mr. Meeds. A wife may be the Attorney or agent of her husband and as such she may bind him by her acts and may in some sense be a witness against, but never for him. I am also of the opinion on that the charge is not such as could be proved by Book-Entry. 2nd. The second item being of the same description is rejected for the same reasons. 3rd. and 4th. These charges are unsupported by any evidence. 5th. This item respects the rent of the House on the Bay where Meads and Craig Kept their Coffee House and the rest of which was together with the yard & Co. occupied by Mrs. Mead's as a Boarding House. The rent paid for the premises to Keating Simons & Son was $1100 from 1st June 1919 [sic] to 1 June 1820. There is no proof as to what Share of the rent Craig and Meeds were to pay. I am therefore compelled to decide upon the testimony as to the relative value, and I do accordingly declare that the Partnership is justly charged with one half say $550. But Craig occupied the lower part of the house only about three months for he died on or about the 25 of August. Meeds therefore as the surviving partner had the possession and use of the lower part of the House and he is therefore debtor to the Estate of Craig for 9 months' rent at the same rate: of course he can only charge the Estate of Craig with one half of 3 month's rent or at $550 per annum equal to $68.75. This charge must be rejected for another reason: at the death of Craig it was a partner ship debt and the property administered upon by Meeds was the private property of Craig and is therefore liable in the first instance to pay his private debts. The present representative of the Estate is in every person authorized to settle its concerns, and she will be liable to the partnership creditors if there be assets in her hands

[Page 189]

after the separate debts. 6th. This item is rejected for the following reasons, because it is a partnership claim. 2nd. Because it was in the lifetime of Craig and was probably either settled by mutual contributions as by Craig who had property, while Meeds was bankrupt having taken the benefit of the insolvent debtor's act on the 17 May and the account having been paid on the 11th June and 7, 8, & 9th. The items are admitted by the Proctor for the Administratrix. 10th. On the testimony of Captain Young I allow $46 instead of present charge of $93.50. 11th. Twenty dollars are allowed instead of this charge of $23.50. 12th, 13th, & 14th. are admitted. 15th. This item is rejected for want of proof. 16th. This is admitted. 17th. This is rejected for want of proof. 18th. This account was before the partnership of Meeds and Craig and was paid before the death of Craig. 19th. 3 more are admitted, no proof of the rest. 20th. One dollar fifty cents are admitted, no proof for the rest. 21st, 22nd, & 23rd. These are rejected because of unsupported by any evidence. 24th. This is rejected on the principal already decided of the performance of separate over joint creditors. 25th. This is admitted. 26th. This is rejected as partnership debt. 27th. This item must be rejected because it is an account against W. M. Meeds only. 28th. This must be rejected because it is a joint debt. The result of this examination is that the whole Amount of which the first administrator and examination is that the whole Amount for which the first administrator and his Securities can claim credit in making up the present account is two hundred and two dollars and 46 1/4 cents as will appear by the account herewith. It appears then that at the end of the year after his administration commenced viz. on the 20 day of September 1820. The administrator had a balance in hand of $1527.71¼. This money has not been accounted for. There appears to have been no good reason why the administrator kept it unproductive in his hands and I must conclude under the proofs and circumstances of the case that the balance was appropriated by Mr.

[Page 190]

W. M. Meeds to his own use or to purposes not sanctioned by Law. The administrator therefore is chargeable with interest on said balance from the expiration of one year after his administration to wit: from the twentieth of

September 1820. The Securities being answerable for the default of the administrator. I do therefore decree that Alexandria Ingram and George Timmons as Securities of the first administrator Meeds do pay to Mrs. Jane Rothwell the present administratrix the said Balance of $1,727.71 3/4 with interest thereon from the last mentioned day together with the cost of these proceedings. James D. Mitchell, Ordinary

John Nevill's Case. In the Court of Ordinary, Charleston District. July 9, 1825. Hunt for the Will. Lance contra.

This case came before the Ordinary at the Instance of James O'Brien, the next of Kin of the dead. who sued out a Citation to have the proved in solemn Form. Two of the subscribing witnesses to the Will, (the third being out of the State) with several other persons who were acquainted the circumstances connected therewith, were examined. and after due consideration of the evidence, the Ordinary will give a brief explanation of the motives which was governed him in the decision. Mr. William H. Brown, the first subscribing witness appears to be the witness upon whom the next of Kin relies chiefly in the support of his case: he appears to be under the impression that the testator was not in his senses and has given his reason for thinking so: there are other witnesses, Mrs. Scott and Miss Collins who were also of this Opinion: but in the contrary P. Hackell, another of the subscribing witnesses was clearly of opinion that he was in his mind and declared

[Page 191-- follows page 192 on microfilm]

he would not have signed it if he had conceived the testator out of his senses. In corroboration of this testimony: there are many witnesses and Particularly I shall advert to the testimony of the Revd. Mr. McEncroe and when we remember the correct and perspicuous manner in which he had stated the facts and circumstances connected with the case, the particular instrumentality he had in the transaction, the experience and consequent capacity in matters of this kind arising from the nature of his office, all lead to expect more circumstantial testimony and which must give more satisfaction on the elucidation of the matter: Mr. McEncroe states that at that request of the testator he had his Will Prepared ten days before the execution: that it was read to him then, and he again immediately before the execution read it twice over to him: that he did not in the least agree that the testator was incompetent to sign and he would deemed criminal to have suffered it under such circumstances under the view of the testimony cannot but confirm and establish that Will. James D. Mitchell, Ordinary.

By James D. Mitchell, Esq., Ordinary. To Henry J. Chalmers, Administrator of the Estate and Effects of Sophia Chalmers, late of Charleston, Widow, deceased.

At the Instance and request of Holmes and Waring, Proctors, for John Ball and Isaac Ball, otherwise called John Ball and Isaac Ball, Executors of the

Estate of John Ball. deceased, you are hereby cited and admonished personally to be and appear before me in the Court of Ordinary to be held at Charleston on Wednesday, the third of August at Eleven o'clock in the forenoon then and there to show cause why you should not make and render before me a just true and faithful account of

[Page 192]

your administration of the said Estate since the eighteenth day of April 1823. Here of fail at your peril. Given under my hand and Seal this twenty eighth of July Anno, Domini 1825 and the 50th of American Independence. James D. Mitchell.

South Carolina, Charleston District. In the Court of Ordinary, August 1825

At the instance and request of Holmes & Waring, Proctors for John and Isaac Ball, Executors of John Ball, deceased, Henry J. Chalmers, administrator of the Estate and Effects of Sophia Chalmers, late of Charleston, Widow, deceased, was cited to appear before me on the third day of August in the year of our Lord, one thousand eight and twenty-five to show cause why he should not render an account of his administration of the said Estate and the said Henry J. Chalmers appeared to his account passed in this Court on the eighteenth day of April 1823 in which there appears a balance in favor of the said Estate of Sophia Chalmers of one thousand and forty nine dollars and fifty seven cents and also to certain accounts before the Honorable the Court of Equity for an account of the said administration, and it appears that the said John and Isaac, Executors aforesaid, have obtained a Judgement in the Court of Common Pleas against the said Henry J. Chalmers, Administrator aforesaid, for the two hundred sixty seven dollars with interest from ninth of February 1819, and also thirty two dollars cost of Suit, I do hereby do decree that the said sum of two hundred and sixty seven dollars with Interest from the ninth day of February 1819 and thirty two dollars be paid over to the said John and Isaac Ball, Executors aforesaid, together with cost in this Case. James D. Mitchell, Ordinary. See pages, 191, 192, 193, 236, 206.

[Page 193-- follows page 194 on microfilm]

In the Case of Mary Ann Dewes, deceased. In the Court of Ordinary. Charleston District, November 18th 1825.

Mrs. Rachel Long admitted to be sworn by the opposing counsel on showing her relationship to the intestate Mary Ann Dewes: upon which administration was granted to her as next of Kin in preference to a Stranger. Mrs. Rachel Long sworn and states that the Grandmother of Mrs. Long and Mary Ann Dewes, the intestate married first Mr. Bee and after his death a Mr. Howard. By Mr. Bee she had the father of Mrs. Rivers and the mother of Mrs. Dewes, the intestate: and Mr. Howard, her second husband, the mother of her present witness (Mrs. Rivers is dead), Rachel Long.

South Carolina, Charleston District. By James D. Mitchell, Esq. Ordy.
To Henry J. Chalmers, Admor of Estate & Effects of Sophia Chalmers, late of Charleston, Widow, deceased. At the instance & request of Thomas O. Iliad, Proctor, for James Buckham, you are hereby cited to appear before me in the Court of Ordinary to be held at Charleston on Wednesday the 30th day of November inst. at eleven o'clock in the forenoon then and thereto make & render before me a just, true and faithful account of your administration of the said Estate. Hereof fail not at your peril, given under my hand and Seal this 18 November 1825 and in the fiftieth year of American Independence. James D. Mitchell

South Carolina, Charleston District. By James D. Mitchell, Esq. Ordy.
To Henry James Chalmers, admor of the Estate & Effects of Sophia Chalmers, late of Charleston Widow deceased. At the instance and request of Thomas O. Elliott, Proctor, for Saunders, Glover & Co., you are hereby cited and admonished personally to be and appear before me in the Court of Ordinary to be held at Charleston on Friday next

[Page 194]

the 10th day of March instant at 11 o'clock in the forenoon then and there to make and render before me a just, true and faithful account of said Estate. Hereof fail not at your Peril. Given under hand and Seal this 6th day of March 1826 and in the fiftieth year of American Independence.

In the Court of Ordinary. Henry J. Chalmers Admor of Sophia Chalmers Ads Sanders, Glover & Co. And the said Henry J. Chalmers Administrator of all and singular the Goods and Chattels, rights & Credits of the said Sophia Chalmers, deceased, come and answer to the Citation served on him in this Case and says that he fully administrated all and singular the goods which belonged to the said Sophia Chalmers in hands to be administered except one thousand dollars ____ cents and will appear by reference being had to the accounts of Administrator thereof filed in the office of the Court of Ordinary pursuant to the act of the Legislature of this State is such cases made and provided which balance is applicable to, and liable for the payment of prior claims according to the law regulation Executors and Administrators in this State. And the said Henry, J. Chalmers, Admor as aforesaid further states that afterwards to wit on the 21st day of November 1822 a decree of the Honorable court of Equity was pronounced whereby the Estate of said Sophia Chalmers was sold by the Commissioners in Equity and the funds directed to be applied as therein mentioned whereby the Administrator of said Estate wholly directed under and by order of said Court. Wherefore the said Henry J. Chalmers insists that in action can or ought to be had or maintained against him and so forth. Henry J. Chalmers

[Page 195 --before page 194 on microfilm]

In the Court of Ordinary. Charleston, March 31, 1826. James E. Mashburn & Catherine his wife vs John Schroder & Jacob A. Boyer, Admors Catherine Wartenburg and their Securities.

This case comes before the Court on a Citation against the administrators of Catherine Wartenburg deceased and their Securities to account for the administration and assets of the Estate in their hands, Catherine Wartenburg, Widow, died in 1821, intestate, leaving three children viz Catherine now the wife of James H. Mashburn, Maria who died shortly after in her minority, and Mary, an illegitimate child. The whole Estate therefore descended to Mashburn and wife. They filed a Bill in Equity against John Schroder and Jacob H. Boyer who had jointly administered on Catherine Wartenburg's Estate for an account & settlement of her Estate. Among other items charged in the administrator's account was one for the maintenance and support of Mary, the illegitimate child. This Item. was objected to by Mashburn and wife as inadmissible. The said Mary being in law filia nullius. But the Court of Equity after argument, Decreed that the parent was liable for the maintenance of her illegitimate child and the items in the Administrator's account admissible a balance of $178.29¼ was admitted to be due by the Administrators on the 23d June 1823, but by changing the illegitimate child's maintenance up to the present time conformably to the Decree, it appears there would be only a balance of $40.29½ due. The illegitimate child Mary, is about six years old has lost her mother, has no known father and has no property or means of subsistence. Mashburn & wife now claim from the Administrators and their Securities the payment of the balance due in the account. This Case is too plain to admit of a doubt, though by the common an illegitimate child is called Filus nullius and filius populi, as few civil rights is subject to many incapacities and can inherit nothing

[Page 196 -- before page 195 on microfilm]

yet by its humanity it does not permit the ties of nature to be so easily dissolved and therefore makes it the duty of parents to maintain and support such children during infancy. Blackstone Con. 458. But were my opinion different I should feel bound by the decree of the Court of Equity which is a case between the same parties (except the Securities) and in the time point has settled the question. In conforming therefore with that decision, I must order the balance now in the Administrator's to be retained.   James D. Mitchell, Ordinary

Jacob Henry Boyer vs John Schroder, the Admor of Jacob Frederick Boyer & his Securities. In the Court of Ordinary. May 3, 1826.

This case came before The Ordinary under the following circumstances. A decree had been obtained in the Court of Equity by Jacob Henry Boyer for a third part of his father's Estate against John Schroder, the Administrator of

Jacob Frederick Boyer, deceased, $1,444.91 with Interest from 20 January 1818. It was objected on the Part of John Schnell, one of the Securities, that it ought not be conclusive against him because he was not a party in that case that case and craves leave to make his defence before this Court. He urges that J. H. Boyer has already received a portion of his claim in various ways: that he received goods, furnished and furniture and that he boarded with Schroder by living at his house almost constantly and that Schnell ought to be allowed something in consideration of these things. But it does appear to me that the defence has not been sustained in many of these points: for although a very considerable degree of dependence and living on Schroder by Jacob H. Boyer has been made out, yet it was chiefly as the brother of Mrs. Schroder and in as a friendly manner

[Page 197-- after page 212 on microfilm]

in which he was in that account received which induced Schroder so to entertain him and even if the principal of allowance for board and goods furnished under the circumstances were allowed, it would be difficult to ascertain, the amount which Schnell should be allowed: and indeed if Boyer were really indebted on that account it appears by documents exhibited that Schroder is very much indebted to him, and I cannot conceive it my duty to investigate matters foreign to the Case before me: but appears that Schroder has substantiated the amount Boyer received in furniture of the Estate which he should be allowed $137.91 and the, he ought not to be charged with interest until 1 January 1819. It appears then I must decree for Boyer in the sum of one thousand and seven dollars with interest from the 1st January 1819 to time of payment with cost.   James D. Mitchell, Ordinary

To Mrs. Ann Glover Holmes of Charleston, Widow, executrix named in the last [will] and testament of James Holmes, deceased, who was administrator with the Will annexed of John Holmes, deceased. At the instance Bentham & Dunkin, Proctors for Thomas H. S. Thayer and wife and Francis Rivers & wife, you are hereby cited and admonished personally to be and appear before me in the Court of Ordinary to be held at Charleston on Friday next the second day of June next at eleven o'clock in the forenoon then and there to show cause why you do not render a just, true and faithful account of the Administration of John Holmes, deceased, who was Administrator of John Holmes, deceased, with the Will annexed. Given under my hand and Seal the 29th day of May 1826. John D. Mitchell, Ordy.
See next page for John Holmes.

[Page 198]

Francis Rivers & wife vs Ann C. Holmes, Exix John Holmes, decd., who was Admor cum testamento annexo of John Holmes, Senr., Decd. In the Court of Ordinary. June 2, 1826.

In this case Ann G. Holmes the defendant at the instance of Francis Rivers & wife to render an account of the transactions of her dec'd Testator as Admor of John Holmes Senr., deceased. And it appears to my satisfaction that her deceased testator as Admor aforesaid was indebted to the said Francis and Susannah, his wife, in the Sum of two hundred forty dollars and five cents on the 12th May 1826 which sum is accordingly decreed with that date. James D. Mitchell, Ordy.

Thomas H. J. Thayer & wife vs Ann G. Holmes, Exix John Holmes decd., who was Admor of John Holmes, decd., cum testamento annexo. In the Court of Ordinary June 2, 1826.

In this Case Ann G. Holmes the Defendant was summoned at the instance of Tho. H. S. Thayer & wife to render an account of her deceased testator as administrator on the Estate of John Holmes, Senr., deceased: And it appeared to my satisfaction that her deceased testator as admor aforesaid was indebted to the said Th. H. S. Thayer & wife in the Sum of four thousand five hundred and fifty two dollars five cents on the 12 May 1826 which Sum is accordingly decreed with Interest from that date. James D. Mitchell, Ordy.

In the Court of Ordinary June 6, 1826. In the matter of John Elcock, deceased. This Case was bought before the Ordinary under the following circumstances. A paper purporting to be a Will of John Elcock was propounded for probate having only two witnesses, the same was attested in the usual manner by E. M. Baynard, Esq., one of the subscribing witnesses: it bore on the sixth day of March 1823 and it was distinctly by the witness to have been executed about that time: it was offered for Probate by King on the around that although the testator died after 1st of May 1825 (about a fortnight ago) that as the Will

[Page 199]

[was] good when it was executed ought now to be received. The Ordinary was of the opinion that by the principal of law a Will is ambulatory and cannot take effect until the decease of the testator that in this case John Elcock died long after the act requiring their witnesses had gone into operation that consequently it is the [duty] of the Ordinary to refuse the Probate. James D. Mitchell, Ordy.

In the case of George Osborn Nichols, deceased. Exparte Mark L. Williams on Petition for Letters of Administration of the Estate and Effects of George O. Nichols, deceased. Caveat by Benjamin Theus. Mary Nichols, the wife of George O. Nichols, previously Mary Chaplin was the sister of Mark L. Williams' wife and died on the sixth of November 1826, leaving four children, Mary Chaplin and Sarah Chaplin: Children of the first husband who are still alive and have been inmates of the applicant's family since their mother's death. George O. Nichols died 7 Nov. 1826, and of the two children by one died on the 18 and the other 24 of 1826. Benjamin Theus, the caveator married the sister of George O. Nichols. The Estate consists of Hogs, cattle, sheep, a horse and gig, some household furniture and plantation utensils. Mrs. Nichols while married to Nichols bought three negroes and took the bill of sale in her own Name, with his knowledge, she executed a mortgage for part of the purchase money, about one fourth had been paid. The Question submitted to this Court is whether the half Sisters of the deceased, children of George O. Nichols taken in exclusion of the Aunts, the caveator withdrawing his Caveat if the succession is in the half sisters. I have heard Argument and examined the Law upon the point. The fifth claim of the Act of 1791 for abolishing rights of Primogeniture and the distributing of the Intestate's Estate, provides that if the deceased leaves a widow and brothers or sisters of the half blood that the Estate shall be distributed shall be distributed between them, one moiety to the widow and the other moiety to the half blood. Now it is apparent

[Page 200]

that the last takers (the children of Nichols) had left widows, the clause of the act would provide in express terms for the case at bar: and in the 8th section. It is enacted, that if the Intestate leaves no widow the provision made for her. Shall go as the rest of the estate is directed to be distributed in the clauses in which the widow is provided for. This clause removed the only point of difference between the case provided for in expressed terms in the 5th section between the case at bar and therefore is a direct provision for the case at bar: the Caveat is dismissed and administration is granted to Mark L. Williams, the applicant. James D. Mitchell, Ordy.

Charleston, February 1st, 1827. In the Court of Ordinary. In the matter of Joshua Player Legare, deceased.

The Case comes before the Ordinary on Motion by Col. Hunt as Proctor for John & Rebecca Deliesseline, late Legare to revoke the administration granted F. G. H. Gunther on the Estate and Effects of Joshua P. Legare, decd., on the ground that being the widow of the deceased, she was entitled to the administration in her own right and as mother of his infant son and that the Administration was obtained without her knowledge by the present administrator who has been guilty of Mal administration, subversive of the interests of the widow and child by confessing to a judgment under which the land was sold and prays that the administration be revoked and granted to her. Mr. Pepoon in behalf of the administrator insists that the administration has been regularly granted and that no mal-administration has been committed and offers to relinquish the administration to the widow on payment of the debts which being declined the matter was

[Page 201]

submitted to the Ordinary. in viewing the Case the Ordinary must observe that if the widow had intimated her intention to administer on the Estate no difficulty would ever have occurred, but her remaining silent so long after the decease of her husband without having taken the precaution to apprize the Ordinary of her reason for delay and creditors urging their rights induced the Ordinary to commit the letters of Admon: but it is now necessary that the creditors should be in the administration to maintain their rights and having discovered that the Estate is more considerable than was represented and as it is presumed that the interests of the minor, and of the widow would be better protected in the hands of the widow. I conceive a duty to revoke the admor to Mr. Gunther and to appoint the widow to be Administratrix. James D. Mitchell, Ordy.

June 8, 1826. South Carolina. John Deliesseline being duly sworn says that he was entirely ignorant of any application being made for the Administration of the Estate of Joshua P. Legare until the sale of his Estate was about to take place. John Deliessiline Sworn before me. Rebecca Deliessiline the former wife of Jos. P. Legare says that Edward M. Legare her husband's brother never advised to administer on the Estate but in the contrary told her she must not that there was no use and the mother of her also expressly persuaded her not to administer: she never [asked?] to administer and had no notice that any was attempting to do so. She has been kept entirely ignorant of her rights and believes that the purpose of obtaining the administration was to destroy the rights of herself and child. Rebecca Deliessiline

In the matter of Thomas Drayton's Will. for decree see original Will where it is filed. Hunt for the Will. Pettigru & Holmes contra. In the Court of Ordinary, Charleston District, September 26, 1825. This case comes before the Ordinary under the following

[Page 202]

circumstances: Thomas Drayton made his Will in 1820 which he duly executed in which he nominated his son William Henry Drayton to be his Sole Executor. That afterwards he caused a paper to be prepared by a confidential friend which it appears to have been fully his intention to have executed as his Will in which his Son in law Thomas Grimke is named the Sole Executor which paper marked No. 6 after having some alterations and an unexecuted Codicil introduced was to have been his final determination on the subject of his Will. The object of making another Will was apparently to appoint a different Executor. It was at this crisis that Mr. Drayton preserving his disorder to be increasing, hastened to Charleston to submit his case to medical aid: but the physician here declining to undertake it he suddenly resolved to the North for that purpose: just before his departure he writes a letter to his friend in which he complains of his remissness in not having the paper ready as he was fearful least he should die with a Will such as he did not wish. Mr. Drayton sailed to the North before Mr. Wilson received the letter and shortly after died there not having executed the draft of 1824. Under these circumstances the paper No. 6 was propounded as a revocation of the Will of 1820 marked A or to be proved as part of it. Much argument was adduced in favor of these propositions: but it appears to me they are founded on a State of things prior to the Act of 1824 and consequently now inadmissible in this Court. The Act of 1824 was certainly designed to put at rest and silence all subtleties of arguments on the subject of Will. Since it expressly declares "that from and after the 1st day next all wills and testaments of personal property shall all be executed in writing and signed by the testator or testatrix by some other person for his or her; presence and by his or her express direction: and shall be attested and subscribed in the

[Page 203]

presence of the said testator or testatrix by three or more credible witnesses, or else they shall be utterly void and of no effect." I cannot therefore under any sense of duty admit the draft of 1824 to probate and must allow of the Will of 1820. I feel however a relief in the consideration that a superior Ordinary may afford that redress of which the case may be sustained[?]. James D. Mitchell

In the matter of Thomas Drayton's dec'd Will. See 201, 202, 203. In the Court of Ordinary, Charleston District. August 7, 1826.

Pettigrue & Holmes for the Motion. King contra.

This matter came before the Court on the application of Thomas Wilson for Letters Testamentary and a Warrant of Appraisement to take an Inventory of the Estate of Thomas Drayton who as Executor of William Henry Drayton who was Sole Executor and residuary legatee of said Thomas Drayton, deceased. The Motion is opposed by Mr. King on the ground, that William Henry Drayton having died before Probate he was not intitled to do so and that administration cum testamento annexo must be granted some fact of the case must be referred to for the better understanding of the Court. It appears that William Henry Drayton propounded the Will of Thomas Drayton deceased, to be proved and unexecuted paper was offered as a revocation of a part of the aforementioned Will and after some examination of Mr. Wilson it was submitted to the Ordinary who rejected the paper purporting to be a revocation. The Will of 1820 which was regularly executed was so capable of being established, that the parties admitted the same and submitted it to the Ordinary to make a decree who accordingly refused the unexecuted instrument of 1824 and allowed of the Will of 1820: An appeal was then made against the decision on the ground that the Ordinary erred in deciding that the Act of Assembly of 1824 relative to Wills of personal property requiring three

[Page 204]

witnesses was conclusive and notice was served on the Ordinary that no qualification be granted to William Henry Drayton before a final determination of the question on an appeal. The appeal was subsequently argued in the Court of Common Pleas and the decree of the Ordinary confirmed. William

Henry Drayton died soon after without having taken the oath prescribed by the Act of Assembly and before Letters Testamentary were issued to him on this motion now before the Court relied on the circumstances of their being no probate and Letters Testamentary which were considered as all important and cited a case from Dyer's Reports, P. 372, Isted V Stanley stating that when the Executor dies before proving the Will his Executor cannot take upon himself the execution of the first Will and that administration of the goods of the first testator with the Will to it is to be committed to the Executor by the Executor of the residue of the goods of the first testator (The legacies performed) were bequeathed by his last Will to the first, Executor, or to such other persons to whom the residue is bequeathed otherwise to the next of blood to the first testator demanding it. and also relied on the Executor's oath of the Act of Assembly of this State never having been taken by William Henry Drayton. The first Question arising in this Case is weather Probate had been granted of the Will of Thomas Drayton. William Henry Drayton, the Executor named therein propounded in the Court of Ordinary for Probate and after argument the Will was admitted to Probate. An Appeal was made to the Common Pleas according to the Act of Assembly and upon the hearing thereof, the Decree was confirmed. And no further Appeal took place and the parties acquiesced. These facts appear to me to establish the Probate of the Will, and though the letters Testamentary were not issued to William Henry Drayton still that circumstance

[Page 205]

did not affect the validity of the Probate. Nor indeed they constitute any part of the Probate technically. The appointment of an Executor by a testator is the sanction and authority under which he acts and the letters testamentary confer no rights or power but are only evidence _____ the competent jurisdiction of the Executor having assessed the administration or the Estate Commission vested power and is only evidence of appointment _____ State 1 McCord 233. From the circumstances it does not appear that William Henry Drayton died before the hearing of his testator's Will, but that he died long after it was established in the Court of Ordinary and even after it was confirmed by the Court of Common Pleas. William Henry Drayton being then very sick and shortly after died and it is now to be inquired into whether the want of the Probate or Letters testamentary can work such an effect as to call this case a dying without Probate. The following authorities in the opinion of the Ordinary must sustain the Will as sufficiently proved to carry all its and among others the right of Transmitting the Executorship if the Executor proved the Will of testator and dies, his Executor shall administer to the first testator. Comyers Digest Title Admon &c. If an Executor proved the Will and afterwards make his Executor and die his Executor shall be Executor to the first testator. Conyers Digest: Title Admor No. 6. in the Case of Wankford vs. Wankford 1 Salk 300. Mr. Justice Gould said it appeared that though, it has been proved the Will yet he had administered and by that means had put it out of his power to refuse the Executorship and that the proving of the Will was only to signify to the Spiritual Court that there was a Will because in case there were none then there was a dying and the commission of administration belong to them. He said that an Executor was a complete Executor to all purposes but bringing of actions before Probate: he may release an action, may be sued, may alien or give away the goods or otherwise intermeddle with them. Salk. P. 300.

[Page 206]

Now though the Executor ceases by the death of the administering Executor on the case, yet he being Executor of his administering that as by consequence had its operation of a release already. Salk. 308. In this Case William Henry Drayton had made his election by establishing the Will before the Ordinary thus by a manner taking himself the Onus executianes testamenti, and had he not been under the impression that the Appeal suspended his qualifications he no doubt would have taken the usual Executor Oath and consummated the Executorship by receiving the Letters Testamentary: he was clearly entitled to have done so at any moment after the establishing the Will in the Court of Ordinary, he seems to have been impressed with this conviction as it manifest from his doing an act, to have done which effectually he ought to have qualified before the Ordinary for he had by administering in various ways put out of his power to have ever refused the Executorship. It appears to me that it was a vested right and by operation would transmit the Executorship. There is much to regret for the absence of the Letters Testamentary: yet it is to be remembered that the Executor interest is derived from the Will and not from the Probate or Letters Testamentary. In this case it is believed no serious inconvenience can arise from the want because from a late constitutional decision there would be no occasion for a new Probate. "That there was no question that the Executor of an Executor represents the first testator and may declare without naming or noticing the first testator" 1 Noll & McCord Reports P. 77. It is ordered and decreed that Thomas Wilson be admitted to qualify as Executor of Thomas Drayton as Representative of his testator William Henry Drayton, deceased. James D. Mitchell, Ordinary

[Page 207]

By James D. Mitchell, Esquire, Ordinary. To Henry J. Chalmers, administrator of the Estate and Effects of Sophia Chalmers, deceased. At the instance and request of J. T. Gadsden for the Bank of South Carolina, you are hereby cited and admonished personally to be and appear before me, in the Court of Ordinary, to be held at Charleston on Wednesday next the thirtieth of November instant, at eleven o'clock in the forenoon, then and there appear[?] and render before a just, true and faithful account of your administration of the said Estate. Hereof fail not at your Peril. Given under my hand and Seal this 18th. day of November in the year of our Lord one thousand and eight hundred and twenty-five and in the fiftieth years of American Independence. James D. Mitchell, Ordinary.

South Carolina, Charleston District In the Court of Ordinary. August 30, 1826. At the instance and request of J. and T. Gadsden, Proctors, for the Bank of South Carolina. Henry J. Chalmers, the administrator of Mrs. Sophia Chalmers was cited at the said Court to show cause why he should not render an account of his administration of the said Estate. The administrator appeared and referred to his account past the eighteenth of April 1823 by which it appeared that the sum paid and allowed amounts to Four hundred and seven dollars ninety three cents leaving a balance in his hands of one thousand and forty-nine dollars fifty-seven cents. The sums credited to the Estate in this amount consists of sums received at different times for the rent of Houses and the wages of slaves. On the 20th of February 1822, a Schedule and appraisement of the personal Estate and Effects of the said intestate was rendered in and has been duly filed and recorded, the appraisal value of property therein specified amount to the sum of Seven thousand six hundred and fifty dollars, a list of certain articles of household furniture not appraised is added to this Schedule of Inventory on the eighteenth day of November 1822 an Inventory and appraisement of the personal Estate and effects of the said Estate and duly filed and recorded consisting of Items therein mentioned and certain articles of household furniture, the

[Page 208]

appraised value of which is stated to be two thousand seven hundred and thirty-one dollars seventy-five cents. The above assets are made known to the Court, these assets are properly applicable to the payment of the debts of the Estate for which the administrator is justly chargeable. The reference made to the decree of the Court of Equity cannot prevent or debar the Court from requiring administrator to account before it, when an application is made by a creditor of the Estate. It appears that the said Bank of South Carolina received a Judgment bearing date of 16th day of July 1825 against the aforesaid Administrator on the conditioned for the payment of the sum of five hundred and twenty dollars with lawful interest from the date thereof: the said bond is the ninth day of March 1819. Upon a consideration of the matters in this Case appearing to the Court. It is ordered & Decreed that the said Henry J. Chalmers do pay unto the said Bank of South Carolina or their Attorneys the sum of two hundred and sixty-nine dollars the balance in the Bond in which there is Judgment with the interest from, the 8th. day of July 1820 and the cost of the said Suit. James D. Mitchell, Ordy.

South Carolina, Charleston District. In the Court of Ordinary August 30, 1826. At the instance and request of Thomas O. Elliott, Proctor for Saunders, Glover & Company. Henry J. Chalmers the Admor of Mrs. Sophia Chalmers was cited at the said Court to show cause why he should not render account of his administration of the said Estate, the said Administrator appeared and referred to his account past on the 18th. day of April 1823 by which it appeared that the sum paid and allowed amounts, to four hundred and forty-seven dollars ninety three cents leaving a balance of one thousand and forty-nine Dollars fifty-seven cents. The sums credited to the Estate in this account consists of sums received at different times for the rents of Houses and the wages of slaves on the 20th. February 1822 a Schedule and appraisement of the personal Estate and Effects of the said Intestate was rendered

[Page 209]

in and has been duly filed and recorded. The appraised value of property therein specified amounts to the Sum of seven thousand six hundred and fifty dollars, a list of certain articles of Household furniture not appraised is added to the Schedule of Inventory. Afterwards on the eighteenth day of November 1823 an Inventory and appraisement of the remainder of the personal Estate ____ of the said Estate was rendered and duly filed and recorded consisting of slaves therein mentioned and certain articles of Household furniture the appraised value of which is stated to be two thousand seven hundred and thirty-one dollars seventy-five cents: the above are assets made known to this Court: these assets are properly applicable to the payment of the debts of the Intestate for which the administrator is justly chargeable: the reference made to the Decree of the Court of Equity cannot prevent and debar this Court from requesting an administrator to account before it when an application is made by a creditor of the Estate. It appears that the said Saunders, Glover and Company received a judgment bearing date the eleventh day of February 1822 against the aforesaid administrator. Bond conditioned for the payment of the sum of two thousand seventy dollars with Interest from the date thereof. Date of said Bond is the twenty-seventh day of July 1821 and the cost of the said suit. James D. Mitchell, Ordy.

By James D. Mitchell, Esquire, Ordinary.
To Mrs. Esther Parsons, Executrix of Joseph Parsons, late of Charleston deceased, and Frederick Sledings, his wife Exix of Joseph Dorrill. at the instance and request Pettigru, Proctor, for John Walker, assignee. These are to cite and admonish you personally to be and appear before me in the Court of Ordinary to be held at Charleston on Tuesday next the twenty-ninth of August instant at eleven o'clock in the forenoon then and there to show cause why Daniel Joy for whom Joseph Parsons and Joseph Dorrill were bound as Sureties in his Bond as Administrator of Charles Whitesides, deceased, has not rendered before me as account of the Estate of the said Charles Whitesides, deceased, or why you should not render an account for him.

[Page 210]

Given under my hand and Seal this twenty-second day of August in the year of our Lord one thousand eight hundred twenty-six and in the fifty-first year of American Independence. James D. Mitchell, Ordy.

In the matter of Charles Whitesides, deceased. In the Court of Ordinary, Charleston District. August 31, 1826. Daniel Joy to whom on the tenth day of July 1810 administration of the Goods &c not administered by Charles Whitesides by Moses Whitesides was committed, has died Intestate: no administration has been given to any one of his Effects and it is proved that he did not have Assets to pay the funeral expenses. The Sureties to his Administration Bond were Joseph Parsons and Joseph L. Dorrill who are also dead. On the 10th day of July 1810 Daniel Joy returned to the ordinary a schedule of the Assets of Charles Whitesides not yet administered which came to his hands on that day consisting of Bonds taken by Moses Whitesides for the sale of the personal property amounting to $1,984.63 besides the interest. Daniel Joy never gave an account to the office of his Administration. Charles Whitesides left a widow who after his death married one Jacob Gotfriet Diekert and afterwards one John McIntosh and 2 half brothers, Daniel Joy and William Joy and one half sister, Charlotte Severance. John McIntosh & wife assigned to John Walker their undivided moiety of the Estate of Charles Whitesides and William Joy and Charlotte Severance assigned to him their share being one sixth respectively, he is therefore entitled to five sixths of the Estate as the assignee of the widow and part of the next of Kin and demands an account according to the condition of the Administration Bond. Daniel Joy being dead and having no personal representative, the representatives of the Sureties have been summoned by Esther Parsons, Executrix of Joseph Parsons and Frederick Stedings of Joseph Dorill: Mr. Walker exhibits

[Page 211 -- after page 212 on microfilm]

the Schedule filed in this office of Assets of Charles Whitesides' Estate received by Daniel Joy and demands five-sixths of the Amount. Frederick Stedings appeared in Court and has shown no cause against it. The Claim is resisted by Mrs. Parsons and it is objected that no Suit will be in the Court for an account of the Estate of Charles Whitesides because that Estate is not represented. But the suit is not against the Estate of Charles Whitesides: it is against the Sureties of Daniel Joy. The objection to the suit, if it were to hold would show that a distributee could not sue in this Court. But in Semkin W. Powers Nott. & McCord's 213. It is said that this Court must take cognizance of all matters relative to the Estate and it is the duty of the Ordinary to decree distribution. If the Ordinary can decree distribution, a distributee may sue, for no distribution can be made except at the suit of a distributee. This jurisdiction of making distribution is also exercised by the Court of Equity and there Bills are every day filed by distributees. Cooper Equ. PL. 39. But if the distributees may sue they can sue no one in this case but the Securities and it is clearly proved that there is administrator or Executor of Daniel Joy and that he did not leave any Assets. And in Lyles V. Brown, State Rep. 31. The jurisdiction of the Court against Securities of an administrator where the administrator is dead and has left no Estate is laid down and admitted. I therefore sustain the jurisdiction. It is also objected that Mrs. Parsons is not nor never was the personal representative of Charles Whitesides and never intermeddled with his Estate that she knew nothing of the alleged Security and pleads lapse of time and the statute of limitation against any claim she accepts also to the jurisdiction of the Court to compel her to answer. The Ordinary can discover in these objections which ought to correct the decree for it is clearly proved that Joy administered on the Estate of Charles Whitesides and

165

that Joseph Parsons became one of the Sureties and that Daniel Joy has never accounted for the assets which came into his hands and has serious doubt: consequently the Estate of Joseph Parsons is liable: Further the Ordinary is of the opinion

[Page 212]

that she cannot in this case avail herself of lapse of time and of the statute of limitations being on an admon Bond within twenty years, nor can she accept to the jurisdiction of this Court which has been confirm by late constitutional Decisions. For these Reasons I decree for the Admor. and order Esther Parsons, Executrix of Joseph Parsons and Frederick Steddings and wife pay to the said John Walker out of the Estate of said Joseph Parsons and Joseph Dorrill one thousand five hundred ninety-eight Dollars and fifty-three cents with interest from the 14 June 1805 the day on which the Bonds began to [run?] and forty seven dollars with interest from the 13 of April 1810. James D. Mitchell, Ordy.

In the Case of John Kelone, dec'd. In the Court of Ordinary, Charleston District. September 22, 1826. At the instance and request of Clarke, Proctor for William. A. Caldwell, Creditor of the deceased Lente Mira Kelone, otherwise called Bennett, Administratrix of the Estate and Effects of John Kelone, late of Charleston, deceased, who was cited to appear before me in the Court of Ordinary on the twenty first of September 1826, to show cause why she should not make before me a just & true account of her administration of the Estate of the said John Kelone deceased, and after service duly proved hath not appeared and it appearing that the said William A. Caldwell hath a Judgment in the City Court against the said Administratrix of fifty-one dollars seventy-six cents and twelve dollars & fifty cents cost, I do hereby order and decree that the Administratrix unto the said William A. Caldwell his debts and Costs aforesaid with interest from the date thereof to wit July 22, 1826 and the cost of this Suit amounting to four dollars. James D. Mitchell, Ordy.

South Carolina. Charleston District. In the Court of Ordinary, Charleston District. September 22, 1826. In the Case of Sophia Chalmers deceased.

[Page 213 -- before page 212 on microfilm]

At the instance and request of Thomas O. Elliott, Proctor for James Buckram, Henry J. Chalmers, Administrators of Mrs. Sophia Chalmers, deceased, was cited at the said Court to show Cause why he should not render account of his Administration of the said Estate. _____ Administrator appeared and referred to his account passed on the eighteenth day of April 1823 by which it appears that the sum paid and allowed amount to four hundred and seventy dollars ninety-three cents leaving a balance in the hands of one thousand and forty-nine dollars fifty cents: the sum credited to the Estate in this account consists of Sums received at different times for the rents of Houses and the wages of slaves. On the 20 of February 1822 a Schedule and appraisement of the personal Estate and Effects of the said Intestate was rendered in and has been clearly filed and recorded. The appraised value of property therein specified amount to the sum of seven thousand six hundred and fifty dollars: a list of certain articles of Household furniture not appraised is added to the Schedule or inventory: afterwards on the eighteenth day of November 1823 an Inventory and appraisement of the personal property of the said Estate was rendered on and duly recorded consisting of slaves therein mentioned and certain articles of House Hold furniture and the appraised value of which is stated to be two thousand seven hundred and thirty one Dollars and seventy-five cents. the above are assets made known to this Court these Assessments. are properly applicable to the payment of the debts of the Intestate for which the administrator is justly chargeable. The reference made to the decree of the Court of Equity cannot prevent or debar this Court from requiring an Administrator to account before it when an application is made by a Creditor of the Estate. It appears to my satisfaction that the said James Buckram obtained a Decree into Court of Common Pleas in January Term 1825 against the foresaid Administration for the payment of the sum of fifty-one dollars and fifty cents and ten dollars for cost of said Suit.

[Page 214]

Upon consideration of these matters appearing to the Court, It is Ordered and Decreed that the said Henry J. Chalmers do pay and satisfy unto the said James Buckram the said sum of fifty-one dollars and fifty cents and ten dollars for cost of said Suit. James D. Mitchell, Ordinary.

South Carolina, Charleston District. By James D. Mitchell, Esq., Ordinary To Mary Schwartz Qualified Executrix under the last will and Testament of John Schwartz, late of Charleston, Grocer, deceased. At the instance and request of John C. Jones a qualified Executor of the said deceased you are hereby cited and admonished personally to be and appear in the Court of Ordinary to be held at Charleston on Wednesday next on the ninth day of May instant at 11 o'clock in the forenoon then and there to show cause of any you can you should not make and render before me a true, just and faithful account of your Administration of the said Estate. Hereof fail not at your Peril. Given under my hand and Seal this second day of May anno Domini 1827 and in the fifty-first year of American Independence. James D. Mitchell, Ordy.

State of South Carolina. By James D. Mitchell, Esquire Ordinary, Charleston District. To Mrs. Lachicotte.

At the instance and request of John C. Hobrecker by his Attorney, John H. Sergeant, you are strictly charged and required all manner of excuses being laid aside personally to be and appear before me in the Court of Ordinary on Thursday next the thirty-first day of May instant, at 11 o'clock in the forenoon then and there to show cause why you have not taken out Letters of

Administration on the Estate and Effects of your late husband, P. H. R. Lachicotte, late of this City of Charleston in the district aforesaid, deceased. Hereof fail not at your Peril.

[Page 215]

Given under my hand and Seal in Charleston this twenty-fifth of May in the year of our Lord eighteen hundred and twenty-seven and of the Independence of the United States of America the Fifty-first. Sargeant Pffs atty. Ordinary office.

State of South Carolina, Charleston District. Court of Ordinary. Before James D. Mitchell, Ordinary, for the said District. Be it remembered that Mrs. Marie Frances Feliutite Lachicotte, widow, having been duly cited personally to appear before me to show cause why she hath not taken out Letters of Administration upon the Estate and Effects of her late husband, P. H. R. Lachicotte, deceased, doth now appear in proper person and being duly sworn and examined upon the premises and to declare the truth thereupon doth say that hath not any property, personal in hand power or possession belonging to her said late husband and that she knows of no real or personal property belonging or which belonged to him at the time of his decease except a certain claim for Indemnity an the Saint Domingo claims to be paid or already paid to the French Government for the use of the late proprietors and inhabitants of that Island and which she intends prosecuted in France by Messrs. Du Montier & Gangaud as will for herself and the other claimants and relations connected with her said late Husband, deceased, as for the Estate of her said late Husband and that as soon she shall have discovered information upon the extent and amount of said claims for Indemnity as it is her intention to administer upon the said Estate. M. F. R. Lachicotte.
Sworn before me the 31 May 1827. James D. Mitchell, Ordy.

South Carolina, Charleston District. To Mark Marks, Admor of the Estate of Daniel Joy, late of Charleston, deceased. You are hereby cited and admonished personally to be and appear before me in the Court of Ordinary to be held at Charleston on Wednesday next the nineteenth day of December instant at ten o'clock

[Page 216]

in the forenoon then and there to show cause if any you can why you should not pay over the amount decreed by the Ordinary in the Case of Charles Whitesides, deceased, against the Sureties of Daniel Joy, deceased, Admor of said Whitesides: Hereof fail not at your peril. Given under my hand and Seal eighteenth day of December anno domini one thousand eight hundred and twenty-nine and in the 52 year of American's Independence. James D. Mitchell, Ordy.

In the Court of Ordinary. In the matter of Daniel Joy, deceased, Charleston District, Dec. 19th 1827. On the 10 June 1810, Administration of the Estate of Charles Whitesides not administered by Moses Whitesides was committed to Daniel Joy, and the same Daniel Joy returned an Inventory of said Estate which came to his hands consisting of Bonds &c taken Moses Whitesides for the Sales of the personal Estate of the Intestate mounting to $1,984.63 besides interest. Daniel Joy never accounted, has since died intestate. Administration of his Estate has been granted to Mark Marks who has made his returns to the Court showing that the said Daniel Joy left no assets. Charles Whitesides left a widow who after his death married one Jacob Godfied Deikert, and afterwards John McIntosh and two half brothers Daniel Joy and William Joy and one half sister Charlotte Severance; John McIntosh & wife assigned to John Walker their undivided moiety of the Estate of Charles Whitesides and William Joy and Charlotte Severance assigned to him their Shares being one sixth respectively; he is therefore entitled to 5/6 of the Estate of Charles Whitesides and in his own name and on behalf and in the name of the next of Kin demands an account of the Administrator of Daniel Joy of the monies belonging to the Estate of Charles Whitesides which came to the hands of Daniel Joy, Administrator de bonis non. The foregoing facts are fully [proved?]. The Administrator of Daniel Joy being cited shows that he inquired of the Widow, and next of Kin of Daniel Joy and can obtain no information of any debts of Charles Whitesides paid by him: nor of the Bonds, Notes or mentioned in the Inventory returned by Daniel Joy. It is clear therefore

[Page 217 --before page 216 on microfilm]

that the Estate of Daniel Joy is answerable for the full amounts of the Bonds & Notes which came to his hands. I do, therefore order the said Mark Marks to pay to the actor John Walker out of the Effects and Estate of Daniel Joy $1,598.53 with interest from the 11th June, 1805 the day on which the interest on the Bonds and Notes began to run and forty-seven dollars with interest from the 13 April 1810. James D. Mitchell, Ordinary.

Henry Murray per pro: ami James Duffy & Esther his wife Admor & Admix Roger Murray, decd. In the Court of Ordinary, Charleston District. January 14, 1828.

James Duffy and Esther his wife, Admor & Admix of Roger Murray, deceased, were cited to account for their Administration of the said Estate: The following account was relied on. 1. That Inventory & appraisement amounting to $422.65. 2d. A permission to sell from the Court the personal property of Roger Murray's dated Nov. 3, 1824. 3d. The Acct. sales produced & proved by the Auctioneer amounting to $363.05 and 4. Vouchers of sums paid away on account of debts and Charges due by the Estate. The above account was resisted on several grounds, but principally to show that the above sale was illegal and void that the property still continued the estate of Murray and that the actual value of that Estate, at any given time subsequently to the Administration must be accounted for by the respondent. Much evidence was introduced in behalf of the applicant to show that the Estate of Roger Murray which consisted principally of a Stock of groceries had been used in trade by the Admix as well while she, with widow of Murray, as during her intermarriage with a Mr. Fitzgerald and it was proved that the Stock had in the course of trade realized some time about the day of December 1815, the sum of eight hundred dollars in Cash, besides a small quantity of groceries saved from the fire which happened just before and some household furniture which had been the property of Murray in his lifetime. The balance of the Stock and the furniture

[Page 218]

was estimated about $400. It was contended by the applicant that this sum $800 having accumulated out of the funds out of Murray's Estate & in the course of trade carried on by the Administratrix was to be accounted for as assets and to support this argument. Toller's Law of Executors. P. 165, 167 and quoted which appears to me to establish that position: and it was alleged that the balance of Stock saved from the fire estimated at $200 must be likewise accounted for. It appears to me that there was two questions to be decided in this Case, first, whether the Sale referred to was valid or void. 2. If void what was the value of the Estate at any given time Subsequent to the Administration. The following exception to the sale are taken which appears to me to invalidate it. 1. The purchase was made by Admix through her Agent Mr. Ryan for the benefit of herself & child. See the evidence of Condy and Ryan. 2d. The price was inadequate, refer to the Testimony of Mr. Taylor who declared he would have been glad to purchase the Estate of Murray at $1,000. Mr. McNance who said the Affidavit was worth $1000: or Mrs. Howe who said the property was worth $1000 of Mrs. Howe who said the property was worth fifteen hundred dollars, of Col. Philon, who would not say what the property was worth, but that Murray was apparently in easy circumstances and rented a House from O'Connor's Estate to which he was Executor, never had to call twice for the rent, which was for the first two years $300 and afterwards about $200. For the law on the first and second exceptions, See 4 Equi Reports, P. 486, 502, 504, 506. The 3 exceptions was that the terms of the Sale prescribed by the permission were not compiled with: the terms were Case and the Auctioneer expressly states that he receive no cash but took Ryan's bid for cash. In matters of the Ordinary that he had concurrent jurisdiction with the Court of Equity and therefore for the above reason decides that the Sale was illegal and void. The second question is as to the value of Murray's Estate at any given time subsequent to the Administration. The evidence proved that after Murray's death that the Store carried on

[Page 219 -- before page 218 on microfilm]

South Bay as in the lifetime of Murray. The Admix continued to buy and sell with the funds of the Estate until she married Fitzgerald, then Fitzgerald and herself carried on the Store until in process of time they had accumulated $700 Cash besides which there was $200 and $100 received for _____ which she had after the fire in December 1825: and the Admix declared at the time that it was from the Estate of Murray and it was proved that Fitzgerald had no visible property before he married the widow and therefore could have carried nothing to the funds of the Estate. These sums of $800 in cash and $200 in stock, I think are assets of the Estate which the Admor & Admix must account for from the time December 1825. From the Vouchers and evidence produced before me it appears since the above date the sums paid Admor & Admix in discharge of debts. or reserve to pay that amount to $27.77 which must be allowed as a fair account as far as it goes for the Admor & Admix and the Applicant is entitled to two-thirds of the balance. The Account must be formed according to the principals of this decree and I do Decree for Henry Murray the Sum of five hundred and twenty-one dollars and forty-eight Cents. James D. Mitchell, Ordy.

State of South Carolina, Charleston District. Personally appeared before me Elizabeth Dukes, who being duly sworn deposeth, that the property belonging to the children of Jerry Wright is in a fair way of being spent contrary to the Will of the said Jerry Wright and the intendence of the law. These are therefore to request the inference of the Ordinary of Charleston District in behalf of the children of the said Jerry Wright. Elizabeth (X) Dukes. Sixth of February 1829. Witness: Powell Jones.

South Carolina, Charleston District. In the Court of Ordinary. March 19th 1828. Before James D. Mitchell Esquire, Ordinary. At the instance and request of J. H. Sargeant, Esquire, Richard Teasdale, Administrator of the Estate and Effects of John Teasdale,

[Page 220]

late of Charleston, Merchant, deceased, was on the twenty-fourth day of February last duly cited and admonished to be personally before me in the Court of Ordinary at Charleston on the fifth day of March instant at Eleven o'clock in the forenoon then and there to show cause if any he could why he should not make and render a true, just and faithful account of his administration of the said Estate and Effects at which time and place the said Richard did not make appearance by himself in person, but made default: Whereupon Mr. Barker, Attorney at Law, stated to the Court that Mr. King had been specially employed in this Case and being occupied in the Court of Appeals was not able to attend: Whereupon on motion of Mr. Barker that the time for the appearance of Mr. King should be enlarged and extended to the twelfth instant, the same was granted. Whereupon at the last mentioned day to wit the twelfth instant Mr. King appearing as the Proctor of the said Richard produced in Court an account signed by said Richard exhibiting the same as a true, just and faithful account of the said Administration agreeably to the requisition at the said Citation. Whereupon Mr. Sergeant moved for an adjournment till the morrow when he would cause the personal appearance of Mr. Teasdale: Whereupon the Court adjourned accordingly and on the morrow, to wit, the thirteenth day of March instant Mr. King appearing as aforesaid as the Proctor of Mr. Teasdale stated to the Court that Mr. Teasdale was gone out of town yesterday before he was able to give him notice of the necessity of his personal appearance and therefore moved for further extension of time till Wednesday next the nineteenth instant to which Mr. Sargeant objected; Whereupon the Court granted the motion and adjourned accordingly. And now at this day the nineteenth instant Mr. Teasdale with Mr. King his Proctor appeared in Court

[Page 221 --several pages before 220 on microfilm]

and the accounts which has been left by Mr. King on the twelfth instant was referred to and produced accordingly: when it was proposed by Mr. Sargeant that the same should be sworn to and that the oath should be in the words of the Admor. Bond whereupon Mr. Teasdale read the Conditions of the said Bond and the oath was administered to Mr. Teasdale accordingly by the Ordinary. After which Mr. Sergeant that the Vouchers should be produced as well to sustain the credit side of the account as the debit side and also objected that there was no Inventory and no appearance to which Mr. Teasdale said there was nothing to make an Inventory of as all the Household furniture belonged to his Mother and insisted the said account was a full and perfect account of his Administration and swore to the same before me the ordinary. Whereupon as there were no Vouchers or other account exhibited the said account was ordered to be filed as it had been originally produced with the signature and Oath of Mr. Teasdale as aforesaid.

Given under my hand and Seal this nineteenth day of March one thousand eight hundred and twenty eight. James D. Mitchell

In the Case of Jones Nelson, deceased.
State of South Carolina. Personally appeared before me Levi Crose who made oath & saith that after having obtained Administration of the Estate of James Nelson, deceased, he proceeded to collect in the Effects of the said estate had been conveyed away by Bills of Sale and Voluntary deeds: and the said deeds & Conveyances were made without consideration and intended to protect the property from the just claims of the creditors: That by making application to some of the persons holding their negroes he obtained possession of one family and that there are now certain negroes, the bonafide property of the Estate which are now in possession of other persons under the Bills of Sale which are voluntary and void and Mr. W. R Nelson holds a Deed of

[Page 222]

Gift of Negroes and other property belonging to the said Estate: which Bill of Sale so as exhibited by the said Mr. Nelson and the property claimed by him under the said Deeds your deponent for this saith that there is a judgement for Sixteen hundred dollars in favor of John W. Clarke: and that herefore of any portion of the Estate should be withdrawn for the payment of the debts, his debts which he lost. Levi Crose.

Personally appeared before me. March 19, 1829. Tho O. Elliott, J.P. Mr. Elliott moves on the ground of proper attention to the Collection of Effects that the present Admor should be continued and that Mr. Nelson should be joined in the same administration with the creditor being now in possession of the Administration. 1. Because the Administration had been granted already to another and should not now be destroyed. 2. That William R. Nelson holds a voluntary Deed for the property of the Estate and first claimed the property that he holds this voluntary Deed from Mr. Crose and was refused to him by him until the debts are first paid. Personally appeared before me T. O. Elliott who made Oath that Mr. W. R. Nelson claimed the property of Nelson for which he holds a voluntary deed in the presence of this deponent T. O. Elliott. Sworn to before me this nineteen March 1829. J. Clarke, J. P.

South Carolina. William R. Nelson being duly Sworn maketh, Oath and saith that he has a paper purporting to be a Will executed by his late brother James Nelson: that he came to Charleston: he happened to be Present when Mr. Crose's appraisers were proceeding with the appraisement: that upon said occasions finding some of the articles contained in said Deed about to be appraised he inquired of Col. Elliott who was present whether those ought to be appraised as they are mentioned in the deed: that Col. Elliott replied to him that his rights to the property would not be impaired by the appraisement that a day or two after this he spoke to his

[Page 223]

Council in regard to said deed who informed that this deed was of no validity: that since that time he has not pretended to set up any thing like a claim upon said Deed. William R. Nelson. Sworn to before me the 19 March 1829.

Joseph H. Foster p'r his Guardian Jotham Lincoln vs Alexander Black. In the Court of Ordinary, Charleston District. April 15, 1829.

This was a citation issuing out of the Court of Ordinary citing and administering Alexander Black, Administrator of Nathan Foster to appear before me in the Court of Ordinary to make and render a true, just and faithful account of his administration of the said Estate. At the time appointed the said Alexander Black did appear and exhibit an account current between the Estate and Joseph H. Foster the minor son of Nathan Foster. It appears that Nathan Foster at his death left a widow and one Son Joseph H. Foster that the said widow has since died and her proportion of her husband's Estate; she devised to various Legatees. It further appeared by vouchers and the admission of parties that the other Legatees of the Estate of Nathan Foster had received their distributive portions and were satisfied, that was a balance still due the said Joseph H. Foster of three thousand four hundred and seventy five dollars and fourteen cents which said Sum is the amount of two-thirds of the Estate of Nathan Foster after all debts paid & interest on the net amount of the proportion or Share of the said Joseph H. Foster. The accounts exhibited have been made up with great care by a regular accountant and the amounts stated, acquiesced by all the Legatees and distributions and the account on which the decree is founded a copy of which is made a part of this decree has been furnished by Mr. A. Black, the administrator and is admitted by the guardian of the minor to be correct. I am therefore of opinion that the said Joseph H. Foster is entitled to receive from his father's Estate the sum of three

[Page 224]

thousand four hundred and Seventy five dollars and fourteen cents with Interest on the same from the 15 April 1829 until paid. And that Sum I do hereby order direct and decree the Alexander Black, Administrator, as aforesaid to pay unto the said Joseph H. Foster as his Distributive Share of his father's Estate. James D. Mitchell, Ordinary.

In the matter of William Mims deceased. In the Court of Ordinary April 16, 1829. This Case comes before the Ordinary in behalf of Sarah Ann & Mary Mims, minor children of Drury Mims, late of St. James Parish, planter, deceased, to cite Caswell Mims, Administrator of William Mims to account and pay the amount to which they are entitled to Wit: one fourth of the thirds of the said Estate: and the said Caswell Mims with a view in an amicable settlement of the Estate admits and confesses on the sixteenth day of April 1829, that the sum of Five hundred and Sixty three dollars is justly due by him as Administrator of the said William Mims, deceased, to the said Sarah Ann and Mary Mims as Distributees of the said William Mims, deceased, and I do hereby order and decree that the said Caswell Mims, Admix as aforesaid paid to the said Sarah Ann and Mary Mims, the said sum above stated five hundred and Sixty three dollars. James D. Mitchell, Ordinary. N.B. Agreement filed with account No. 1665.

In the Case of Martha Mackay, deceased. In the Court of Ordinary May 22, 1829. Answer to the appeal entered against the Ordinary's order for revocation in this Case on the 19 May 1829. First the Ordinary directed the attention of the Court to a petition and affidavit filed in this court in answer to the first article which will evince that he was not the only mover in the Case.

[Page 225]

2ndly. In consequence of the foregoing Petition and affidavit, a special citation had been issued out of the Court to cite John L. Crawford to show cause why he should not give further security on the administration be revoked, the same was lodged in the Sheriff Office for service: The Petition for relief having been withdrawn in the mean time and the citation returned Non est Inventus, the Ordinary inferred that it would [be] useless under the present circumstances to proceed until he had received further information and the matter was suspended. 3rdly. On the first of April 1829 Mr. Elliott sued out another Citation to the same effect which was returned personally served on the

Admor requiring him to show cause on the 15 April which service proved on the 10 April to have been made. The day of the 15 April arrived and the Admor did not appear but made default. Mr. Elliott shortly afterward moved a revocation and while the Ordinary was deliberating on the matter Mr. Finley moved that an order or decree should be to pay the money then in the hands of Mr. Elliott formerly the Attorney of Crawford into the hands of Mr. Ferrell, the present Attorney, in fact of Crawford upon which it was which it was proposed should be appointed Admor on his giving Security which was declined. Mr. Elliott came into court and delivered the funds into the hands of the _____ the Administration: There being no one disposed to take the administration and the present Admor incompetent. The contents of the original petition and affidavit could not escape the observation of the Court although it was withdrawn: which is willing to abide the order of the Court above. James D. Mitchell, Ordy.

[Page 226]

In the Case of John Holmes, Senr., deceased. Thomas H. Thayer, Admor de bonis non John G. Holmes Senr decd. vs Ann G. Holmes, Exix.
In the Court of Ordinary. May 23, 1828.

In this Case Ann G. Holmes, defendant, was summoned at the instance of Thos. H. Thayer, Admor, with the Will annexed of the goods & chattels of John Holmes, Senr., unadministered by John Holmes, decd., to order an account of the transactions of her deceased testator as admor of John Holmes, Senr., deceased, and it appeared to be satisfaction that her deceased testator as admor aforesaid was indebted to the said Thomas H. Thayer was Admor as aforesaid in the sum of nine thousand two hundred fifty nine dollars eighty three cents on the 12 May 1826 which sum is accordingly decreed with interest from that date (decree with papers). James D. Mitchell, Ordinary

In the Case of John Scott, Carpenter. In the Court of Ord'y, Charleston District. May 30, 1829.

Richard Connelly who administered on the above Estate was called upon to show cause why his Letters of Admor should not be revoked upon the ground that Letters had been Previously granted to Francis Sylvester Curtis upon the estate of John Scott, Factor, with the will annexed. It was admitted on the part of Mr. Curtis that the John Scott upon whose Estate he administered was not a carpenter: but it was contended that his Letters of Administration being upon record in this office and having never been revoked it was necessary for Mr. Connelly to show that the John Scott upon whose Estate he administered was not the person upon whose Estate Mr. Curtis administered that the circumstances of his being named a carpenter was not of itself sufficient evidence to establish the fact of their different persons: It was contended on the contrary that the onus probandi laid upon Mr. Curtis to prove that the John Scott upon whose Estate he administered was the same person upon whose Estate Mr. Connelly had administered and so I decided it came out in the Course of the course of the investigation that the Negro Jenny whom Mr. Curtis claimed & who was returned as the property of the Estate of John Scott upon which he Mr. Connelly administered was not the property of said John Scott or rather Mr. Connelly admitted he had not been able to ascertain that the said negro Jenny was the property

[Page 227]

of John Scott upon whose Estate he had administered. Philip Moore Sworn. Never knew a carpenter of the name of Scott in Charleston: witness has been a lumber Merchant since 1811: had transactions with most of the Carpenters of Charleston. Witness thinks that if there had been a carpenter of that name since he had been a lumber merchant he would have known it: witness has been in business in Charleston as a Cabinet maker since 1793: in 1811 he became a lumber Merchant that during the whole time since 1793 he had never known or heard of John Scott, carpenter: he thinks it probably he would have heard or known it had there been such a one. Was there not a person kept the jail named Scott who was a Carpenter? Answer he does not know he knew two John Scotts neither of whom was a Carpenter; the first John he knew was a negro, the second a planter on James Island he might have become a factor, but does not know the fact. He had a large property and ran it through: does not think he ever was a Carpenter, adjourned to 10 o'clock on Thursday the 4 June. June 4, 1829. It is admitted by Mr. Connelly that John Scott upon whose Estate Curtis was Admr with Will annexed was the same person upon whose Estate Connelly has taken out Letters of Admor contending never the less that he has been properly appointed by the Ordinary. Mr. Thomas Bennet Sworn. Was acquainted with John Scott: he resided in witness' family and was first or second cousin to witness' wife; has seen Mr. Scott write and does believe from seeing Scott write that the Bill of Sale produced to witness and before the Court dated 19 July 1806 from John Scott to Jenny Pearce of a negro boy named James is signed by John Scott and is his handwriting. I knew Jenny Pearce to whom said Bill of Sale was executed believes she was foster mother of John Scott. She was free: John Scott was much attached to her, he more strongly infers that the signature to said Bill of Sale is John Scott's from the circumstances of the attachment that he entertained for Jenny Pearce the object of said Bill of Sale was to secure the said boy James to her during her natural life on account of

[Page 228]

the affection which she had for him and for the services which he was able to render her. The witness does not from his own knowledge of the execution of the Bill of Sale produced to him, but strongly infers that it was his deed from his knowledge of the attachment which John Scott had for her: that John Scott rendered her many Kindness: it is in witness' recollection that she requested John Scott to give said boy to her and thinks it probable from all circumstances that he would have done such an act: Witness has a vague impression that John Scott intended to make conveyance. Did not know the boy James but knew there was such a Boy: Witness does not believe that John Scott was intimate in the family of Mr. Curtis. The decd. left a widow. Knew after the death of John Scott that his widow resided in Mr. Curtis' family: Believe that it was the intention of John Scott to limit the said boy to Jenny Pearce during her life time so as to place him beyond the reach of his admors exors. or creditors and that he should revert to his family after his death: John Scott left no child. Witness does not know with certainty what property John Scott possessed at his death, but thinks he then possessed of a Sloop and 8 or 10 negroes. Thinks he was worth at that time between 5 to 7,000 dollars, but does not know what debts he owed.

Mrs. Martha E. Gibbes: Knew John Scott but not intimately: cannot tell when he died would not pretend to say, Saw John Scott at my father's house. Thomas Hollingsbee on James Island. He came to visit Jenny Pearce who lived very near my father and on account of my father being intimate with his father he spent the day above alluded to partly at my father's house and partly with old Jenny, he was there

[Page 229]

more than once within my knowledge, Has seen him occasionally there: that is at Jenny Pearce's & my father's: John Scott was much attached to Jenny Pearce who was his foster mother, his mother having died in her confinement with him. Jenny Pearce's mistress was John Scott's grandmother Knew the boy James and his mother, who was the youngest daughter of Jenny Pearce, her name was Bella, James was with Jenny while Scott used to go over to see her he was always from his birth with Jenny who was very much attached to him: he was with her at the time of her death: Jenny Pearce's house was his general place of residence. Knows nothing of the Bill of Sale, never heard that Jenny Pearce's claim to said boy was disputed: since 1808 she lived in Witness's place and James with her. He was a fisherman and would occasionally be absent. but, considered. Jenny's residence as his home. Bella, the mother of James, was John Scott's property. She was the devised to Mr. Scott from his grandmother, Mrs. Francis Pearce who died about 37 years ago. James was born after the death of Mrs. Pierce. Jenny Pierce was made free by the will of Mrs. Pierce. By which Bella was given to John Scott. Witness knows that John Scott sold Bella and her other child, a daughter, which distressed Jenny very much and she came to town to see John Scott in order to know whether he intended to sell James. Witness does not know the transaction of the Bill of Sale produced but firmly believes from the circumstances of John Scott's attachment to Jenny and her distress of mind that he executed said deed. Robert Gibbes sworn. Has resided on James Island off and on 54 years: knew John Scott when he was small. Knew Jenny Pierce and her grandson James. James always lived with Jenny from a child to the time of his death. they were much attached to

[Page 230]

one another, Jenny died on January last, Knew Jenny Pearce a great many years, no one claimed James that I know of, always considered him as Jenny's property knew Bella she belonged to Mrs. Pearce, Is certain she went to John Scott after Mrs. Pearce's death as his property, old Jenny in the latter part of her life was maintained by James R. Jenny. William Jones Sworn. Knows Richard Connelly. Knows that Connelly has been here since 1815, does not believe that he was here before that time; never saw him in Charleston before. It was admitted on all sides that John Scott, carpenter, was the same person with John Scott, Factor, and the latter Administration was granted under a wrong impression and therefore revoked.

In the Case of Shadrack Williams, deceased. From the testimony of Mr. Jacob Keen taken in this Case coupled with the documents produced in this Case, it appears that the cattle mentioned in the Inventory sold for $439.50, the Bed for sixteen dollars. The other articles appraised at $10.50; so that the whole Estate amounts to four hundred and sixty-six dollars $466. It further appears that the Intestate left seven children his heirs at Law, two of whom have since died intestate unmarried and without issue: each of the Heirs are therefore entitled to one fifth of the Estate: two of them it appears have been settled with. The remaining three to wit: Martha, Mary and Frances have not been settled with. It is therefore ordered and decreed that Abraham Hood, the Administrator of Shadrack Williams, do pay to each of them

[Page 231]

the said Martha, Mary and to the Guardian of Frances the sum of Ninety three dollars and twenty cents with interest from 15 May 1816 together with the cost of this Suit. James D. Mitchell

In the Case of Jeremiah Wright. State of South Carolina, Charleston District. By James D. Mitchell, Esq., Ordinary

To Sarah Brazil formerly Sarah Wright and John Brazil, Administrators of Jeremiah Wright, late of St. Stephen's Parish, deceased. You are cited and admonished (at the instance and request of William Dukes and Elizabeth his wife) personally to be and appear before me in the Court of Ordinary to be held at Charleston on Tuesday the thirtieth day of June instant at eleven o'clock then and there to show cause if any you can, why you should not make and render before me a true, just and faithful account of your administration of the said Estate. Hereof fail not at your Peril. Given under my Hand and Seal this sixteenth day of June in the year of our Lord one thousand eight hundred and twenty-nine and in the fifty-third year of American Independence.

St. Stephens Parish, Charleston District. To James D. Mitchell, Esq., Ordinary. Personally appeared [before] me William Gaskin who being duly sworn made oath that he personally cited John Brazil to be and appear at Charleston in the Court of Ordinary held at Charleston on Tuesday the thirteenth of June last, when to give a true account as the within directs. Sworn before me, John Calvin, J. P.

The Citation was left in Court on the 25 Aug 1829. The parties cited never appeared and the case was abandoned by the citing party who did not proceed in the case.

In the Case of John P. McNeill deceased. In the Court of Ordinary, Charleston District, June 9th, 1829. This is a Case on an application to cite

[Page 232]

A. McNeill Burke, the Admor of John P. McNeill, deceased, to show cause why the Administration should not be revoked on the ground that the deceased at the time of his death was resident of Natches in the State of Mississippi; and the Executor had qualified thereon and that there were no assets of John P. McNeill within the State of South Carolina. The Ordinary is of the opinion that if there had been a will authenticated in the manner prescribed by the act of Congress and that Exors applied for probate it would have been a good cause for revocation of the Letters of Administration: but that he cannot recognize the Will now before the Court as possessing those forms required by the Act of Congress. There being no Will on record of John P. McNeill in this Court a general Administration on the Estate was granted the parties applying are not yet provided with such a Will as can be recognized by the Court: the Court is ready to revoke as soon as it is warranted by the circumstances of the case: as to the circumstance of their being no assets returned it has been the usual practice in the Court formerly and latterly to grant for special purposes when the Administrators upon taking Administration have declared on oath that there was no personal property belonging to the Estate. James D. Mitchell, Ordinary.

The Executors of John P. McNeill protested against the jurisdiction of the Ordinary of Charleston District to grant Letters of Administration on the Estate of John P. McNeill in the state of South Carolina and reserving to themselves the right to apply or not for a probate of the Will in said state, gave notice to the Ordinary that they will proceed a certified copy of the said will duly authenticated in form of law and will then apply for a revocation of the

[Page 233 --several pages before page 222 on microfilm]

Administration of A. McNeill Burke on the Estate of John P. McNeill in due form. Benjamin P. Pepoon, Proctor, for the Exors., 10 June 1829.

In the matter of Amarinthea Screvin, deceased. In the Court of Ordinary, Charleston District, August 24, 1824. On motion of Hunt & Shand, Proctors for William Stuart, Administrator de bonis non of the said Amarinthea Screvin, deceased. A Special Citation was issued on the 7th day of July last against John Mayrant Junr., the Administrator of the late Dr. Thomas W. Wright and also Mrs. Sarah E. Wright, which said Dr. Thomas W. Wright and Sarah E. Wright on the ninth day of January 1824 became Administrators of the Goods and Chattels of the said Amarinthea Screvin, deceased, requiring them to appear before the Ordinary for Charleston District on Friday the 21st of August instant to render a true, just and faithful account of their Administration aforesaid, and on the day last named neither the said John Mayrant, Junr., nor the said Sarah E. Wright did appear, neither had they or the said Dr. Thomas W. Wight in his life time rendered Schedule, Inventory or Account of the said Administration and therefore the Proctors for the said William Stuart, Administrator de bonis non moved for a decree against the legal representative of the said Dr. Thomas W. Wright and the said Sarah E. Wright of the Penalty of the Bond given to the Ordinary, there being no other means of fixing the sum due to the Estate and by the Court now here it is considered & adjudged that the condition of the said Bond is forfeited that the said Dr. Thomas W. Wright in his life time did not neither has his personal representative accounted any Inventory as required by the condition of said Bond, and the Court accordingly Decrees and Adjudges that the said William Stuart, Administrator de bonis non aforesaid do recover

[Page 234-- page before 233 on microfilm]

against the said John Myrant, Junr., Administrator of Thomas W. Wright and also against the said Sarah E. Wright the sum of eight thousand dollars.

In the Case of Christopher Rogers, deceased. State of South Carolina, Charleston District. Charles Rogers, son of Christopher Rogers deceased, being duly sworn deposes, That on Saturday afternoon the 10th of January last, his father, then on his death bed, he having died the next morning at ½ past 5, declared to Dr. J. W. Schmidt his attending physician, that he had given his Will to Mr. J. Glen, an officer in the Planters & Merchants Bank, and that it was in a brown box inclining to Black: That this deponent was present and heard him say so: that his father was then aware that he was expected to die shortly, having been told so by Dr. Schmidt and the Minister of his Church having left him but a short time before this deponent further says that afterwards and on the same Evening he repeated to him, that he had made his Will and that Deponent would get it at a proper time and when he should want it: that his father had previously declared to him that he had made his Will to his satisfaction: This deponent therefore prays that Ordinary would grant a Citation calling upon the said J. Glen to produce the said Will and have the same produced and proved, he prays that the Administration granted upon this Estate of his said father may be revoked. Ch. Rogers Sworn to before me this 4 September 1829. James W. Gray, Not. Pub. & Q.U.

South Carolina, Charleston District. By James D. Mitchell, Esq., Ordinary

To John Glen, an Officer in the Planters & Mechanics Bank, Charleston. You are hereby cited and admonished personally to be and appear before me in the Court of Ordinary to be holden in Charleston on Friday next eleventh

[Page 235 --before page 234 on microfilm]

day of September instant at Eleven o'clock in the forenoon then and there to produce for probate the last Will and Testament of Christopher Rogers, late of Charleston, Gentleman, deceased. Hereof fail not at your Peril given under my hand and Seal at Charleston this Fourth day of September in the year of our Lord one thousand eight hundred and twenty nine and in the fifty fourth year of the Independence of the United States of America. James D. Mitchell

South Carolina, Charleston District. By James D. Mitchell, Esquire, Ordinary, To Mary Ann Rogers, William Rogers, Robert C. Brown and wife and Dr. W. J. Schmidt. At the Instance and request of John Glen: You & each of you are hereby cited personally to be & appear before me in the Court of Ordinary to be holden at Charleston on Tuesday the 15th day of September inst. at eleven o'clock in the forenoon & then & there to testify the truth in a certain case depending between Charles Rogers & John Glen on the part & behalf of the Defendant. Hereof fail not, Given under my hand and Seal this fourteenth day of September in the year of our Lord 1829 and in the 54th year of American Independence. By James D. Mitchell, Esq., Ordy.

State of South Carolina, District of Charleston. To John Ferguson, Administrator, of the estate of David Muir, late of St. Paul's Parish, planter deceased. Whereas Angus Stewart, the Security for the said Administrator hath represented to me that he conceives himself in danger of being injured by his said Securityship and hath petitioned for relief. These are therefore to cite you and admonish you personally to be and appear before me in the Court of Ordinary to be held at Charleston on Thursday the 8th day of October at 11 o'clock in the forenoon then and there to show cause if any you can, why you should not make and render before me a true, just and faithful account of your administration of the said Estate, and why such order or the decree should not be made as will be sufficient to give relief to the Petitioner. Given my hand and Seal this 29 day of September 1829 and in the 54 year of American Independence.

In Reply to the within Citation served upon me

[Page 236 -- before page 235 on microfilm]

in the matter of David Muir's Estate, I hereby that it is not my intention to continue to act as Administrator, But to close the same so as I have acted and to renounce the administration allowing those interested to nominate some other person to take the same to which appointment I will make no objection. Signed: John Ferguson

In the Case of Sophia Chalmers, deceased. In the Court of Ordinary, Charleston District, October 7th 1829. At the instance and request of Mary Ann Miles by her Proctors, Thomas S. & Henry Grimke, Henry J. Chalmers the administrator of Mrs. Sophia Chalmers, was cited at the said Court to show cause why he should not render an account of his Administration of the said Estate. The Administrator appeared and referred to his account passed on the 18th day April 1823 by which it appeared that the Sum paid and allowed amounts to four hundred and seven dollars ninety three cents, leaving a balance in his hands of one thousand and forty nine dollars fifty seven cents. The Sum credited to the Estate on this account consists of sums received at different times for the rent of Houses and the wages of slaves. On the 20th February 1822 a Schedule and appraisement of the personal Estate and Effects of the said Intestate was rendered in and has been filed and recorded, the appraised value of property therein specified amount to the Sum of seven thousand six hundred and fifty dollars [also] and an appraisement[?] of certain articles of Household furniture [now] appraised is added to the Schedule or Inventory, on the 18 November 1822: an Inventory and

[Page 237 -- before page 236 on microfilm]

appraisement of the remainder of the personal Estate & Effects of the said Estate and duly filed and recorded consisting of Slaves therein mentioned and certain articles of Household furniture. The appraisement value of which is stated to be two thousand seven hundred and thirty one dollars seventy five cents. The above assets are made known to this Court. The assets are properly applicable to the payment of the debts of the Estate for which the Administrator is justly chargeable. The reference made to the decree of the Court of Equity cannot prevent and debar this Court from requiring an Administrator to account before it when an application is made by a creditor of the Estate. It appears to my satisfaction that Mary B. Miles recovered a judgement in October term 1825 for the Sum of Three hundred twenty one dollars ninety cents with interest from the twenty first day of July one thousand eight hundred and twenty four until paid and thirty five dollars and thirty six cents for the cost of said Suit. James D. Mitchell, Ordinary.

In the Case of Sarah Mason, deceased. To Peter T. Marchant, admor, Sarah Mason. Sir, you are hereby cited to appear before me on Thursday the 22 day of October inst. at 10 O'clock in the forenoon in the Present year to prove the account current you have filed in the Case of the above Estate and to vouch the several particulars contained in the same. Given under my hand this twentieth day of October anno domini 1829. James D. Mitchell, Ordy.

In the Case of John M. Verdier, deceased. South Carolina, Charleston District. By James D. Mitchell, Esq., Ordy. To John M. Verdier of Beaufort, Attorney at Law. At the instance and request of John Porteous, Esquire, you are hereby required personally to be and appear before [me] in the Court of Ordinary to be held in Charleston on Friday the fourth

[Page 238 -- before page 237 on microfilm]

day of December next at 11 o'clock in the forenoon then and there to show cause why you have not taken Letters of Administration on the estate & Effects of John M. Verdier, late of Charleston, planter, deceased, agreeably to the Citation issued out on the third day of November in the year of our Lord one thousand eight hundred and twenty eight last. Hereof fail not at you peril. Given under my hand and Seal this twentieth day of November in the year of our Lord one thousand eight hundred and twenty nine and in the fifty fourth year of American Independence. James D. Mitchell, Ordinary

South Carolina, Beaufort District. Personally served John M. Verdier with a copy, this 30 November 1829. R. Fuller. John Porteous, Q.U.

In the matter of Thomas Craig, deceased. In the Court of Ordinary Charleston District, December 4, 1829. This is a Case arising from the Administratrix having a demand against the Estate of her Intestate, which she is required to prove before the Court. It appears that Thomas Craig boarded for many years with the Administratrix as by the testimony of Miss Reilly from 1821 to 1818 off and on and was boarding there before that time: she thinks he must have been there certainly about four years, of which two years and some months were unpaid mounting to $1162.85. The Intestate appears to have been Debtor to Reilly by entry in his Books in Craig's own hand writing for cash _____ and various articles furnished amounting to $132.56. Also for Boarding & lodging in 1818 of twenty one weeks and some days amounting to $217.13 so that the whole Sum substantiated to which the Administratrix is entitled amounts to $1,513.49½. I therefore Order and Decree that she retain the amount of her debt from the Estate of Craig, fifteen hundred and thirteen dollars forty-nine cents & a half. James D. Mitchell, Ordy.

[Page 239 -- before page 238 on microfilm]

In the Court of Ordinary, Charleston District, December 1, 1829.
In the Matter of Christopher Rogers, deceased. The Case came before the Court under the following circumstances: a Citation issued from this Court on the affidavit and at the instance of Charles Rogers, a son of the deceased, citing and admonishing John Glen who it was believed was an Executor named in the last Will and testament of Christopher Rogers, late of Charleston, Gentleman, deceased, to appear before the Court of Ordinary to show cause why he should not produce the said Will for probate. At the time appointed Mr. Glen appeared with his Council and for answer to the said Citation stated he has not nor ever had any Will of the deceased in his possession. Testimony was then produced to substantiate the following facts, that Christopher Rogers during his last illness in view of his approaching dissolution and on the subject being brought to his mind by the attending physician whose duty induced him to declare the previous state in which he was, stated he had made a Will and given it to the care of Mr. John Glen, an officer in the Planter and Mechanics Bank. The witness Dr. Schmidt in consequence of the information he had

received went to the Bank and made inquiry of Mr. Glen who disclaimed all knowledge of it and reference he had to Mr. Ravenel, the Cashier, who searched for it and declared that there was no paper of that nature or any other belonging to Mr. Rogers which intelligence Dr. Schmidt communicated with Mr. Rogers and said that if he had put his will in the Bank he must have taken a receipt for it. Mr. Rogers said he had the receipt was down stairs in a desk or drawer; the witness with the family ransacked every place in vain and told Mr. Rogers that it could not be found. Mr. Rogers answered that it would be found in

[Page 240 -- before page 239 on microfilm]

time when he was dead. The physician stated that when Mr. Rogers said this he was in a perfect state of mind. A certificate was produced from the transfer clerk that Mr. Rogers owned eight shares in the Planters and Mechanics Bank and sold them on the twenty first of May 1828. Such appears to be the substance of the testimony on the part of the applicant. On the part of the respondent the declaration of Mr. Glen was the only testimony on the nature of the case that he can offer in answer thereto and he expressly stated that he never had any confidential communication with Mr. Rogers, never received any paper on anything else from him for safe keeping: that he never was at his house: never visited him nor was Mr. Rogers ever over his threshold and his Son Mr. Charles Rogers on his declaration states that he never knew of any intimacy there. Upon the whole in reviewing the evidence it does appear that Mr. Rogers had impressed his family with the belief that Mr. Glen was in possession of his Will and surely that circumstances together with a sense of duty towards his father may have justified Mr. Charles Rogers in the investigation which he has instigated. Yet on the other hand there does not appear anything but the declarations of Mr. Rogers which would have created a belief that so great a trust would have been committed to Mr. Glen, nor does any intimacy between them lead us to have expected it. It is therefore difficult to account for the appointment, but from the high estimation in which he held Mr. Glen or from the eccentricity of his character generally which should have caused him to name a stranger in the refusal of his son under circumstances to accept the trust. There are no circumstances but the declaration of the deceased which have transpired in the case before the Court, which would warrant inferential suspicion that Mr. Glen had motives to secure

[Page 241 -- two pages before page 240 on microfilm]

the will and the Ordinary under these impressions must dismiss the Citation. James D. Mitchell, Ordy.

In the Case of Benjamin Jewel, deceased. January 1, 1830. Special Citation granted W. Lance, Proctor, to cite Benjamin Jewel, Admor, Benjamin Jewel, decd., to show cause on the sixth instant why the Letters of Admor. granted should not be revoked and granted to Col. Magwood in behalf of the widow.

In the matter of Rebecca Rose, deceased. In the Court of Ordinary, Charleston District, January 23, 1830. From the testimony adduced in the case: I see nothing to induce me to revoke the probate of the Will and the Letters testamentary granted under it to George Timmons. There is no evidence that testatrix was not in her senses when she signed it and she must have known it was her Will. As to the effect of the Will, if there be any matter requiring a construction of it this is for another tribunal. The examination of such a question is not in the Jurisdiction of the Ordinary, I therefore pronounce my decree in support of the Will dated 9 September 1829. James D. Mitchell, Ordy.

In the case of Robert Henley, decd. In the Court of Ordinary, Charleston District, March 10, 1830. This Case was brought before the Court by a Citation sued out by Mrs. Mary Manson on the fourteenth of January last as a Creditor. A Caveat was entered against the administration on the twenty-first of January by Col. Hunt and the Case came on for hearing on the 22 January and was adjourned from time to time to afford an opportunity to hear from the relatives of the deceased; on the tenth of March, Mr. Macrady in behalf of Mrs. Manson and Col. Hunt the Caveator appeared in Court; Mr. Macrady insisted that the Administration should

[Page 242]

be granted to Mr. Manson as Creditor: there being no reason shown to the satisfaction of the Ordinary why longer postponement should take place, as a considerable time had elapsed since the death of the Intestate and no measures have been taken by the relatives to bring the matter to a close. Whereupon granted Administration to Mary Manson she being the greatest creditor applying for the same. James D. Mitchell, Ordinary

In the Case of Frederick Beard, decd. Special Citation granted to Mr. Philips to cite Mrs. Grace Strobell to appear on the 24 March instant, to show cause why the admor granted her should not [be] revoked. Mr. Philips afterwards consented to let the admor remain and it was consented to that he might bring the Suit in name of her husband and herself.

In the Case of Rebecca Rose, decd. A Special Citation to cite George Timmons, Exor., to appear on the 14 March instant to show cause why an Order of Sale granted in the said State should not be revoked.

[pages before 242, in a different handwriting]

South Carolina, Charleston District. It has pleased my Heavenly Father to remove from our midst my estamable & long valued friend Mrs. Jane Keith, widow of the late Dt. Isaac Stackton Keith, who whilst alive appropriated the largest portion of her estate in advancing the cause of her Redeemer on Earth & in her Will disposing of her estate to a large circle of friends & the Balance or rest & residue she has given to me in trust however, "to be disposed of as she (I) alone shall think but for the glory of God on earth & the extention of the Redeemer's Kingdom in the World."

Again in a Codicil attached to her Will and made a part of the same, she makes to me this additional bequest: "I do here by give to my friend Miss Sarah B. Stevens all my wearing apparel, Books, all other matters and things not heretofore disposed of." From these two clauses some diversity of opinion may arise and in the event of my death before I shall have executed the Trust reposed on me by my friend Mrs. Jane Keith which I deem sacred and with a view of enforcing the executors of the same if it shall please my Heavenly Father to call me home to Him, before I have done so, I make this instrument of writing which I declare to be a codicil to my last Will & Testament dated the _____ and direct the same to be taken as a part of my aforesaid last Will & Testament.

If the foregoing trust shall not have been executed by me in my life time, I charge my estate with all that I may have received or my Executors may receive on account of my estate as residuary legatee of Mrs. Jane Keith, who in her life time was entitled to a legacy from her sister Mrs. Mary Maxwell of Philadelphia and as residuary Legatee under that Will & who was also entitled to the Rest & residue of his sister Miss Elizabeth Husehanis' Estate also of Philadelphia or to any other sum or sums of money I may be entitled to under the two clauses of the Will & Codicil of Mrs. Jane Keith except the Books [apparently the page or pages following are missing]

[From torn pages in back of Original Book:]

In Witness whereof I do here unto subscribe my name and affix my Seal in Paris this seventh day of April in the year of one thousand seven hundred and eighty three. Sigr. Seal and Delivered (Seal) Montmorency P'ce. de Luxembourg (Seal). In the presence of us: Archd. Redford, Geo. Fox

Know all Men by these presence that I Ferdinand Grand, Banker, in Paris named in the proceeding letter of Attorney to me executed by the above written Prince of Luxembourg, do by and in virtue of the power and authority to me thereby given substitute place and appoint Edward Bancroft of Westfield in the State of Massachusetts Bay Doctor in Physic and fellow of the Royal Society of London in my stead to exercise the several powers therein described and do hereby give, grant, assign over and Convey to him the said Edward Bancroft all the Singular the Rights, Powers and Authorities to me given and Conveyed by the said letter of Attorney, hereby ratifying and Confirming all that he, the said Edward Bancroft, shall do or cause to be done by his substitute in virtue of the said letter of Attorney and of this Act. _____ my name.

I do approve and confirm the Substitution made and Contained in the preceding Act. Paris, April the Seventh 1783 Mont. Montinresey, Pr. de Luxembourg Witnesses Archd. Redford, George Fox.

Philadelphia [illegible]. This day appeared Archibald Redford and George Fox both of this City, Gentlemen, and subscribing witnesses to the within Act or letter of Attorney and its supplementary parts and severally made Oath that they were present at the Execution thereof in Paris and said the within named Montmorancy Prince of Luxembourg and Ferdinand Grand, Sign, Seal, and deliver the same as their Act and Deed respectively and that the names Archibald Redford, George Fox substituted there. Several times as witnesses to the Execution of the said letter of Attorney and the supplementary part thereof are the hand writing of the Deponents respectively. Sworn before me the subscribing Chief Justice of the State of Pennsylvania and Doctor of Laws in Philadelphia this the twenty third day of December in the year one thousand seven hundred eighty three. Tho. M. Keen, Archd. Redford, George Fox.

Said State of South Carolina or of the Government whereof the said Alexander Gillon jointly or separately the full Sum of three hundred thousand Livers lawful money of France to me due and owing by Virtue of the Act or Control made as aforesaid on the thirteenth day of May in the year one thousand seven hundred eighty, and in the Virtue of the power given as thereof mentioned to the said Gillon by the said State of South Carolina, and having received the said sum or any part thereof to give valid and sufficient [illegible] or discharge for the same in my Name and stead: And I do also authorize and empower my said Attorney in my Name to Commence and prosecute to find Issue and Suit or Suits either in Law or Equity which to him may appear Convenient for recovery the said Sum of three hundred thousand Livers with the interest thereof, and to make one or more Attorney or Attorneys, Solicitor or Solicitors in such Suit or Suits as he my said Attorney may commence, maintain and prosecute in Virtue of the Several Powers herein described and given. and the same to dismiss or charge at his pleasure by appointing others in there stead and generally to do and perform all and all manners of Act and things, forms and proceedings which to him may seem expedient, in reason, law, or equity for ascertaining, adjudging, setting and completely. Signed, Sealed and Delivered in the presence of us. Archd. Redford, Geo. fox.

CHARLESTON DISTRICT JOURNAL OF ORDINARY 1812-1830

MARRIAGE LICENSES 1812-1823
Charleston, S. C.

Men / Women	Abode	Occupation	Reverend
1812			
Dec. 24 Maurice Moriarty	Charleston	Gentleman	
Jane Brady	Charleston	Widow	Dr. William Best
1813			
Jany 5 Richard Pearce	Charleston	Merchant	
Harriet Petsch	Charleston	Spinster	Mr. James D. Simons
March 5 Henry Cowing	Charleston	Merchant	The Rev. Dr.
Ann Wagner	Charleston	Spinster	Theodore Dehon
March 20 Edward Power	Charleston	Merchant	Mr. Christian
Eliza Catherine Wolf	"	Spinster	Hanckel
Nov. 26, George Morgan Gibbes	Charleston	Planter	Rt. Rev.
Eliza Gardenia Garden	Charleston	Widow	Theodore Dehon
1814			
Dec. 7 Francis C. N. Lafond	Charleston	Goldsmith	Christopher
Sophea Smith	Charleston	Widow	Gadsden
March 19 Charles Humphrie Tunis	Charleston	Carpenter	
Margaret Ann Mitchell	do	Spinster	Dr. John Buchan
1815			
Feby 2 Matthew Braid	Charleston	Carpenter	
Elizabeth Hudson	do	Spinster	Dr. Aaron Lilas
11 Nathaniel Holt		Soldier	
Anne Cherrytree	do	Widow	Mr. Alexr. Talley
Nov. 6 Effingham Wagner	Charleston	Merchant	Rt. Rev.
Franciade M. Godard	do	Spinster	Dr. Theo. Debs
10 Robert Hasell Quash	St. Thomas Par'h	Planter	Revd. Christopher
Hannah H. Harleston	St. John B'y	Spinster	Gadsden
1816			
Dec. 11 Christopher Williman	Charleston	Esquire	Rt. Revd. Dr.
Sarah Simpson Baron	Charleston	Spinster	Theo: Dehon or Rev. Andrew Fowler
Feby 5 Peter Mitchell	Savannah	Merchant	
Carolin Susan Putnam	Charleston	Spinster	
John Hynes	St. Jas. Parish	Planter	Rev, Dr.
Martha Moore	Pendleton dist	Spinster	William Percy
May 11 Joseph Smith Gibbes	Charleston	Planter	
Amelia Sarah Shoolbred	Charleston	Spinster	do do

21	Peter Thomas Ryan	Charleston	Merchant	Rt. Rev. Bishop
	Elizabeth Hall Mortimer Chasn		Spinster	Theo Dehon
25	Ashbel Bulkley	Charleston	Merchant	
	Ann Eliza Fanning	Charleston	Spinster	....

1816
June 4

	Holm, Andrew	Charleston	Mariner	
	Middleton, Ann	Charleston	Widow	Flyn, Andrew
	Torre Della Antonio	Charleston	Merchant	Gallager,
	Ryan, Margaret Ann	do	Spinster	Simon Felix

Sept. 17

	Grayson, John	Do	Mariner	Christopher
	Frances Ann Harvey	do	Spinster	Edward Gadsden
24	Wagner, George	do	Merchant	Right Revd. Dr.
	Charlotte Ogier Martin	do	Spinster	Theodore Dehon

Nov. 15

	Alex'r Baron Wilson	do	Squire	The Revd. Dr.
	Sophia Frances Perry Shepheard Do		Spinster	William Percy

Dec. 5

	Wilkie, James	do	Esquire	Right Revd. Dr.
	Mazyck, Sarah	do	Spinster	Theodore Dehon

1817

	Philemon Dickenson Rea	do	Storekeeper	Dr. William Percy
	Lake, Jane	do	Spinster	Rector St. Philip

July 11

	David Pluck[?]	do	Physician	
	Sarah Sampen	do	Widow	Revd. Thomas Frost

May 22

	William Flack	St. Paul's Par.	Planter	Revd. Dr. Simon
	Julia Gallager	Charleston	Spinster	Felix Galleger

Octbr. 1

	David Carmichael	Charls	Merchant	Rev. Dr. John
	Catherine Sarah Swift	do	Widow	Buchan

Mar. 3

	Richmond Kinloch	do	Millwright	Revd. Frederick
	Jophia Jeannette Hopton	do	Spinster	Dalcho

1819
Sept. 29

	William Lucas	Chars.	Esquire	Revd. Mr. Robert
	Charlotte Hume	Chars.	Spinster	S. Symes

1821
Aprl. 2

	Joseph Snow	Province R. I.	Mariner	Rev. Mr.
	Louise Henderson	New York	Spinster	Artemis Baies

1822
Jany. 2

	John Lascellas Nowell Chas.		Esquire	Rev. Dr. C.
	Sarah Ann Wheeler	Charles	Spinster	E. Gadsden

1823
Mar. 2

	John Willcock	Charl'n	Bricklayer	Revd. Christian
	Sarah Adams	Charleston	Spinster	Hanckell

(omitted)
1819
Dec. 26

	John Eberley Halsall	Ch.	Butcher	Revd. John
	Elizabeth Venters	do	Spinster	Bachman

INDEX

INDEX

INDEX

INDEX

INDEX

www.ingramcontent.com/pod-product-compliance
Lightning Source LLC
Chambersburg PA
CBHW070909270326
41927CB00011B/2509